A DIFFICULT COUNTRY
The Napiers in Scotland

A DIFFICULT COUNTRY
The Napiers in Scotland

Priscilla Napier

London

MICHAEL JOSEPH

First published in Great Britain by
MICHAEL JOSEPH LTD
52 Bedford Square
London, WC1
1972

7181 1052 8

Set and printed in Great Britain by
Ebenezer Baylis and Son Ltd., The Trinity
Press, Worcester, and London, in ten on
twelve point Times Roman on paper
supplied by R. F. Bingham Ltd., Croydon,
Surrey, and bound by James Burn, Esher,
Surrey

To my son
Miles Napier

This is a difficult land. Here things miscarry,
Whether we care, or do not care enough
The grain may pine, the harlot weed grow haughty,
Sun, rain, and frost alike conspire against us:
You'd think there was malice in the very air.

        *   *   *

We have such hours, but are drawn back again
By faces of goodness, faithful masks of sorrow,
Honesty, kindness, courage, fidelity,
The love that lasts a life's time. And the fields,
Homestead and stall and barn, springtime and autumn,
(For we can love even the wandering seasons
In their inhuman circuit.) And the dead
Who lodge in us so strangely, unremembered,
Yet in their place. For how can we reject
The long last look on the ever-dying face
Turned backward from the other side of time?
And how offend the dead and shame the living
By these despairs? And how refrain from love?
This is a difficult country, and our home.

                    From 'The Difficult Land' by Edwin Muir

Contents

1*

List of Illustrations

Foreword

In this book I have kept the spelling of early days when quoting from contemporary documents, because it is phonetic, and retains, though probably only faintly, the flavour of Scots fifteenth century speech. When in doubt, read it aloud, and the meaning becomes clear.

I am greatly indebted to Nigel, Lord Napier and Ettrick, for lending me original documents in his possession, for permission to quote from them, and to reproduce a number of pictures of his. Also for drawing my attention to sources of information of which I was ignorant.

Warm thanks also to those who have risked the post and sent me letters or unpublished memoirs for this and other volumes, particularly Mr Ivan Napier, Sir Joseph Napier, Bt., Captain Lennox Napier, Royal Navy, the late Brigadier Arthur Napier, Lady (William) Luce, and my son, Miles Napier. Gratitude as well to the Bodleian Library, the National Library at Edinburgh, and the Public Record Office, institutions whose calm and comfort and whose helpful staff too often get taken for granted.

John Simpson, of the Department of Scottish History at Edinburgh University, most kindly read the manuscript against time, and corrected many a slip: sadly, I thought it best not to follow his advice and keep the noble original spelling of all the Scots poetry, some of which is very obscure in the original, but to go for that stronger impact which immediate comprehension would bring to English minds. I am most grateful to him, and only sorry that lack of time (mine) prevented his taking the thing at a canny pace and me from having the benefit of his more overall advice.

My thanks to Faber and Faber for permission to quote from 'The Difficult Land' from Edwin Muir's *Collected Poems 1921–58*, to Mrs. W. Brownlie Hendry for a quotation from 'John Napier of Merchiston' by W. Brownlie Hendry published in *History Today*,

April 1967, to the author and the Hamlyn Publishing Group for a quotation from Eric Linklater's *Edinburgh* and to Rosalind Mitchison for a quotation from her *History of Scotland.*

And apologies to all those people, roughly five million in number, who know more about Scotland than I do. This book is not for them, but for the general English reader, the thousands of people in England of Scottish descent whose knowledge of Scotland is even less than mine.

This is Vol. I on the Napiers. Vol. II, *The Sword Dance*, came out last year; Vol. III, *Raven Castle*, is due next year.

Family histories have a certain melancholy resemblance. 'Universally respected' (which means that no active harm was known of him in the three surrounding villages) 'Elias Brunch was laid to rest in the spring of 1711.' Good luck to him; but what has this to say even to fortunate beings with Brunch blood in their veins? Shady events, we know, will be glossed over: vainglory, like bracken fronds, will keep popping up all about. Too many twentieth-century biographies of distinguished admirals and generals insist that they came of a long line of fox-hunting squires when all their friends know that dad and grandad in fact were horse-copers, trailing round the midlands from back-door to back-door through the long Victorian years on the off-chance of doing a deal. All the more honour to the heroes for doing what they did—but we are never told these realistic items. A genteel myth pervades all. People's forbears have to be working class, wicked aristocrats, or respected gentry. They are rarely allowed to be what they generally were—solid middle class.

Round about page 74 of a family history we stop trying and drop off into a dreamless sleep. Too many indistinguishable characters will bear the same name. But do they also, strangely, bear after hundreds of years, the same characteristics? The griping hands of heredity will gladly be shrugged off by those who much dislike their own forbears, and most of us have a great-uncle or aunt at thought of whom the mind automatically switches off in self-defence. But there they are, with their good and their awkward impulses, pushing us all along; lodged in us unremembered, but goodness, lodged.

In the thirty generations between now and the Norman Conquest we must each have 1,073,741,824 progenitors, and as there were only at most five million inhabitants of this country even at the time of Queen Anne, we must all be related to each other. Far enough back we are one vague herd; struggling to survive and unlikely to succeed; blown in waves like the sand through those endless European forests down the centuries by one route and another, towards the semi-colon and full-stop in the Atlantic known uninterestedly by the civilized Mediterranean world as Albion and Ierne. Anyone here for a century and not descended from William the Conqueror, Hengist, Horsa, Malcolm Canmore, Llewellyn ap Rhys, or the High Kings of Ireland is probably a museum piece. The traceable, legitimate descendants of, say Edward I, must by now amount to many thousands of people, who are as likely to be cutting cane in Queensland or peddling petrol on the Pacific shores of North America as they are to be living in the English shires. The wind of centuries seeds us here and there, sprouting up the normal family complement of rogues and nonentities, towards remote and chancy fields, in which perhaps some vital shoot awaits its resurgence. But do the oats stay oats, and will the barley seed always throw barley?

What *had* to persist until the last century was robustness, hardihood: nothing else could survive. For the most part weak lungs and imperfect hearts went the way of all flesh before they were old enough to procreate. The time-honoured lot of women was to bear up to a score of children, and raise, if they were lucky, a half of these. The survivors would be dogged, wily, and physically and nervously resilient. So much for genes, the hand which we are dealt: many other factors operate in the playing of it. Were all old families a bloody lot, scoring, in *sauve-qui-peut* fashion, on a lone hand? Up to a point, or they would never have survived. But like most judgements by category, this one does not bear close scrutiny: it took all sorts to make even a world of barons. Good or bad, it is reasonable to suppose that in a long insular history, through those eternal mudbound winters of the countryside, a pronounced individuality or eccentricity grew up and became confirmed amongst those large isolated families. The countrymen and customs of Devon are still plainly different from the countrymen and customs of Northumberland, in spite of mass communications; and how much more so in the past? The frosty nights closed over those stone-cold houses, with their roaring fires and their icy intervals between; over the quaking marshes and the soggy woods that lay outside: families, driven in almost wholly on themselves and constantly marrying their first or second cousins, became more markedly individual than would now be thought sociologically desirable. Some of them became very rum indeed. Brave, clever or mad, and however deflected or enriched by the introduction of wives from all over, through these entrenched name-conscious families some kind of a theme-song appears to run.

Were the Russells always uniquely like Russells, and like no one else, the Churchills always combative, the Cecils always clever and collected? Are the Fitzgeralds forever romantic, from John, rescued as an infant from his father's burning castle by a tame ape in the thirteenth century to Silken Thomas, 10th Earl, hanged at Tyburn in the sixteenth; from handsome doomed Lord Edward Fitzgerald in the eighteenth century to America's twentieth-century Fitzgerald Kennedys, all crowned by charm and intelligence and riddled by rashness and disaster? Have the Homes stayed level-headed ever since Flodden? Are the misfortunes of the Beresfords due to the gypsy's curse, or does their own cheerful and changeless intransigence enter in? Did some who shall be nameless always grasp, always twitch, always turn their coats? Would the Huxleys have been scientific however they were brought up? Did the Forsytes—that imaginary family whom so many people claim as their own—stomp right down the ages insisting that what they had they held? Are the Sitwells indoctrinated into being Sitwells or does it come quite naturally?

Although in remote ages the bards used to give the family forebears a nightly run-through, it must be many centuries since the young were prepared to listen; interest in ancestry rarely sets in before the forties and never until character has been fully formed. Tradition of course impinges upon the young, and especially in the choice of a profession, but does it alter the complicated structure of a human being and make it other than itself? The mind within the mind will still live on. In those rare cases where people consciously try to imitate their forebears it at once becomes apparent and ludicrous, like Mussolini trying to be Julius Caesar. Do some characteristics natively persist, and if so, why some and not others? Do the waves of history, washing over one family, leave it roughly the same shape?

Certainly the quirks of a national character endure, whether induced by climate or heredity. In 991 the Danes, in process of ravaging England's eastern counties, landed on an island in the Blackwater estuary near Maldon in Essex. The isle was joined to the mainland by a narrow causeway, along which, when the ebbing tide made it possible, the Danes advanced upon the English army gathered on the strand. As they could only proceed three abreast, the English were able to pick them off without difficulty. Stop, said the Danes, this won't do: you are not giving us a sporting chance. To be sure you are right, said the English: step ashore in safety and we will fight you fairly on level ground. Whilst they were marking out the pitch and doubtless rolling it, the Danish army proceeded to land unmolested. Once ashore they formed ranks, inflicted a smart defeat on the English, and killed all but about seventeen of them. This happened 1,000 years ago, could happen again (*mutatis mutandis*) tomorrow, and could happen nowhere but in England.

By the twelfth and thirteenth centuries the French were already dedicated solely to French *gloire*, were already saying *Non* to all forms of co-operation. How different are the combative and churchy Irish from themselves in 1100? Or the Welsh, defying the Saxon from their mountains, refusing to speak his tongue, chanting their melancholy songs in their incomparable voices? How different are the Scots, still, in the form of their plaids, wearing the toga of civilized Roman Britain in defiance of all later comers? There are sensible and patriotic Scots who believe that in independence Scotland would even now stultify herself in clan rivalry. Why anyone worries about loss of national identity in a united Europe I know not: it is as tough as mountain beef.

It is possible to nourish a valuable individuality without also guarding a narrow separateness: so much has civilization done for us. The key to all Scots history is the power of kin; and much blood flowed therefrom; but much civilizing influence also. Kindness is kindredness, is behaving to humanity in general as we effortlessly behave to our nearest. And civilized behaviour as it is now increasingly realized, is learnt or unlearnt early, in the home, from kith and kin.

One way or another the Napier family embody many of the vagaries and vicissitudes of clan life—the valuable individuality, the spasmodic reaction to civilizing influences, the power of kin. Their history throws a small sidelight on the history of Scotland itself; and it is hardly possible to tell the tale of the Napiers without the history of Scotland with which it constantly became involved.

As far as examining the continuing power of heredity is concerned, no study of any family could be complete over the centuries: we do

not know nearly enough. The Napiers are interesting because they
so repeatedly died in the noon of life, leaving small boys who
scarcely knew them to struggle up alone, swayed by heredity rather
than by living example. Other families could have more stirring tales
to tell, blazons of greater intellectual brilliance; this simply claims
a temperamental persistence, a likeness in thought and belief; what
Sarah Napier, in 1780, called 'a peculiar turn of mind'.

Like so much, it starts in Scotland. Apart from a few Picts milling
about the Antonine Wall, the bright beacon of Iona, and the reign
of Macbeth, this is a country which for most English people rolled
off its ice age only just in time to provide a stamping ground for
Edward I, and vanished into obscurity again until Mary Queen of
Scots was born to reward the English with a satisfying target for
moral disapproval. But other things in fact went on.

A word of warning. However much or little tradition affects character, education surely swings the point of view. History, as taught in
around 1916, took a singular form. There were, for instance, no
women at all in it: for seven or eight hundred years the English got on
perfectly happily without them. Alfred the Great's mother, Matilda
in her nightgown escaping through the snow, Elinor of Aquitaine
coping with her sons, made lightning appearances; but in the main,
women, like carpets, were only introduced into England in the reign
of Queen Elinor of Castile; and, like carpets, took a great while
before they won general acceptance. The movement gained impetus
with Queen Philippa pleading for the burghers of Calais, and again
with Joan of Arc (owing to the bad behaviour of her French judges
and her English executioners); but not until the time of Queen
Elizabeth I was it openly recognized that women were here to stay.
Even the men fell into limited categories; being all either kings,
bishops or barons. Apart from a revolt or two, the peasants could
only rarely be glimpsed in the middle distance, wearing nightcaps and
tilling for dear life, until they disobligingly upset the economy by
succumbing to the Black Death; though they were permitted to
spring briefly into a mitigated limelight at Crecy in order to discredit the French chivalry with their longbows.

In my years at Oxford, women in history were allowed to drift
rather more into focus; and even the peasants advanced a cautious
step nearer the centre of the stage, particularly as several millions of

them were at this time being starved to death in communist Russia in order to prove to them how much better things were since the revolution. It was also made clear at the university that what really matters about history is the number of barrels of herrings exported from Lowestoft in 1382, and not the colour of Henry II's hair. But early indoctrination dies hard; there are more men than women in this book, and a sad dearth of peasants. And the only herrings are red ones.

Part I

The Lennox Fountainhead

I

Into the mouth of a Scottish prince, facing the Roman army, Tacitus puts the most famous anti-imperialist taunt in history: 'They make a desolation and call it peace.' He was Calgacus, leader of a confederation of Caledonian tribes, and defeated by a Roman army under Agricola at Mons Graupius in A.D. 84: no one knows for certain where this was, but the most likely place is Knock Hill, near Keith, in Banffshire. As Agricola was the father-in-law of Tacitus, this writer probably records at least at second hand, and the noble pre-battle oration he attributes to Calgacus may also have a basis of truth: 'We, the fine flower of Britain, are treasured in most inviolate places, out of sight of the shores of subjection, keeping even our eyes free from the defilement of tyranny. We, the last men on earth, the last of the free, have been shielded till today by the very remoteness and hiddenness for which we are famed . . . But today the last of Britain is laid bare, beyond us lies no nation, nothing but waves and rocks, and the Romans, more deadly than they . . .' The legionaries, Tacitus reports, had to fight in Scotland in particular and in Britain in general at this time 'for life itself before we could think of victory'. And it is into the mouth of another Scottish prince, living nine hundred years later that Shakespeare puts the most baneful speech in literature: 'Out, out, brief candle!' Macbeth, son of the Mormaer of Moray, had in fact as good a claim to the throne or a better one than King Duncan whom he murdered; and it is unlikely that he suffered those pangs of conscience with which Shakespeare, five hundred years later, immortalized him. But both Tacitus and Shakespeare divined important Scots characteristics—a lively conscience, and with it a tendency to despair; and a still livelier love of freedom; and with both a tendency to break easily into ballads and poetry of an incomparable kind.

*

Relieved of its ice age, Scotland had proudly risen twenty-five feet higher above sea level and nearer the heavens, a few fishermen had come to live along its estuaries and edges, whalers and foresters with axes drifted in from the Baltic and from northern Europe, neolithic men brought corn and cattle, and iron age succeeded bronze. The Romans came fleetingly, built a string of forts and a great legionary base just north of Perth, captured young men from the Lothians who appeared on the battlefields of Syria, and Caledonian bears from the Highlands who appeared in the arena at Rome, dug and built the Antonine wall from Clyde to Forth, and gradually left. Christianity wafted into Galloway and Iona; the Norsemen came, spoiling or conquering the fringes of Scotland, and were slowly assimilated. In A.D. 843 King Kenneth McAlpine united Picts and Scots; Britons of Strathclyde and Angles of the Lothians were pushed or cajoled in by degrees until the stage was set for the Macbeth drama two hundred years later.

Shakespeare illustrates a certain English smugness in describing the goings on in Scotland under Macbeth, who in fact ruled comparatively well, ensured seventeen years of peace from civil strife, and was a generous benefactor of the Church:

> 'Alas, poor country,'—mourns Ross
> 'Almost afraid to know itself! It cannot
> Be call'd our mother, but our grave: where nothing,
> But who knows nothing, is once seen to smile;
> Where sighs, and groans, and shrieks, that rend the air,
> Are made, not mark'd; where violent sorrow seems
> A modern ecstacy; the dead man's knell
> Is there scarce ask'd for who; and good men's lives
> Expire before the flowers in their caps,
> Dying or ere they sicken.'

Scotland had its bad times; but was it in fact much more violent, treacherous, cruel than England or any other country in the throes of finding itself? Climate and terrain may have made the fine flower of Britain appreciably leaner, grimmer, tougher than their southern neighbours, but their violent sorrow could be replaced by violent joy, their good men's lives, however brief, had as great an impact here as elsewhere; and their results at least did not expire before the flowers in their caps. True enough that people died before they sickened: how sad a thing is that?

From the Macbeth drama emerged triumphant King Malcolm Canmore (Bighead), who married a saintly but rather managing Englishwoman called Margaret: his younger brother Donalbane also survived. Margaret was sister to Edgar Atheling, who was then battling ineffectively for the English throne to which he was the rightful heir, and mother eventually to the wife of Norman King Henry I of England. Through Margaret the old Saxon line of kings was perpetuated in the royal house of England, surviving the childless demise of Edgar Atheling and the defeat of Harold Godwinson at Hastings, and lasting to date.

It is interesting to trace the slow bubble in families where something is cooking, from the first upward burst of an able and ambitious man; through the building up by son and grandson or wily tenacious daughter; the greed and the intelligence and the canny marriages; the luck and the skill and the seized opportunities of a gradual establishment. No such process is possible with the Napiers, who appear to spring fully characterized from the brow of history, in the person of Archill, a nobleman of Northumbria, fighting doggedly for a cause already well and truly lost two years back.

The time is 1068; the place Yorkshire (a part of Northumbria, which stretched from the Humber to the Lothians). An illegitimate Norse duke, domiciled in northern France, and backed by, of all people, the pope, had landed a year or two previously on the south coast; and after a successful tussle there, had actually had himself crowned King of England at Westminster. Against this state of affairs Archill was, very naturally, contending; for if you accommodate yourself to this type of event there is no knowing where it will all end. For Archill, not accommodating, it ended on the banks of Loch Lomond.

He had lost the battle. 'Tunc Archillus,' wrote Ordericus Vitalis in 1068, in one of those helpful pieces of Latin chronicle that make us all feel we have had a classical education, 'tunc Archillus potentissimus Nordohimbrorum cum rege concordiam fecit.' He was presently forced to yield up his tracts of land north of the Humber, leave his eldest boy as a hostage, and take himself and his depleted army to the court of King Malcolm Canmore of Scotland, whose wife, Margaret, was sister to the Saxon heir to the English throne, Edgar Atheling, on whose behalf Archill had been fighting.

Queen Margaret and her husband (generally and understandably known in that order) received Archill well, and he soon found himself in possession of Dunbartonshire and most of Stirling, scenically more splendid than Northumberland and North Yorkshire, but agriculturally less rewarding. He had married the daughter and heiress of the Celtic ruler of these shires, the Mormaer, or sea steward. These lands around Loch Lomond were known as the Levenax, a word which means 'the field of the quiet stream', and which was eventually shortened into Lennox; and on many documents of King David I of Scotland, first and ablest organizer of Scottish land tenure, Alwin MacArchill, grandson of Archill, is known as Earl of Lennox. This relationship, like much in the twelfth century, is undocumented; but the Gaelic bards called all subsequent Earls of Lennox 'Siol Arkyll', and the bards had a way of knowing more than got down on parchment.

The Scots, as if bent on confusing us, all came from Ireland, while the Picts came from places east, and were in time overwhelmed by Scots, leaving scarce a trace of tongue or legend; and are only to be remembered by the Pictland Firth, corrupted in time into the Pentland Firth, and by their astonishing stone carvings. The local family of Scots into whom Archill married had once been Kings of Munster and went on nostalgically giving their children Irish names like Corc or Maldwin. He was lucky to stake out his claim when he did, for the Norman followers whom King David of Scotland imported from his Huntingdonshire estates lagged in the ever-running status race and the exciting snatch for power. They were not *comites* unless they married the heiresses of the Celtic earls, and therefore not *regaliter*, small time kings with powers of life and death in their own domains.

Government was based on land: life was held together by kinship: power, as in Moslem princedoms, could pass from cousin to cousin by a system known in Scotland as tanistry: affairs, as in the Sicilian or American Mafia, were conducted by personality and sleight of hand more than by legal niceties. And yet religious belief, the certainty that the universe was peopled and ruled by transcendent beings invisible to man, was almost as much a part of human composition as were their lungs and legs. Norse belief had seen human life as the flight of a bird through a warm and lighted hall, fluttering momentarily out of eternal darkness and cold and doomed to return into the same; an existence dominated by harsh and hostile fates. The

notion of a Christian God, like the sound half-heard of some divine
hunting horn in a silent and enormous forest, haunted men's hearts;
piercing their minds like a slant of sunlight between those dark
hillsides; promising, to those who would pay the subscription of
faith and obedience, a lasting sojourn in the warm bright hall. The
cold and dark had turned from menace into affection. Maybe
the continence and abstinence Christianity demanded seemed, in the
light of its promises, no more galling than the continence and
abstinence involved in life with Che Guevara in the Sierra Maestra
ranges of Cuba. Life glowed with a promise of freedom from doom.
Men felt the presence of God as they felt the air on their faces. They
lived hand to mouth, rejoiced by hope, tormented by almost incessant
fear; but unplagued maybe by those great bogies of industrial
civilization—boredom, accidie, burnt-outness. They endured what
to us would be a hell of physical misery; but were not left stranded
on the deserts of a causeless despair.

The Lennox lay along the Highland line; its ruler had one foot
planted in the mountains and the other on the plain, could fortify
himself on the islands of Loch Lomond and endure an indefinite
siege. The Mormaers, now become Earls of Lennox, had their
purpose in the scheme of things. Sudden raids or even large scale
invasions from overseas were still frequent enough to make needful
the power of local lords who could repel them: they formed a strong
local garrison, and a local administration, hence the royal tolerance
and even encouragement. Dying in 1153, Alwin MacArchill was
succeeded by his son Alwin, 2nd Earl of Lennox, and father of nine
sons by his wife Eve, daughter of Lord Menteith. The eldest,
Maldwin, succeeded him, and the fifth, Gilchrist, was outlawed after
a fracas with the Church, and somewhere down the line amongst
Aulay and Corc and Dugald and all the other younger brothers was
Donald, from whom the Napiers derived one of those pleasing
legends that are handed down from father to son and enchant a
whole family for hundreds of years, faithfully repeated from illiterate
parent to illiterate child and slowly acquiring the sanctity of accepted
truth. It was not written down (few laymen *could* write before the
sixteenth century) until 1625, when the Napiers who had settled in
England applied to the head of their family for an acknowledged
right to bear his arms. His answer was a document directed through

them to Sir William Segar at the College of Heralds in London.

'Know ye that I, Sir Archibald Napier of Merchistoun in the Kingdom of Scotland Knt, Deputy Treasurer and one of his Majesty's Privy Council there. Forasmuch as my entirely beloved kinsmen Sir Robert Napier Knt and Bart, Sir Nathaniel Napier Knt, Nicholas Napier of Tintinhull Esqre, John and Robert Napier of Puncknowle Esquires, being desirous of being confirmed of their pedigree and descent from my house, I have to satisfy their lawful and laudable request herein declared the truth thereof, and the original of our name, as by tradition from father to son we have generally and without any doubt received the same. That one of the ancient Earls of Lennox in Scotland had issue three sons, the eldest succeeded him in the earldom of Lennox, the second was named Donald,* and the third named Gilchrist, he for killing two of the Abbott of Paisley's servants for fishing in the river Linfren lived outlawed all his lifetime amongst the hills of Arrochar, his father gave the lands of Kilpatrick to the Abbey for satisfaction of the offence.

'The then King of Scotland having wars did concreate his lieges to the battle, amongst whom was the Earl of Lennox, who keeping his eldest son at home sent his second son to serve for him with the forces that were under his command. This battle went hard with the Scots for the enemy pressing furiously upon them forced them to give ground until at last they fell to flat running away which being perceived by Donald he pulled his father's standard from the bearer thereof and valiantly encountering the foe being well followed by the Earl of Lennox's men he repulsed the enemy and changed the fortune of the day, whereby a victory was got. After the battle as the manner is everyone advancing and setting forth his own acts, the King said unto them Ye have all done well but there is one amongst ye who hath Nae peer, and calling Donald into his presence he commanded him in regard of his worthy service and in augmentation of his honor to change his name from Lenox to Napier and gave him the lands of Gosford of Fife and made him his own servant, which discourse is confirmed by sundry of my old evidences and testimonies wherein we are called Lenox alias Napier . . .'

The most surprising thing about this pleasing tale, firmly believed in by all Napiers, and greeted with increasing derision by most of the experts, is that it may be true. A twelfth-century charter confirms that

---

* Donald has now been rationalized by Sir Archibald into the second son.

there was a contemporary 'Donald, son of the Earl of Lennox, from whom came the Napiers', and in an age when hardly anyone could write and those who could were quite unable to spell, only one distinguishing mark stands out—unmistakable and jealously guarded as a signature tune—a coat of arms, visible to all in battle, legible by all on documentary seals. By this alone can continuity be traced with any certainty; and when next century the Napiers emerged into the clear light of written record, the arms they bore and the seals on all their documents were the arms of Lennox, cadenced for a second son: a saltier engrailed, cantoned with four roses; the cross supposed to have been won by crusading Malcolm de Lennox. All names come from somewhere; are jobs, places, patronymics, peculiarities. In England a nap or nape was the top of a hill: were the Napiers simply always tall or big-nosed? But the word was not used in Scotland. In England the king had a royal naperer to look after the linen, just as he had a butler, steward and constable. There is no record, although there is a possibility, that the King of Scots had such an official; and this, although not advanced until the 1860s, is to some historians the preferred explanation of the name. But certainly as early as the fifteenth century the family explanation was widely accepted. The accuracy of father to son testimony is always suspect to historians because it is not susceptible of proof, but over and over again archaeology has confirmed that which expert dogma swept aside as impossible. Intelligent illiterates—many still exist, in the Greek islands and elsewhere—do not know much history but what they know they remember and pass on to their children. A piece of local knowledge so transferred from father to child for two thousand years and condemned by the learned as impossible, received dramatic confirmation by the diggers not long ago in Greece.

Experts have cast doubt on the Bruce–Comyn story* on the grounds that Bruce and Kirkpatrick would have spoken Norman French instead of Lowland Scots. But how is it possible to dogmatize about who spoke what language on any given occasion more than two hundred years after the Conquest? Nothing is more stubborn, more blandly uncomprehending than an Englishman or Scot confronted by a language he does not wish to understand: whatever they spoke among themselves the Anglo-Normans would have

---

* Bruce, rushing from the Franciscan church of Dumfries where Comyn, Balliol's nephew, had summoned him for a conference, 'I doubt I ha' slain the Red Comyn!' Kirkpatrick, 'Doubt ye? I'll mak siccar!' (secure).

bowed to some extent to this mulish deafness and picked up enough over two hundred years to communicate with their men. Bruce and friends must have all had Lowland Scots nannies, and addressed their troops in the vernacular. The British, only intermittently in India, acquired plenty of Hindi quite early on and frequently addressed each other with words or phrases in Indian tongues.

If the Napiers were Naperers, why should they have pretended otherwise, in an age of vainglory when personal attendance on a king was the sure road to fame and fortune for a younger son, the coveted role *par excellence*? The Butlers, the Chamberlains, the Durwards, Marshalls, Constables did not pretend to be anything else; the Stewards in fact adopted that name in preference to their own, which was Fitzalan, and became, by marrying the king's daughter, the royal house of Stewart. Naperer was a proud office in England; as late as 1820 Lord Petre, no upstart, applied (unsuccessfully) for the office of Hereditary Naperer at the coronation of George IV. Naperer, if it had been true, would have seemed grand enough. There was no need for one of those flash inventions of a romantic origin so dear to the sixteenth century.

Who now can know the truth? But as long as any of them could remember the Napiers had been Ne parium, Ne par, unequalled; and one of them, living near Peebles, even spelt his name, rather vaguely, Peerlus. John Napier's book was published in France as the work of Jean Nompareil; and in 1627 there was a mocking popular rhyme all ready for the first Lord Napier:

> Napier is a peer, yet Nae peer is he
> Napier has nae peer, yet a peer is he . . .

What were they like, our infinitely remote grandparents? What feelings heaved the hearts under those mailed or leather jerkins, what thoughts spun in the minds behind those ferocious barred visors? They are shadows; visible only by their reactions to the events which swirled round them; knowable only through the stark times in which their lives were lived. Difficult as it is to discover the motives of fully documented characters living in our own era, how can we tell which ones drove the unlettered subjects of seven hundred years ago? To consider individual lives in these early centuries is like flying over a great continent blanketed in cloud; from the occasional glimpses afforded us we draw conclusions, probably false, as to the nature of the terrain. To complete the confusion, Edward I took all Scotland's state documents away with him to Westminster in 1290, where it is no surprise to learn that they remained in someone's in-tray until 1937, by which time all but nine of them were lost.

Living in the late eleventh century, Saxon Queen Margaret of Scotland, we know, fed three hundred poor men every day. The same ones? How selected? Could a poor man move on and come back again and be re-victualled next week? Margaret's sons, instead of being called Donalbane, or Macbeth, or Indulf, as customary, were christened Edward, Edgar, Edmund, and Ethelred, after her own family, Alexander after the pope, and David after the son of Jesse, names hitherto unused in Scotland. Oh, dear, the bossy English! She made a further impact upon Scottish life by insisting that everyone should go to church on Sundays. She also built the delectable little Norman chapel on the rock of Edinburgh Castle, which in spite of having been used as an ammunition store in the seventeenth century and now being permanently apse-deep in tourists, still exudes a deep archaic holiness. Margaret's real break-through was her canonization, the first mother of eight (or mother of anybody much) to be made a saint. Brought up in Hungary, she was European-minded, civilizing, read from gold-lettered gospels and lined her draughty palaces with silken hangings; perhaps communicated with relations and did something to dispel the legend put about the continent by Roman Procopius that the air in Scotland was so lethal that no one could survive there for more than half an hour. Good or ill, her memory lives.

'There was a gravity in her very joy, and something stately in her anger,' reported Turgot, prior of Durham, who knew her well. 'In her presence no one ventured to utter even one unseemly word.' It sounds the least bit intimidating and difficult to live with; the comments of husband Malcolm Canmore are not recorded (the moment he died the Scots reverted to Donalbane, free from Norman or English tendencies).

Upon the Lennox family her impact was lasting. They owed their petty kingdom of the Lennox to their faithfulness to her family, or to marrying the daughter of the Mormaer of the Lennox, or to both. The glimpses of them are tantalizing and brief. Difficult to tell from the available facts whether the pre-Stewart Lennoxes were more, or less, brave, scheming, pious, loyal, treacherous, or impulsive than other Scots lords of the time; but there is at least the suggestion of a race often preferring public weal to personal advantage, and in long-memoried Scotland a kind of romantic legend gathered around 'the Lennox of Auld'.

History, coming down to us mainly in its Sunday newspaper aspect, gives us notions that are probably slanted. Life in twelfth-century Scotland is blurred in mists as thick and unpredictable as the Atlantic clouds that cloak her high hills, unless there is an incident so horrific or ennobling that the tale is re-told and in time written down. The long winters lie like shrouds over these early Lennoxes and Napiers, living between the valley bogs and barren hill-tops, living by still or stormy lochs that hang in silence under dark clouds, among surrounding snow, treading through black winter heather that clots above the thin bog-ice. On the steep braes the murk rocks push through snowfall and echo back no human sound. By dark gnarled oaks and scattered birches, clinging along the white hillside, lived men in rough stone crofts; their lords in icy fortresses only a whit less bare. Family and clan cohesion was their sheet-anchor; loyalty or death their alternatives—the shared hearth through the interminable winter nights, the shared crust in the hungry months before the new grass showed. Not all of it is gloom: at nights they sing and dance and listen to the harper's ballads, and in summer they round up the red deer and slaughter a score and feast themselves full; and when did they learn to distil their whisky? A kind Atlantic wind blows in the spring rain, and men and waters are on the move again, with a glint of steel and of flowing river among the glens and lowlands, thin hardy spearsmen, small but dangerous against the hugeness of their empty landscape, off and away to replenish the scanty larder (preferably at English expense), leaving old men and boys to tend the cattle, and often never returning; fugitive high in the Eildon hills where the Roman garrison of Trimontium had so nearly starved a thousand winters ago; or dying and stripped on a sunny hillside on the not yet settled Border, with ravens swooping and the untroubled larks singing overhead to ears that could no longer hear them.

Yet not all of history is Sunday newspaper stuff. Slowly the valley bogs of Scotland are drained—a task not completed until the eighteenth century—and the scrub is cleared and the little fields creep out towards the foothills; wooden buildings give place to stone; King

James I of Scotland—resolute, red-haired, a poet; married to John of Gaunt's granddaughter, Joanna Beaufort. *Scottish National Portrait Gallery.*

James II of Scotland —James of the Fiery Face. Like all the first Jameses and Mary Queen of Scots, he had red hair; but so, judging by the rude comments of French soldiers during the Hundred Years' War, and by almost all Elizabethan portraits, had practically everybody in the British Isles in these centuries. *Scottish National Portrait Gallery.*

James III of Scotland—from an altarpiece by Hugo van der Goes. James enjoyed the company of architects and musicians, and was accordingly very unpopular. Like all the first four Jameses he died a violent death, killed at Sauchieburn. His son, James IV, who kneels behind him, became a magnificent renaissance prince, clever and active, but was killed at Flodden. *Reproduced by gracious permission of Her Majesty the Queen.*

David I, son of Malcolm, mints coins, founds burghs, organizes both knights and priests to take their part in his administration; and slowly the towns and churches rise behind great walls of limestone or granite, behind creaking oaken doors. Slowly civilization, like an infinitely graduated dawn, rolls onwards through cloud-enshadowed hills. The prayers rise up from the chill dark chapels, turning men's minds from avarice and bloodshed, if only for twenty-five minutes; and men remember that ex-warrior prince, Saint Columba, who came unarmed to their ferocious heathen land, softening their *samurai* qualities with the great Christian virtue of hope; and gentle Saint Maluag of Lismore, wafting across from Ireland on a south-west wind like a breath of summer, preaching his incomprehensible doctrine of love and forgiveness to beings who reluctantly found that they had these qualities somewhere concealed about them. Almost in spite of themselves the old sanctified fears and hatreds of Valhalla and other contemporary beliefs lose their long grip, and God, or if you prefer long words and scientific explanations, the element of benevolence in the collective subconscious, takes hold; and disinterested kindness, like a delicate plant unlikely to survive a harsh climate, very slowly unfurls.

A nameless voice drifts out of the smoky halls, above the trampled evil-smelling rushes and the strewn bones on the floor, singing a marvellous and still-remembered ballad, of love and treachery and death, moving the hearts of the rude to strange unearthly thoughts. And always, everywhere, as if it were a natural growth like nails or hair, there is courage and hardihood, because nobody grew up unless they were robust; and everywhere a fierce determination, in the teeth of all adverse weather, of all darkness and all dearth, to survive, procreate, stake a claim and defend it at any cost.

Are all mountain people so fierce? Is the early history of the Swiss, the Kashmiris, the Bolivians, as dogged and embattled? Do violent gradients make for violent deeds? For everywhere, in the news flashes that come down to us, there seems to be blood. Slowly and hardly the flow diminishes; blood in a thick ceaseless stream on field and fell and upland, blood soaking into the grassy sheep-nibbled hills of the Lowlands, into the dark peat-bogs and the little patches of trampled green oats; blood clinging on the banks of heather, on the tawny deer-grass of the high hills; splashing the walls of Stirling Castle, trickling over the grey stone cobbles of Edinburgh's spiny central ridge; while a people of exceptional fire and vigour comes

2

imperceptibly to terms with itself, and even with its redoubtable and scarcely less bloodstained southern neighbour. No two people have cut each other in smaller pieces with fiercer glee than have the English and the Scots of the twelfth and of the fourteenth century (down to chop Newcastle, up to chop Berwick); and despairers over Jew and Arab could take heart from their tale.

Occasionally, a shaft of light breaks through our ignorance. In the twelfth century Maldwin, 3rd Earl of Lennox (married to Elizabeth, daughter of Walter the High Steward by his wife Beatrice, daughter of Gilchrist, Earl of Angus), grants fishing rights over Loch Lomond to the Abbot of Paisley, the Cluniac Abbey that Walter Steward had founded, and the right to dry nets and build huts on its shores; and a slanting eastern ray over the waters reveals them covered in little boats full of the Abbey servants fishing the loch, or spreading their nets on the beaches below tent-shaped, heather-thatched, round huts, rather like an African kraal. What about all Maldwin's eight younger brothers? By the law of averages seven of them must have wanted that fishing. By the same law two at least of them must have had red hair, and the accompanying temperament. One, at least, rebelled. The fog rolls down again; and a few years later, among the steep hills of Arrochar, Gilchrist of Lennox who fell foul of the Abbey servants over the fishing and lives a fugitive from clerical vengeance, leans down to gralloch a stag. Why doesn't brother give the abbot a couple of farms and have done? And perhaps he does. Gilchrist shared his exile with wolf and lynx and bear, as well as deer: further north the sad bellow of an elk could still be heard in the high hills. In between his hunting activities, Gilchrist found time to found the clan Macfarlane (his son was called Bartholomew, Pharlane in Gaelic), thus becoming the ultimate author of all those biscuits.

Repeated grants of property to the Church evidence a piety that the Lennoxes shared with other contemporaries;—Campsie to the Cathedral Church of Glasgow, Kilpatrick to the Abbey of Paisley, and twelve more farms before 1200, lands around Luss to the Dean of Luss in 1224, Roseneath to the Abbey of Paisley, the right to net salmon on Gairloch (but every fourth fish is for the owner), 'pasture of the land of Levenax in pure and perpetual alms,' further grants to Glasgow Cathedral and fishing up to tide level on the Leven. The deeds go on: lands to the Abbey of Arbroath, for the soul of King

William the Lion and for the souls of Maldwin, 3rd Earl's father, mother, all ancestors and all descendants, the right to pasture eight oxen and two horses at Bonhill, liberty to take stone and wood for building and fire. (Fishing and forestry rights, then as now, occupied a good deal of Scottish attention.) What dictated all these benefactions? these gifts of great chunks of fertile land, from which mankind parts so hardly? Christ had taught men—however rarely they obeyed—to be merciful, and to be brothers to each other. How deep did this message bite? Were these gifts insurance policies for the next world? Led by the desire to keep in with a powerful institution? Inspired by Christian charity, and a recognition of the bounty of Heaven? Impossible now to tell; and may even have been difficult for the Lennoxes to be quite certain themselves.

How they affected the recipients is equally unsure. Were there gleams of avarice from keen eyes under tonsured heads, the folding of fat abbot hands in satisfaction over a full paunch? Was there the subtle corruption of increasing power? But this was a great age of faith, the 1200s, the century of the long blazing summers when grapes ripened in the open vineyards as far north as York, the century of full-hearted giving, whether connected with climate or not. Two years after Maldwin de Lennox's grant to the Dean of Luss, St Francis, once a rich young man, had died in poverty outside the walls of Assisi. And men with wheel-barrows and pulleys, living out their lives in reed huts held together with clay, were building cathedrals all over Europe before whose skill and beauty succeeding centuries would stand in speechless awe. Up went Coutances, Wells, Bourges, Lincoln; the hewn stones of Salisbury, Burgos, Beauvais; the heady towers of Rheims. The Scots were not less generous or faithful than the rest, though few and poorer.

Another version of the legend of Nae peer suggests that it was acquired now, fighting King Haakon of Norway in the 1260s, under King Alexander III of Scotland, in the Lennox countryside where the Norwegians invaded, which would make it more likely. 'There is a certain substance in this story of Donald,' Lord Lyon King of Arms guardedly admitted in 1966. Nae peer is one of those jolly pieces of nonsense, like Alfred and the cakes, which nobody can either prove or disprove but which probably hold a core of fact within them.

*

By the end of the thirteenth century the mists were clearing. In 1280 Johan le Naper, owner of lands in Dunbartonshire, a son? a grandson? of Donald Lennox alias Napier of the legend, is mentioned in a charter of Malcolm, 4th Earl of Lennox, and with other local landholders witnesses another a few years later; a hand comes out of the dimness and seals with the Lennox arms after his clerk-written name. Was he Johan the nonparell or Johan the naperer, and if the latter, what was he doing farming in Dunbartonshire and not holding the towel for King Alexander in Dunfermline town? Scotland's earliest known poem celebrates these last happy years of 'Alysandyr oure Kyng', when Scotland was 'led in luve and le' (peace), when there was abundance of 'ale and bread, Of wine and wax and gaming and glee', before

> Oure gold was changyd in to lead;
> Chryst, borne in to Vyrgynte,
> Succoure Scotland, and remede
> That stad is in perplexyté.

Well might she be perplexed. Something fey and fated seems to hang over the early history of Scotland; as if those three witches of Macbeth's had kept their cauldron permanently on the brew. The luckier English, banged into a sort of cohesion by those well-fibred, long-lived Plantagenets, and by the greater ease of their communications, were to miss at least some of the internal wars that bring such misery to all, but especially to the poor. But in Scotland no sooner do things begin to look up a bit, no sooner does peace raise its sweet head and warm up life for the generality, than fate intervenes. On a wild March night of 1286, King Alexander III, widower of Edward I's sister, hastening from council in Edinburgh to join his new young wife, Yolande, at Kinghorn, crosses by Queensferry in a rising storm and, spurred on by love and haste, rides his horse over the cliff in the darkness and fog. Rock and sea devour him, and all is to do again.

II

A little girl of seven now stood between Scotland and chaos. Both Alexander's sons had died, his only daughter had married the King of Norway, and after giving birth to this vital infant, she, too, had died. The little girl, Margaret, the Maid of Norway, was the last descendant of King William the Lion, second son of David I.

Malcolm, 4th Earl of Lennox, swore to support this baby girl as Queen of Scotland, and in March of 1290 rode south to England to negotiate her marriage with Edward I's son; a marriage that could have left unwritten the carnage and hatred of two hundred bitter years. That summer the English sent a ship to Norway for her, well supplied with sugar-loaves and gingerbread and raisins and figs, for no trouble was too much for the little girl who was to unite two kingdoms. But the King of Norway doubted them. Moved by some unknown and fatal impulse, or perhaps by simply not wishing to say goodbye to her, he delayed all summer, and sent her to Scotland in a ship of his own. It sailed on September 20th, although the shrewd and sea-faring Norwegians, in a century so much more weather-dependent than our own, must have known about the equinoctial gales. Soon the poor little girl was long past sugar-loaves, and died at sea, 'between the hands of the Bishop of Bergen'. A Scottish escorting ship, commanded perhaps by Sir Patrick Spens, was lost in the storm—'Half owre, half owre, to Aberdour,'—and Scotland's woes had begun. The ballad, written much later, rings with the authentic sadness that this loss brought:

> To Norroway, to Norroway,
> To Norroway o'er the faem—
> The King's daughter of Norroway
> Tis thow must bring her hame . . .

But home she would never come.

Another stir of the witches' brew had let loose Edward I of England; a traumatic experience which rocked Scotland like an earthquake shock. Although he wrote in French or Spanish and spoke little English, Edward was the prototype, the first of many organizing Englishmen whose passion for the rule of law blinds them to the unaccountable wish of other peoples to go their own sweet way, however sour it seems to more ordered minds. Why could not the Irish, Welsh and Scots, and eventually the Indians and the Africans, run their countries on common sense English lines? 'And because elections ought to be free, the king commandeth upon great forfeiture that no man by force of arms nor by malice nor by menacing shall disturb or hinder any to make free election,' Edward's judges declaimed to the people of England—if anybody wanted anything better than that he must be daft. To a Scots people bound, in Edward's view, on the joyless wheel of feud and counter-feud he was offering the bright release of justice; that rule of law which to a king so close in time to the night of barbarism seemed no less than a heavenly jewel. In his own mind Edward was the natural suzerain over all the British Isles, successor to King Arthur whose legend haunted his imagination. With their own king as obedient vassal to himself as lawful suzerain, Edward might rule, and in his view, civilize, Scotland. Had not earlier Scots kings done homage? What of those nine legendary monarchs of the north who had rowed King Edgar of England on the Dee? Here was a folk memory to float the imagination upon towering clouds. He would be a kind of Christian Caesar bringing law and order into the junglier parts of his domain. Thus he proceeded; confident, efficient, urbane, and about six inches taller than anyone else in sight; becoming notably less urbane when the Scots failed to see things his way. When they rebelled vigorously against his rule he felt as one who had held out the koh-i-noor diamond and had it slung back in his eye: the results were fearful.

To his servant, Nicholas Trevet, Edward seemed 'great of soul', and by the English in general he was sure to be beloved—a shrewd commander, and a jouster and wrestler of Olympic standards who had won the all-European tournaments and rudely banged the Saracens in the Holy Land; hot-tempered and cheerful and far from stand-offish; wheeling ahead to victory on his great black horse, Ferraunt. With them he could be merciful and cool. In planning cities and castles and in coding law he was as keen-witted as he was in battle or at chess. His queen, Eleanor of Castile, must have heaved a sigh of relief when she arrived from Spain on this life-long blind date (she had only seen him once when she was a very small child) and found him handsome and gay, and surprisingly faithful for one so sexy and energetic. He shared her love for beautiful buildings, ritual and music. Court life at this time was a kind of prolonged and slap-up picnic, and on many of the king and queen's ceaseless and inseparable journeys their harpists, fiddlers and trumpeters went too. At their hunting-box castle of Rockingham in Northamptonshire Edward made Eleanor a garden, put in windows, fireplaces and such like mod cons, a bedroom up a winding stair with a little window from which she could look down into the great hall. She called him 'terrible to all the sons of pride but gentle to the meek of the earth'. Music was a life-long passion: when he was dying on his last campaign Edward made them stop his litter so that he could hear the songs of the Scotswomen reaping in the fields. Dynastically this well-attuned couple were not lucky. Their daughters prospered but their sons were less fortunate: two died as babies, and promising Alfonso as a ten-year-old, and was there something unlooked for in their fourth, handsome little Edward?

The queen's death after thirty-six happy years estranged her husband from the human race: the beautiful stones of his grief rose up from Nottingham to Charing Cross, the still-standing Eleanor crosses for the *Chère Reine* who is unwittingly commemorated by thousands of commuters every day when they take their tickets to her final cross. Edward turned with a new savagery upon his luckless neighbours to the north. Each year he grew more formidable. His neglected five-year-old son quailed before him, and the Dean of St Paul's, predecessor of John Donne and of Canon Collins, dropped dead of shock when confronted by Edward in argument. The Scots were made of sterner stuff. To them and to the Welsh he became a never forgotten menace and anathema, the cruel and hated scourge who never had enough, the Covetous King of Merlin's age-old prophecy.

King Edward was appealed to as umpire, and the question of the Scottish succession opened in a seemly manner: evidence in favour of the fourteen claimants to the throne was carefully examined by a panel of judges and they were short-listed to three. The final choice fell on Balliol, grandson of the eldest of William the Lion's nieces, and much more biddable than either

Bruce or Hastings, descended from younger sisters. Why not, Hastings suggested, follow Scots inheritance law where sisters were concerned, and divide Scotland into its three ancient kingdoms, Lothian, Albany and Strathclyde? Three weak kingdoms would have suited Edward admirably, but he was a tiger for legality. His judges declared the kingdom of Scotland impartible, and he thus, quite by mistake, turned it into a nation.

Some time elapsed before this became a clear issue. Round the douce and wooded shores of Forth and Tay a frail precious core of civilization had been built up under the Scots kings, David I, William the Lion, and the two Alexanders. Many were loath to see it burnt away in war; and with it the loving and le, the ale and bread, the wine and wax and gaming and glee. The chronicler Fordun thought that David I's rule had 'turned the savageness of the Scots into kindliness and humbleness': civil war would predictably turn it back again. Balliol, for all that his father had founded the Oxford college, did not seem a man to die for: his subjects called him 'the Toom Tabard' (the empty jacket), and Bruce was old and made his peace with Edward. No one could know in advance the grim lengths to which the English king would go in gripping his fief. One of the most admired kings in Christendom, had he not sent the Saracens flying in Syria and mediated successfully in a dispute between Aragon and France? He was both strong, and a known statesman. At least once in the course of the dispute he came up with statesmanlike proposals, but as usual in the dealings of the slow-moving English, with countries at their mercy, these did not appear until too late when everyone was unalterably alienated. But Edward's common sense was dazzling: his drive was formidable; some years passed before the Scots realized that for them there were to be no terms.

In 1295 Balliol was so rash as to make a defensive alliance with King Philip of France, with whom Edward was at odds over Gascony. Edward leapt north like a tiger, forced Balliol to abdicate, and made himself master of nearly all Scotland, standing in a brief triumph of sovereignty on the cool and bracing shores of the Moray Firth. 'Arthur himself never had it so fully,' the ballad-makers sang, and two thousand Scots lords, bishops, knights and burgesses, representing all but the whole country, sealed allegiance to Edward in a document known as the Ragman's Roll. A rain-washed uncertain acquiesence hovered over hill and dale. Among the signers were Bruce's grandson, Robert, Earl of Carrick, Malcolm, 5th Earl of

Lennox (who had succeeded his father three years earlier), and his kinsmen John and Matthew Napier. Was it all what the chronicler of Lanercost Abbey called 'mere feigning, their hearts always with their own people'? Or were they playing for time? hoping for peace? believing that this feudal plan would leave Scotland free?

Edward's bossy English officials rapidly dissolved this last dream. Subscribers to the theory that non-Caucasians begin at Berwick, at Dublin, at Caerleon-on-Usk, they soon had all Scotland in a seethe. The angry Scots were led by Andrew de Moray and an enormous young squire from Clydesdale called William le Wallace who struck the first blow by killing the English sheriff of Lanark. Moray and Wallace organized night raids and swooped on English garrisons, vanishing again into the hills and forests: English prisoners and Scots collabos, borne off with them, died the usual ungentle deaths: (Edward had put to the sword every man, woman and child in Berwick.) Scotland is ideal guerrilla country, with the fish of its firths and rivers and the game of its forests, abundant water and fuel, the shelter of rocks, and the warmth of heather. The hills at this time were largely afforested.

At the start of the troubles James the High Steward and Malcolm of Lennox tried to make terms between the patriots and Edward, but that time passed. As soon as the English king left for the Continent, Earls Lennox, Buchan, Menteith, Ross, Strathearn, Atholl and Mar collected a large vassal army and leapt at England, devastating Northumberland and Cumberland and laying siege to Carlisle. Later in the summer of 1297 Wallace out-generalled the English army at Stirling Brig, and his well-led force surrounded and massacred the previously unbeatable armoured knights. Cressingham, a mean and paunchy oppressor high up in the English hierarchy of officials, was literally cut into strips: it was clear there could now be no peace. Lennox, with more to lose than most, threw in his lot with Scots independence: he was followed by few of his peers, who mostly had lands in England they were reluctant to forfeit.

Wallace was proclaimed Guardian for Balliol, and Malcolm of Lennox welcomed him to his castle of Faslane:

> Than to Fasslane the worthy Scot gan pass
> Quhar Erle Malcolm was bydand at defence,
> Right glad was he of Wallace gude presence

Blind Harry wrote. In the high hills behind Arrochar, when things became more difficult, Lennox met Wallace and feasted him and his men, nor was Lennox amongst the Scots lords who joined in the chase and capture of this hero after his defeat by Edward at Falkirk. John Napier, also, with an unerring eye for an admirable character liable to end up on a scaffold, supported Wallace; one of those ruthless leaders loved for their resolution and dash, and not only because, as Blind Harry the poet later wrote: 'Of riches he kept no proper thing, Gave as he won, like Alexander the King.' Handsomely helped on his way by a later poet, Robert Burns, Wallace's courage was rightly to live on as a lasting legend in Scottish hearts, steeling them in dark hours, and toasted in gallons of whisky every last day of November from Melbourne to Milwaukee. King John Balliol, on the other hand, had settled in France and declined to come back. Bruce was the last real hope.

By 1304 Edward had flailed all Scotland flat again; not that it did him much good; the Scots simply scorched their earth and retired into the hills, leaving the English armies foodless in the plains. But even Robert Bruce, grandson of the original claimant, laid down his arms. Scots weakness lay in the rivalry of the two claimants; at a recent meeting the Red Comyn (Balliol's heir) had leapt at Robert Bruce and taken him by the throat. Another lesser roll of allegiance to Edward was signed, but not by John Napier, who was defending Stirling Castle, the only stronghold in the country still in Scottish hands, as lieutenant to Sir William Oliphant.

The siege of Stirling Castle began in April; two hundred men against the concentrated might of England. King Edward, in a mood described by the chronicler as 'full Grim', directed the assault himself. Thirteen 'great engynes' were brought by him to batter down the walls, and the leaden roof of the refectory at St Andrew was melted down to make cannon balls. All day long as the summer light lengthened the great boulders crashed on the walls, the dust flew up, the loosened stones came raining down, and the *loups de guerre* spat out fire; and at night the weary garrison, tightening their belts, began to glance sideways at each other's portions. There were fifty survivors of them; nothing they might do could shake off Edward. Wallace was a hunted man in the hills; was it possible that he could gather enough men to raise the siege? In their hearts they knew that he could not; and at every dawn after the short nights the relentless battering shook the walls with a noise like the trump of doom.

Some time after midsummer news came that Wallace had been captured. He was to have a mockery of a trial in London in August, and be dragged through its streets on a hurdle, to be hanged, drawn and quartered for breaking an allegiance he had never made. His loss sickened Scotland, and the Stirling Castle garrison were now fighting alone, and subjected to Greek fire in increasing volume, for Edward was not one to neglect the latest contributions of technology. He had married again, and perhaps feeling that a wife so emphatically second best deserved a little amusement, the king had an oriel window made in the outer wall of her house in Stirling, so that she and her ladies could comfortably watch the siege of the castle. In August the garrison were starved into surrender; their stubborn resistance had enraged Edward so much that he refused to let them march out with the honours of war. There followed the long trudge south to an English prison. As they clumped gloomily over the Border hills with their innards still deranged from starvation it must have felt like the end of the chapter, if not the end of the book. They were spared the indignity of chains, but John Napier had to pay the English king three years rent of his lands (Charter—October 15th, 1305)—what did he live on meanwhile?

The flame of Robert Bruce was now fitfully burning, and with him Malcolm de Lennox, one of the only three Scots nobles not in English pay, threw in his lot. It was a dicey game; for Bruce was not only a rebel and forsworn; in the early spring of 1306 he had been guilty of sacrilege by the mortal wounding of his Balliol rival, the Red Comyn, in the church of the Greyfriars at Dumfries. Three times Bruce had surrendered to Edward and been forgiven; the sacrilege, probably unpremeditated, had burned his boats. Nothing awaited him or his followers from the English but a gruelling death—*peine fort et dur*—backed by all the fury of outraged religious sentiment. With the courage of desperation Bruce locked up the English king's assize judges in their courtroom at Dumfries, and leaving his followers to cope with the south-west, galloped north through the naked trees of Lanarkshire as if all the hounds of hell were after him, as indeed he may have felt they were. He knew himself the best hope of Scotland,

but without some seal of forgiveness on the stain of his sacrilege he
was a maimed man. At Glasgow was Bishop Wishart, a patriot
supporter; from him Bruce sought and obtained absolution and much
more. He did not wait in Glasgow. From its hiding place the bishop
unfurled the royal standard of Scotland, like a talisman of outlawry
from Edward's suffocating dominance. With Bruce and Lennox and a
few others he bore it to Perth, through a countryside still locked in
winter and garrisoned with Englishmen, to Bruce's coronation at
Scone. It was the Palm Sunday of an early Easter, with snow on the
hills and the branches unbudded, and never a swallow to herald the
splendour of Scotland's summer. The ancient crown had been taken
south to London, together with the sacred stone; a narrow circlet of
gold was hastily knocked up by a local smith. The right of crowning
Scots kings belonged to the Earl of Fife, an eleven-year-old boy in
in the hands of the English: his place was taken by his sister Lady
Buchan, who had stolen her husband's horses to get there, and was
said by the Balliol faction to be the mistress of the man she crowned.
In a hasty defiant trembling ceremony she put the gold circlet on
Robert Bruce's head; he was blessed with full solemnity as King
Robert by Wishart and by the Bishop of St Andrew's, also prepared
to chance his arm in the cause of freedom. Of Scotland's seven earls,
Lennox and Atholl were the only two who dared to swear fealty,
with about a hundred knights and gentlemen, Sir James Douglas,
Simon Fraser and Thomas Randolph among them. 'We are but King
and Queen of the May,' said Robert Bruce's wife, half English and
inclined to make frivolous comments.

She was nearly right. Though Bishop Wishart had absolved him,
Bruce's sacrilege had given his enemies a new impetus. On May 18th
Pope Clement V excommunicated him. Although now in a litter and
too ill to ride, terrible Edward stormed north again, his iron will
eating up the long counties as if they were fields, and by August the
coronation party were scattered to the summer winds. On the way to
safety in Orkney, Bruce's wife was captured at Tain, Mary Bruce and
Lady Buchan were both shut up in cages in Edward's Scottish castles,
and two of Bruce's brothers, Nigel and the clever and learned
Alexander, were hanged, drawn and quartered, as were Atholl and
Simon Fraser. Bruce himself, surprised at Methven, had narrowly
escaped capture and had taken to the heather, and Lennox, too,
was only saved by his hills; it was Arrochar for him once more.
Late in the year he went north across the Highlands with Bruce to

castigate the strong Balliol and pro-English faction of the Comyn and Buchan country in the north-east. The execution of Atholl in London caused a mild furore as there was an old-fashioned prejudice against the public gutting of earls; but the sacred claims of status were honoured by hanging him thirty feet higher than Simon Fraser, a knight.

Something had come alive in Bruce from that sudden killing in the church, from his brave crowning, from the slaughter of his brothers (and perhaps even from the undiscouraged spider he met on Rathlin Island this summer of his flight); something tough, inspiring and undefeatable; and now the English would be in for a traumatic experience. In the end he was to teach them that technology is not all. From the hills he gathered adherents; keeping up relentless partisan warfare on the collabos of eastern Scotland he came slowly to embody the hopes of all his countrymen. In a January midnight of 1314 he waded chest deep through the moat with a scaling ladder to capture the strong city of Perth, and on Shrove Tuesday of the same year Thomas Randolph led a party to the capture of Edinburgh Castle, another moonless night escapade, helped by a soldier who had used this precipitate route to visit a girl friend in the town in days when he had been garrisoned in the castle. In the spring Bruce attacked in the west, and together with Malcolm of Lennox, laid siege to Dumbarton Castle, held for the English by Lord Menteith. Menteith offered to surrender it to Bruce on condition he be given the earldom of Lennox as his reward: Malcolm, asked by Bruce, agreed to these hard terms, perhaps hoping to get his earldom back later. But between them, they conquered the castle without resort to this awkward condition; and Menteith, repentant of his backsliding in the English direction, was offered forgiveness if he would stand in the front rank at the battle of Bannockburn, agreed, and redeemed himself by a noble bash at the English in this capacity.

For now, ten years after the fall of Stirling Castle in Edward I's siege, its English garrison was threatened by the Scots under their indefatigable king, and from its walls the beleaguered soldiers were to witness a shattering event. On Midsummer Day of 1314 the cornered chivalry of England, smartly out-manoeuvred by Bruce, sank into the appalling black marsh around the Bannock burn, and Scotland shook free once more, lucky captors enriching themselves overnight with the ransoms of the few surviving English knights whom they had been spry enough to pluck out of the mêlée.

As often before and since, the English had underestimated their opponents. A light-hearted cavalcade rode towards Stirling in the soft air of midsummer eve: naturally Bruce would be seen off, just as Wallace had been at Falkirk; they would sleep the night in the dry of Stirling Castle, drinking, with any luck, the blood-red wine. Like Napoleon on the morning of Waterloo, they had practically ordered dinner in Brussels. Pennants streamed and armour glinted; the English army could hardly have had more colour and gleam if it had been laid on by Cecil B. de Mille. Watchers on the hills could see the bright panoply of war that so delighted Froissart: 'The fresh shining armour, the banners waving in the wind, the companions in good order, riding a soft pace.' Accoutred on spare-no-expense lines from the yield of rich acres, the English rode light, their heavy baggage waggons creaking along behind. The Scots soldiers carried their commissariat with them, sodden meat, a bag of oatmeal, and a griddle behind each man's saddle: the English, pressed to do like-wise with their flour ration, had instantly complained that the bread tasted of sweating horse and was uneatable; the project had had to be abandoned. The Achilles heel of this glittering force was their new king, Edward II, personally brave and as large and fair and handsome as his father; but both armies had already twigged that something was amiss, and Bruce announced that he feared the bones of the dead Edward more than he feared the living son. Edward II had disregarded his father's injunction to carry those terrible bones before him into battle. His favourite thing, apart from Piers Gaveston, was swimming: at Bannockburn he was quite lucky not to have to swim in full armour.

On rising ground above the rivers the small force of hardened irregulars that Bruce's personality held together waited in the waning light; less than eight thousand to the English sixteen. But armies that we are so bold as to call primitive had one advantage lacking to the later big battalions. They were small enough to be addressed by their leaders on the pros and cons of the next move, told in outline the how and why of approaching battle. So Robert the Bruce, having repelled two attacks and knowing to a T the value of morale, addressed his mottled clan-divided army in the mild evening outside Stirling (if we may believe John Barbour, who wrote in the same century as the fight).

Lordings, he said, we ought to love
Almighty God that sits above
That send us so fair beginning.
It is great discomforting
To our foes, that on this wise
So soon rebutted has been twice;

*   *   *

I trow and know it all clearly
That many a heart shall wavering be
That seemed before of great bounty;
And once the heart is discomfite
The body is not worth a mite.

He took counsel of them all, in the dawn of the next day, and said
he would fight or disperse, as they decided:

We lief your liking to fulfil.

They could fade into the hills, as they had so often done before,
leaving the English to trail home when the food ran out (except in
high summer fodder for their innumerable horses was always a
problem); or the Scots could seize this dangerous chance. All
agreed to fight. As Bruce pointed out, they had three excellent
reasons; they were in the right, the enemy had come 'to seek us in
our awne land'; victory over foes so rich would be plummy; and
above all:

The third is that we for our lives
And for our children and our wives
And for the freedom of our land
Are strained in battle for to stand.

Bruce had seen that the English would have no space to deploy
and make use of their superior numbers if he could catch them in the
bend of the river where they had camped the night. The English
cavalry, as ever, were a group of jolly young sirs avid for honour and
not particular about waiting for orders. As Bruce's schiltrons, like
great solid hedgehogs of spears, moved down the hill, the hot
sparks amongst the English chivalry plunged forward at them and
were there impaled; the infallible English archers had nowhere to fire
except at the backs of their own knights, and, attempting to advance
on the flanks, they were cut down by the small body of Scots horse

which Bruce had kept in reserve for this purpose. Compact and relentless, the Scots spearsmen came steadily on, and there was no mighty and quick-witted King Edward to save the day, only his feckless son, persuaded out when the day seemed lost and speeded on the way to safety by his knights, while the most famous of them, Sir Miles d' Argentine, returned to the shambles, pointing out that he was not spiritually geared for running away. Soon the English were wedged in their narrow space, the screaming horses backed on to the men behind them, and presently there was nothing left of the gleaming army but a desperate floundering mob in the dark peat bog and in the Bannock burn; so many bodies of men and horses that the pursuing Scots crossed over on them. Fifty years after, the poet Barbour, carving the Declaration of Arbroath into a more poignant form and leaving it as a lasting legacy to his countrymen, would write:

> Ah freedom is a noble thing
> Freedom makes man to have liking:*
> Freedom all solace to man gives,
> He lives at ease, that freely lives.
> A noble heart may have none ease
> Nor else nought that may him please
> If freedom fail him; for free liking
> Is yearned for o'er all other thing.

* Choice.

III

It was as brave and skilful a victory as ever was won against heavy odds, and the Scots, like the wild cataract, leapt in glory. Down came all the English castles with a merry thud—'Tour and wall rycht to the ground'—and six years later at Arbroath in 1320 Scotland inscribed her immortal defiance. All, declared those who put their seals to this letter to Pope John XXII (Lennox among them), were bound to Robert the Bruce, excommunicated though he had been for knocking off the Red Comyn in a church, bound 'both of right and by the service he has done, cheerfully enduring all manner of toil, fatigue, hardship and hazard, that he might deliver his people and his heritage from the hand of enemies'. No submission to the rule of England; in ringing words the Scots lords proclaimed that they fought 'not for glory, or riches, or honours, but only for liberty, which no true man would yield but with his life'. It was April, the cold waves pounded on the shore, strengthening the theme of isolation; sea-birds leaned on a wind still sharp with snow. They had been, the Scots told the pope, an independent kingdom for uncounted years, they had long defended their land against Angle, Dane and Norman. From the English they had suffered much; 'from these unnumbered ills' Robert Bruce had delivered them 'with the aid of Him who heals the wounded and makes whole'. And with no other aid, they might have added, but politely did not.

France had dropped them when the going got hard, and so, finally, had the pope's predecessor; even allowing the English to use crusade money to raise an army against them: they were on their own. (Scotland's most effective ally was Piers Gaveston: Edward II's passion for this foreign favourite kept the king and the English lords at loggerheads through the critical first years of his reign.) Be that as it might, 'so long as an hundred remain alive, we are minded never to bow to the dominion of the English,' declared the author of the

Declaration. Dear as King Robert was to them, they would throw him out tomorrow if he attempted submission. They besought the pope to keep on at the English king, until he allowed them to live in peace 'in this narrow plot of Scotland beyond which we have no habitation'. It is a cry greatly more moving than the American Declaration of Independence, and cluttered with no sentimental nonsense about the pursuit of happiness (a by-product state which tends to elude pursuers); yet the non-Scots who have ever heard of it could be counted on the fingers of two hands.*

The pope, now at Avignon and in the hands of the French, replied rather coldly to 'Robert Bruce calling himself king'; but this tireless character remained uncrestfallen, and continued to harry northern England in a series of lightning raids, extracting protection money from English towns even so far south as Ripon, until a battered war-weariness settled upon even the English. In the end a new pope did urge them to make peace, and from Gloucestershire had broken out 'shrieks of an agonizing king': Edward II's French wife Isabella and her lover Mortimer had turned on him and dethroned him: he was being done to death in Berkeley Castle. After his son and successor, the fifteen-year-old Edward III, had reduced himself to tears by his failure to catch and conquer the Scots (he would take it out on the French later), peace could at last be made. 'Final and perpetual peace' it announced itself; hope as ever triumphing over experience. Bruce was recognized as King Robert I; his son David was married to Edward III's sister; and they had such a rollicking wedding at Berwick that the stone walls of the churchyard were broken down and had to be sulkily mended by the parish. (This solution of political problems by the brushing aside of personal inclination is no longer practicable or we could have been in the Common Market in a trice by marrying Prince Charles to de Gaulle's grand-daughter; the old boy would never have resisted it.)

Bruce's re-admission to the fold by Pope John XXII followed; but the longed-for message, trailing leisurely over three countries, arrived too late; the Scots king had died at Cardross in the Lennox, a house he had swopped with Malcolm of Lennox for another. Forgiveness, unlike vengeance, moves slowly. Revenge will swim the swollen ford, while reconciliation hangs around in the riverside inn waiting for the waters to go down. Carrying Bruce's heart, Sir James

* Written before the 650th anniversary commemoration in 1970.

Douglas set off to bury it in the Holy Land; no pilgrimage in search of grace had been possible during the long life of this guerrilla king. Unable to resist a barney, Douglas was side-tracked into crusading against the Moors in Spain, where he died in battle. Throwing Bruce's heart ahead of him into the thick of the Moorish ranks— 'Forward, brave heart, where thou wert wont to go!'—he followed it up; while the Spaniards, more prudently, stayed put. Robert Bruce is an undescribed figure and stays shadowy, aside from the valour and greatness of his achievements, but his great lieutenant, Sir James Douglas, does not. Black-haired, sallow, intrepid and exceedingly good company, he was a *joli-laid* with a magnificent frame; so fine a swordsman that his face was unmarked after a hundred fights; and so compelling a leader that he was said to turn the most faint-hearted into leopards for courage. It is the tragedy of Ireland that they never had a Wallace, a Robert Bruce or a James Douglas, to beat the English at their own game and compel them to a union of equals without the diminution of anybody's individuality.

Bruce's four brothers had died fighting the English, and his son David II had no children, in spite of his jolly wedding. The Stewart dynasty inaugurated itself in a characteristic manner. Bruce's dear daughter Marjory had married the High Steward; a bad fall from her horse caused her death and the precipitate arrival of her son, who became Robert II in 1371, first of fourteen notably charming and accident-prone Stewart monarchs who petered out three hundred and fifty years later in good Queen Anne—only six of them died in their beds.

Malcolm, 5th Earl of Lennox, and married to a daughter of Donald, Earl of Mar, could seal the Arbroath Declaration with a flourish; he was a resistance hero and had been with Bruce through ups and downs, lost cause or winning cause. Bruce re-granted to Lennox his castle of Dumbarton, 'for his good deeds and services often rendered to us,' not all of which had been defensive; there had been a romp into England to devastate Northumberland and Cumberland and besiege Carlisle. The temper of the times was growing less pious; Malcolm was involved in a dispute with the Abbot of Paisley. Some tenants of his, Robert Reddehow and Joanna his wife, were involved in a tussle with the abbot over some land, 'maintaining a protracted obduracy of mind and irreverently contemning the Keys of the

Church as sons of perdition' (in 1294); and Malcolm had had the temerity to have the case tried in one of his own courts, though threatened by the Bishop of Glasgow with twelve local vicars 'clothed in white sacerdotal garments . . . with candles burning and bells ringing . . . personally advancing to the said earl, his depute baillies and others holding the court, warning them by name wholly to desist . . . also to warn all faithful Christians to avoid Robert Reddehow and Joanna his wife, and to place the lands and chapels of such as refused to obey under special interdict'. Two years later Malcolm had another brush with Robert, Bishop of Glasgow; and the Dean of the Lennox was sent to admonish him for trying to bring the Abbot of Paisley into his own civil court over the eleemosynary lands of the Church of Kilpatrick, which Malcolm's predecessors had granted. Who won is not known. But it had begun to appear likely that as soon as the Scots stopped fighting the English they would start fighting the Church.

In later years, growing more pious with age, or perhaps more cautious, Malcolm, 5th Earl, made it up with the Abbot of Paisley, granted more land to the Dean of Luss, and supporting yet another child on the throne (King David II, five-year-old orphan of Robert the Bruce), was killed fighting on his behalf at Halidon Hill in 1333; the brave schiltrons going down before the terrible arrows of Edward III's Welsh longbows, soon to massacre the French at Crécy. Gone was the final and perpetual peace; it had lasted five years. Such was the devastation of Dunbartonshire and Stirlingshire during these next years that the rental of the shires fell to a tenth of what it had been: the misery must have been appalling: perhaps all those well-endowed abbeys gave help; the Church in Scotland suffered no international twinges and was firmly pro-Scots. Whether John Napier returned from English imprisonment to a green if hungry old age in the Lennox is not known. Balliol's son, Edward Balliol, made a bid for the Scottish throne and a desultory war went on everywhere, fought with a ferocity sometimes tinged with humour— Lord Salisbury, kept out of Dunbar Castle for five months by Black Agnes, Dunbar's wife, complained,

> Came I early, came I late,
> I found Agnes at the gate.

Powerful lords looted the customs, and laid hold on other royal revenues. Hundreds were killed, and barbarous enough it seems, but in the east in these same years a grandson of Yenghiz Khan, Timur-i-lang, whom the west called Tamburlaine, had crossed the Hindu Kush and caused the whole of Delhi to swim in the blood of uncounted thousands, although luckily he disliked the Indian climate and went away again.

Donald, 6th Earl of Lennox, who had supported the king against Balliol, was appointed with others to treat with the English in 1357 for the redemption of King David II (captured and imprisoned for eleven years; the sum being demanded was the huge one of 100,000 marks of silver: even only partially paid it hampered Scotland for a century). On May 2nd, 1360, Donald obtained a charter of free forestry from the ransomed king at Perth; and later Donald's only child Margaret was married to a Lennox cousin, Walter of Faslane, who became 7th Earl of Lennox upon Donald's death and who swore allegiance to Robert II, the first Stewart, at Scone on March 16th, 1371.

So many of their kings were either small children, or in prisons, or both, that the power of the Scots earls was at this time little abated, and Walter, 7th Earl was granted the right of "weaponschawings", a muster of armed vassals, over the whole of the region of Lennox. Feudalism in its early stages was a sensible mutual-help arrangement, like life insurance—you dig for me and herd my kine while I protect you from our numerous outside enemies and we both eat in peace—though, like life insurance, it was more closely geared to the interests of its organizers, and in Scotland it was getting out of hand. Agamemnons of a greener Argos, the Lennoxes made the laws and did much as they liked, restrained only by spiritual bonds and the dreaded power of the Church to excommunicate. Here they might have stayed, performing in alliance with their Macfarlane sept the useful public service of containing the Campbells in their neighbouring domain, that had once been the kingdom of Dalriada, but fate ruled otherwise. Producing Duncan, Alexander, Alan, and Walter, the 7th Earl and his wife died around 1388, having, in a very modern manner, resigned the earldom in favour of their eldest son, who, in an ill day, tangled with the house of Stewart, who were to take his earldom from his just heirs and do it little credit.

*

The sun rose fairly upon Duncan, 8th Earl, regarding his large lands from the security of his main stronghold, the castle of Inchmurrin on an island in Loch Lomond. Castle building was still away ahead of sea-siege technique: nothing could shake Duncan here. In 1387 he, too, received a charter of weaponschawing from the ineffective King Robert II (son of Marjorie Bruce, and the first Stewart king). Ringed with his private army and the deep waters of the loch, Duncan, 8th Earl, could have felt he had little to fear; he was strong, proud and immovable as his surrounding hills. With his clan of followers, his long inheritance, his Highlanders at his back and his Lowlanders tilling the plains to the front, he seemed as rooted and triumphant as Ben Lomond, lifting its proud mountain head to his north-east. Like a little king he swept through his domains drawing his due in cain and conveth (which meant corn and hospitality for himself and his following), round the slopes of the hills, through the bogs below the Campsie fells, the cornlands of Fintry. Like a modern Briton or American, he was a racial mixture; an Anglo-Norseman from Northumbria, a Welsh Briton from Galloway, an Irish Scot from the Lennox; with perhaps a dash of the shadowy and artistic Pict thrown in, a suspicion of a spicing from France. (Anglo-Saxon is a nonsense of a modern word, applied by General de Gaulle to modern America or Britain when feeling indignation against them; unfair to Hengist, and unfair to Horsa, who are far from being to blame for everything.)

Duncan took part in no fights or factions, or none that are on record: all his charters are of private feudal transactions—lands to John Kennedy in 1393, lands to Walter Buchanan next year, signed at Inchmurrin. One major weakness troubled Duncan, 8th Earl; he had no sons. He made all as secure as he knew how by marrying Isabella, eldest of his three daughters, to Murdoch Stewart, nephew of King Robert III, in February of 1391 at Inchmurrin. This marriage would unite the earldoms of Lennox, Fife, and Menteith. But Murdoch's dangerous father, Earl of Fife, had been made Duke of Albany by his brother, King Robert III at the same time as the king made his own eldest son Duke of Rothesay: these were the first two Scottish dukes. Albany was the ambitious younger brother of a weak king with only two sons; a situation liable to go to the strongest of fourteenth century heads.

But all seemed set fair for Duncan's posterity. In 1393 he resigned his earldom to King Robert III at Dunfermline, and had it renewed to descend in the direct female line. Failing any children of Isabella's there was his next daughter Margaret, married to Robert Menteith of Rosko (whose only son died young leaving two little daughters, the elder married John Napier of Merchiston, the younger, Haldane of Gleneagles).

Duncan, 8th Earl's youngest daughter was also, with rather less of a flourish of trumpets, married to a rather less glorious Stewart, with the unfamiliar name of Derneley. In any case all this seemed of little importance to old Duncan, as Isabella quickly produced four fine upstanding boys, Robert, Walter, James and Alexander; spoilt, attractive, damaging Stewarts, fated to an abrupt end.

In these years the history of Scotland takes another turn into the murk; the three witches must have given the cauldron another mighty stir. Not only did the Black Death stalk abroad, but weak kings bred dissension, and parts of Scotland were still in English hands, which made it difficult for the Scots to concentrate on anything beyond the immediate problem of getting them out. The willing French were summoned in to help, but at first, 'the Auld Alliance' was a great unsuccess. The French complained of 'hard beds and ill nights,' and the Scots openly asked, 'Who needs them?' Financially, Greek had met Greek: they were instantly at odds about who paid for what. The French insisted on pitched, tournament-type, battles on flat fields where they could deploy their heavy tanks which then took the form of armoured knights: the Scots, used to nipping up and down their steep hills in light armour, knew that their best hope was to harry and guerrilla the English, more numerous and better armed than they were. (The alliance worked better in France, where the Scots fought under Joan of Arc's banner and later formed the Scots Guard of the French kings; though even there the French continued to mutter at the inordinate appetites of Scots soldiers.) But at home Scotland was 'nocht governit'. Throughout Europe there was loss of confidence and deathly gloom from the continuing effects of the Black Death—that pestilence which no prayers could halt—the shock of loss, the mortal depression of the survivors as the black plague kept breaking out anew. Everyone fought, and invading Mongols added to the general slump by closing the eastern trade routes.

Because of King Robert III's invalidism, his brother, Albany (Isabella of Lennox's father-in-law), became Governor of the now unhappy realm of Scotland. It was thought sinister that he had taken the title of Albany, ancient name of the major part of Scotland: what was he up to? More sinister still was the fate of Rothesay, the king's eldest son, a highly unpromising young man, who had abandoned two wives before he was twenty, one of them a Douglas, and who died in mysterious circumstances when in one of Albany's castles with a Black Douglas in charge. There was a strong rumour that he had been starved to death, for the *mores* of the Black Douglases had slipped a little since the days of good Sir James, and of the second Earl who fought Hotspur at Otterburn: ('My wound is deep I fain would sleep.')

The old King Robert III was increasingly ailing—he had been kicked in the spine in his youth by a horse—and now only his second son, the seven-year-old James, stood between Albany and the throne. The king quickly sent James to France for safety; he was captured at sea off Flamborough Head and taken to England where he became a lucky hostage for Henry IV. On hearing this news King Robert employed that useful technique which has been lost to the western world but which still exists in primitive and un-sophisticated races; he turned his face to the wall and died. He had first uttered his own epitaph: 'Here lies the worst of kings and most miserable of men.'

Even if the boy, James, should be ransomed, he would have to face not only the hazards of Albany's protection but also the complicating existence of innumerable second cousins whose right to the throne was in the eyes of many better than his. In his marriages as well as in his rule James's grandfather, Robert II, the first Stewart king, had been singularly inept. Failing to wait for the necessary papal dis-pensation (he and Elizabeth Mure came within the prohibited closeness of blood), the king had four sons and several daughters by Elizabeth Mure in the ten years before they were able to be married; an unkingly circumstance which shocked the Scots as much then as it would now; for since the days of William the Conqueror there had not been very much future in royal illegitimacy: it was on too vast a scale. Marriage legitimized Robert's first family in the end; but their birth out of wedlock gave a powerful lever to other sons, and to his second wife, Euphemia Ross, King Robert had been unquestionably wed. This fact made her innumerable descendants quite unable to settle to a regular job—Douglases, Hamiltons, Stewarts and Malise Grahams, jockeying for position at the expense of all peace and stability—they hung around for two hundred years, haunted by the superior morality of Euphemia Ross and hoping one day to scoop the pool. Nor were their chances slim, in an age of such high mortality: at any minute they might find themselves under starter's orders in the race for the throne. Jameses I, II, and III were all under twelve when they became kings, James IV sixteen, Jameses V and VI were under two; Mary was Queen of Scots at a week old. A solid core of loyalty was indispensable to their survival. Hovering second cousins menaced all these luckless babes, and made life uneasy for practically everybody else. All the same, none of the little Stewart princes were smothered at midnight by their uncles: were the Scots after all more humane than the English?

Humanity on a wide scale did not yet bloom in a world still inconceivably harsh. Monasteries, in their early days, were rare havens of enlightenment and hope; bands of devout and simple men in coarse robes, praying, healing, digging, translating, recording, while the clans came roaring over the hill. Outside them medieval Europe, forested, silent, isolated, was far from being all birdsong, clean air, and unravished woodland. Even unvisited forest held less of mighty trees and level turf and much more of impassable woodland clutter— thorn thicket, dead trunks and branches drowned in bramble, and lethal black bog. The smiling wooded hills of Scotland held innumerable birds and also innumerable wolves and robbers. What with pneumonia and other pulmonary diseases of winter, people were lucky to see another spring: the summer assaults of dysentery, marsh fevers, and after 1348 bubonic plague (which came from the east along with arithmetic, knitting, astronomy and other useful things) made them almost as fortunate to see another autumn with its saving frosts to kill the all-triumphant infections.

The rural poor, if they escaped starvation, had the best survival chances, as they were not menaced by the attentions of medieval doctors, being left to the milder mercies of the village wise-women, who were binding up their wounds with mould-covered rags centuries before the bright dawn of Sir Alexander Fleming and penicillin. And in war the poor did at least escape the knightly fate of being parboiled under their armour whenever the sun came out. It was indeed the survival of the fittest and not always even of them. To grow up at all was still a major achievement; needing co-operative parents, immense determination, the constitution of an ox, and above all, luck.

In the country the peasants had at any rate two-roomed huts, fresh air, room to grow food, and all outdoor space in which to excrete. In towns the rich had cess-pits for this purpose, and the middling well-to-do had privies in the back garden. The urban poor, always the most ill done by, lived in whole families in one unventilated and unlit room off an alley, and were obliged to go some way to the public hole which consisted of loose planks over a pit, into which the luckless, the unwary, or the drunk sometimes fell and were drowned. Mortality in the towns was so high that their populations had constantly to be replenished from the healthier countryside.

As against these miseries, it must be said that everyone enjoyed what totted up to around eight weeks of holiday in the year; the inviolable holy days insisted upon by the Church.

Over this huddled-together, freely procreating, and narrowly surviving world of humanity—like killer sharks above shoals of predatory and bewildered small fish—great lords incalculably loomed and flashed; attacking, retreating, circling for renewed assault like ocean monsters indefatigable in their energies and in their greed. To their contemporaries these activities doubtless seemed quite run of the mill and inevitable; if not exactly agreeable they had become acceptable to the piteous expectations of the poor. And yet, unlike sharks, the great lords who ruled like minor kings sometimes reveal a human face. Granting a net on his water of Leven to the Abbot of Paisley, Malcolm, 3rd Earl of Lennox, in 1230 grants also the protection of his men-at-arms to the monks in the dangerous places where this would lead them. Benefactions extend not only to the locals, but to the monks of Arbroath on the other side of Scotland. No sooner condemned for their careless arrogance than the barons abash us by their lavish generosity, giving away whole parishes, entire rich valleys, as if they were half-crowns. Not all of life is oceanic: a kind of system exists. A charter of Donald, 6th Earl of Lennox, in the 1340s stipulates as the terms of the lease 'to be held of the granter for one cheese for each house in which cheese is made in these lands for the King's army, when need arises'. The lords succoured the abbeys and fed the troops for defence, the abbeys succoured the sick and fed the poor at need. Faith, a powerful mortar, clamped the stones of civilized living and bound men together. And in the darkest hours of terror or tribulation there was the blazing hope of a better life hereafter.

Over this troubled Scotland Albany now ruled as virtual king. It was a Scotland still in dire financial unease: Edward Balliol's partly successful attempt to get back the throne after Bruce's death and the consequent war and harrying, and the huge ransom exacted by the English for captured King David II, had drained the throne of money, slowed down the development of the country, and meant that subsequent kings had not the finances to form a strong government. James I, only surviving son of the melancholy Robert III, and still a small boy, was held prisoner at Windsor. Albany was regent; but without the blest authority of king. Who are the Stewarts, anyway? other Scots nobles, particularly Atholl and Douglas, had long been demanding in loud effective voices. Had not Robert II, when still only High Steward, run away at the battle of Neville's Cross in England and allowed Robert Bruce's young son David II to be captured by the English? Such events were not easily forgotten in a proud harsh age, when physical courage and clan loyalty were the prime virtues; and the other powerful Scots earls, growing over-mighty, moved in still further on the central power. If Albany thought he could usurp, he might have a sharp surprise due.

It seemed clear enough that Albany did not really desire the return of young James I. His scant attempts to buy his nephew out of English captivity were underlined when his own son, Murdoch, captured in battle by Hotspur, was ransomed for an immediate cash payment, instead of the more usual instalment system. The Albanys began to wear the look of those moving in for the kill. At this point Scotland was saved from dissolution into a sea of warring families by the intervention of a poet in his twenties.

A few more grim and dicey years must intervene, while Duncan 8th Earl grew older and perhaps more anxious in his lake fortress on Loch Lomond, and his daughter Isabella ever more rattled about her family. In 1420 Murdoch, who was her husband, succeeded his father as Duke of Albany and became Regent of Scotland without question. More arrogant and much less effective than his father, he cut very little ice as a ruler; it was said that even his own sons made light of his authority. Isabella, who loved them all, seemed powerless to calm them down; swept clean out of her milder Lennox ambience into a Stewart world of ambition and disaster, she may have apprehended but she could not act.

*

For the imprisoned King James was growing up, no fool and no weakling. Looking out of his window at Windsor he had seen Joanna Beaufort walking in the garden:

> '. . . my wits all
> Were so o'ercome with pleasance and delight
> Only through letting of mine eyen fall
> That suddenly my heart became her thrall
> For ever of free will; for of menace
> There was no token in her sweet face.'

This was as well, as there was plenty of menace in every other arc of James's horizon.

He succeeded in marrying her; and from his mild captivity he confirmed the founding of St Andrews in 1412, Scotland's first university. He observed at close hand the power exercised by English kings, and nursed his well-founded suspicions of Albany. He also went on writing poetry; it is thought that the poem 'The King's Quhair' was written by him in honour of Joanna.

> Come summer, come the sweet season and sun!
> Awake, for shame, that have your heavens won,
> And amorously lift up your heades all,
> Thank Love, that list you to his mercy call!

These charming sentiments did not prevent him from keeping a shrewd eye upon the situation in Scotland.

He was not the only poet prince in captivity. Another castle, Bolingbroke in Lincolnshire, sounded to the songs of Charles of Orleans, plucked from under a pile of slain at Agincourt to endure twenty-five years of English imprisonment. Gloomier and perhaps more sensitive than James, '*Je suis cellui au cueur vestu de noir,*' he mourned; and to his young wife, Bonne of Armagnac,

> Pour ce que veoir ne vous puis
> Mon cueur se complaint jours et nuis,
> Belle, nompareille de France.

The prisoner's pangs of jealousy also assailed him,

Soies seure, ma doulce amie,
Que je vous ayme loyaument.
Or, vous requier et vous supplie
Acquittiez vous pareillement.

She wrote back, '*Mon seul amy, mon bien, ma joye*,' but died before his release. It is sad that he and the young King of Scots never came together to exchange their verses, but a getting together of French and Scots was England's major haunt. (The Auld Alliance was going well; had been sealed in blood: Earl Douglas (black) fighting for France, had been killed in the defeat at Verneuil in Normandy by English and Burgundian forces, as had also Earl Buchan.) It is also sad that kings no more write poetry: if the Duke of Edinburgh were to publish a slim volume of verse the share market would drop like a stone and the Bank of England probably have to close its doors.

As well as the latest fashions in poetry, young King James had learned some statecraft in England. His captor, Henry IV, had started life as an earl, had usurped the throne from his cousin, Richard II, and was now established King of England; the Scots king took the hint; from James I onwards the Stewarts stopped being merely the most successful amongst powerful earls and were Kings of Scotland indeed.

Ransomed in 1424, James returned to his own; escorted north by a welcoming party including Duncan, 8th Earl of Lennox, he was crowned at Scone, and at once took steps to put the Scots lords in their places. New and rigorous laws were made to curb such characters as his uncle Alexander, the Wolf of Badenoch, who was ravaging the north coast. 'If God grant me life,' James declared, 'though it be but the life of a dog, there shall be no place in my realm where the key shall not keep the castle and the bracken bush the cow.' Even the potent and unreachable Lord of the Isles was to be brought to heel. A first necessary step was the removal of cousin Albany. Summarily tried, with the king himself presiding, he was beheaded on the hill outside the walls of Stirling, whence, as Sir Walter Scott romantically pointed out, he could see in the distance the great palace he had built and reigned in as a king. With him was executed, for no known reason except the close relationship, his seventy-nine-year-old father-in-law, Duncan, Earl of Lennox, and also two of Albany and Isabella Lennox's sons, Walter and Alexander, described by one contemporary as 'men of princely stature and lovely person, wise, agreeable, and universally beloved', although others held the view that they were too uppish by half, and only got what was coming to them. James, the second brother, alone escaped. Pausing only to sack and burn Dumbarton *en route*, as a last gesture of defiance to King James, he fled to Ireland: his less lucky accomplices were captured and given the wild horse treatment outside the walls of Stirling, below that mound so aptly named the Heading Hill.

As soon as the execution of Albany and family was done, the king's emissaries rode to Tantallon, the dreaded stronghold in East Lothian where Isabella, Duchess of Albany, and now Countess of Lennox by her father's execution, was under durance; waiting in hope for the return of her family. She was, it is recorded, a woman of calm and firm mind; and she had need to be. The messengers cast in her lap a bloody clout, which, when unfolded, revealed the heads of her father, her husband, and two of her sons.

This was policy as well as cruelty. If Isabella could be shocked into crying out against the king, it could be interpreted as treason and her lands could be claimed for the Crown, as well as the already forfeited domains of Albany. But Isabella kept her head, in every sense. 'If these were traitors,' she said, 'the King has rightly done,' thus keeping her lands for herself and her family without admitting any guilt. It has always been tough at the top, with the upper lip forever to be stiffened.

After this bloody start, King James proved himself a just and fearless king, although it is not on record that he wrote any more poetry. He widened the structure of Parliament, insisted that law be the same for everybody, created the central legal machinery which became the Court of Session; and when in 1429 the Lord of the Isles was so rash as to lead the clansmen to the burning of Inverness, James I leapt up the Great Glen, and the mighty Islander soon succeeded Isabella of Lennox as a prisoner listening to the waves beating on the rocks below Tantallon. James I was a lover of the arts, of good living; he was extravagant and perhaps acquisitive. He seemed so to the Church, with whom he tangled when he discovered what immense amounts of Crown property his predecessor, King David I, had made over to them—'he was a sair saint to the Croun,' James pointed out ruefully —and when he opposed the sending of three or four thousand golden florins to Rome from impoverished Scotland every time a bishop was appointed, causing Pope Eugenius IV to complain that the bishops of Scotland, who backed James, were more like Pilates than prelates.

James I gave good justice and laid down that 'a lele and a wys advocate' was to be provided to help 'ony pur creatur' who could not pay one to plead his cause. Within a week of his coronation he had passed through Parliament acts prohibiting private war, riding through the country with excessive followings, and rebellion and failure to give aid against rebellion, under pain of forfeiture of life, land and goods; and appointed 'officers of the law who can and may hold the law to the people.' Like a new sheriff in the Wild West, he would be intimidated by no gangs.

But they got him. Like so many Stewarts, James alas was short-lived. His son James II was only a boy of six when in 1437 his father was murdered, sitting at supper with his wife Joanna in the House of the Black Friars at Perth. 'Thow cruell tirant, quod Grame to hym, thow hadst nevyr mercy of lordes borne of thy blode, ne of none other gentilman that came yn thy dawnger—therefor no mercy shalt thow have here.'

This sentiment was not generally echoed; and in the cataclysm of conspiracy Isabella Lennox took no part. Released from Tantallon some months after her family's execution, she was allowed back to Inchmurrin and lived on for long years. Loch Lomond darkened in winter after winter, spring mornings lit the high top of Ben Lomond, the waters shone with summer, the trees of the lakeside flamed into autumn yet again. Joan of Arc was burned to death in the market place at Rouen, and in blood and tumult Byzantium fell to the Turks, and still Isabella lived on to the sound of the water lapping on the pebbled shore of her island. What did she think of, sitting on a stiff chair in a draughty room, with the ghosts of those severed heads lying in her lap? Her soul, perhaps, mainly: her benefactions were enormous. Like King David I in the twelfth century who

> . . . illumined in his days
> His land with kirks and with abbays

Isabella continued to light up the Lennox. The Church was in trouble, the simultaneous popes had shaken her morale. (England and Scotland, needless to say, backed rival candidates.) A man called Resby had already been burned at Perth for preaching Wycliff's doctrine of the supremacy of the individual conscience to a Scotland that—living in individual valleys—was very ready to listen. Isabella also cherished her son James's seven illegitimate sons, for James Stewart's exile in Ireland, though unmarried, had not been unprolific. (Natural children in the middle ages were almost a privileged class; as they could not inherit anything it was worth no one's while to starve them to death or stab them at supper: these grew up, acquired land, and founded the family of Lennox of Woodhead.) Like other nobles Isabella kept a huge household; there was still very little coin available and if rents are paid in vast quantities of meat, fish, eggs and other foodstuffs there must be somebody there to eat it—the armed followers or servants whose presence, more effectively than the law, secured her rights. Perhaps it was partly to ease out of this overcrowded scene that Isabella shed the load of some of her huge possessions. Though gorgeously robed, sumptuously fed and even sometimes educated, a noble still must move from castle to castle as their privies became intolerable: the noses of smaller fry had perforce to harden; and in the towns disease was still rife.

Isabella's benefactions continued unabated: Kilmarnock to the Prior of Glasgow, 'for the welfare of our soul and for the soul of our dearest husband of blessed memory, Sir Murdoch, Lord Duke of Albany, and for the souls of the deceased Sir Duncan, Earl of Lennox, our progenitor, and for the souls of Walter, James, and Alexander, our deceased sons, and for the souls of all who have died in the faith'; and lands to the collegiate Church of Dumbarton, and money to found three more churches in the Lennox; at Fintry, Strathblane, and Bonhill. All this 'with the consent and assent of our dearest sister-german, Margaret', who also signed with Isabella, and whose grand-daughter had married John Napier.

That the Church was only just holding at bay the older cults, still dreaded the power of witchcraft, was still battling with superstitious terrors as well as with divergent views, is clear enough from the burning in 1431 of Joan of Arc. The English since Crécy and Agincourt had taken too low a view of their French opponents and were certain to consider that anyone who could lead the demoralized French army into giving them a sound thrashing must be in league with the devil. Nothing can excuse her execution by the English forces at Rouen; but the French were seemingly quite as much frightened by this holy and astonishing girl as the English were. Or why did Charles of Orleans, her exact contemporary and a

James V was a son of Margaret Tudor, and father of Mary Queen of Scots. He built palaces, hanged Johnny Armstrong the Border gangster but neglected other abuses. He had ten natural children, and died after defeat at Solway Moss, though only thirty and apparently healthy. *Scottish National Portrait Gallery*

Logarithms John—John Napier, 8th Laird of Merchiston, from an engraving after his portrait by George Jamesone. *By kind permission of Lord Napier and Ettrick.*

ceaseless political correspondent upon Anglo-French affairs, never once mention her name; or the king whose crowning she had made possible not ransom her; or the brave Dunois, in the neighbour-hood of Rouen during her trial and in command of a powerful and disengaged army, make no attempt to rescue her? Of the fifty-two judges who tried and condemned her, fifty-one were Frenchmen. She was tricked by the priests and executed for heresy: it took five hundred years for her to be canonized. And in Paris, during her trial, a whole family were dragged from their house and burnt to death without trial by the French authorities only for saying they thought Joan came from God. These facts have quietly faded from the French consciousness; and it is as if the English had, in 1927, burnt to death Suzanne Lenglen for being better at tennis.

Isabella of Lennox at any rate was taking no chances in the 1400s with the powers of darkness. With land, buildings, endowments, with prayers, masses, chantries, with lavish giving to the Church she would defeat the powers of hell and buy back those loved souls whose headless bodies had tumbled so long ago on the bitter hill outside the walls of Stirling, condemned for treachery and rebellion. She lived to be nearly eighty, fifty years childless—for James Stewart had long since died in Ireland—and a widow; and who now would inherit the Honor of Lennox? Shrewdness and persistence in the form of the Haldanes? Loyalty and integrity in the form of the Napiers? But coming up now on the outside are those dark horses the younger branch of Stewarts; and it takes more than the decapitation of half a dozen of their kinsmen to daunt that élan and that ambition.

Part II

Merchiston and Five King Jameses

IV

Slowly through the fourteenth and fifteenth century, the documents have begun to tell more. A Lennox kinsman, William Napier of Kilmahew in the Lennox, son of John de Napier who defended Stirling, has charters from King David II for lands in Perthshire, from King Robert II in 1376, from Robert III in 1390; a safe conduct in 1398 from King Richard of England for himself and fourteen servants, 'as many horse as foot', to go into that country, where, if he was lucky, he heard some famous voices. The medieval west had long known—none better—how to create in carving and in stone: words and music were now on the way. Soon the dawn chorus of Chaucer and Barbour, of Charles, Duke of Orleans, and of James, King of Scotland, swells gradually into the full-throated roar of a renaissance summer.

No longer quite so hazed, we begin to discern individual faces, to hear separate voices. William Napier of Kilmahew's son, John, perhaps his younger, takes off for Edinburgh, maybe to sell his father's wool, makes good, goes on selling it, stays there. His son, another William, is by 1401 Governor of that frontier fortress, Edinburgh Castle; helps to confront Henry IV of England's invasion; later pleads unsuccessfully as co-heir to the earldom of Lennox, and is lost to sight. The mists from the as yet unfilled in loch at the foot of the castle swirl up around its battlements, and William Napier disappears behind them, living how, dying when? But now at last the light strengthens: our remote parents seem occasionally to take off those stifling visors and come up for air. The long faces of stone or manuscript no longer regard us with a formalized expressionless gaze: limbs are less permanently encumbered in those sweeping cumbersome robes. The miniskirt appears, at least for men, causing no doubt a grave drawing in of breath from the older generation as they contemplated those interminable legs, stockinged in gay colours, and brooded about the morals that went with them.

In 1433 William's son, Alexander Napier, Provost of Edinburgh, holding Merchiston from James I of Scotland, entertains the French ambassador, Reginald Giraud, who came to Scotland in 1435 to escort James I's daughter, Princess Margaret of Scotland, to Paris for her marriage with the Dauphin (who unluckily turned into Louis XI); goes as one of the commissioners for Scotland to meet the English ambassador at Newcastle to arrange a three years' truce. He has not only a name and a place and a time, an inscribed coat of arms and a remembered legend, he has continuity of written record. His son, Sir Alexander Napier of Merchiston, has even, on a pillar high up in St. Giles' Cathedral, a distinctive stone visage. The far distant past suddenly looks out at us with a familiar, mocking, non-medieval face.

For enthusiasts with the battle-axe the party was by no means over, though even feudal rivals, even distantly-based Highlanders had sunk their differences and fought at Bannockburn side by side. The iron of Edward's hammer had briefly banged Scotland into a nation; they never forgot the glowing feeling. Now England, in travail with the birth of the York-and-Lancastrian continuing house of Tudor, was deep in the Wars of the Roses, and their ravaged northern neighbours could take breath at least from invasion. Sir Alexander Napier's Edinburgh, enjoying a lull from being burnt, and even a kind of prosperity, was full of the ring of mallet and chisel as the new stone buildings took shape along the ridge. Froissart, the French chronicler, staying with King David II in around 1360, had noted that though Edinburgh consisted mainly of a single street of thatched wooden houses, the nobles were gallant, the peasants were sturdy, and everybody was hospitable. Fifty years later some of the daub-and-wattle houses which English King Richard II had burnt were being replaced by 'tall houses of hewn stone with glass windows and many chimneys, full of fine furnishings', the Spanish envoy reported. St Giles, briefly to be Edinburgh's cathedral, was being rebuilt; over the fifteenth century the splendid pinnacled crown-spire was gradually rising. The second Sir Alexander Napier of Merchiston was provost for seven years while the choir of St Giles was building, and gave the altar of St Salvador and put his Lennox arms and his own face on the capital of one of the pillars.

As a young man he had been badly wounded fighting for the widowed queen who had been Joanna Beaufort: did her sweet face, after all that had happened since James I had looked out of the window and seen it at Windsor, still hold no token of menace? Her grandfather, John of Gaunt, was famous among other things for being the only Englishman who refrained from burning Edinburgh to the ground when he had the chance, and no very harsh action is recorded of Joanna, who later married another James Stewart, this time the Black Knight of Lorne. She and the new king, six-year-old James II, survivor of her twin boys (the Stewart accident-proneness included a tendency to twins), had been imprisoned by the Livingstones in Stirling Castle, for upon James I's death chaos had come again; the careful house of law and order that the king had built undergoing a series of rude shocks. The little king's powerful guardian, a Black Douglas (black as to hair rather than skin), had died of plague, of the 'pestilence without mercy' type, guaranteed to kill within twenty-four hours all those who caught it. Once this strong if violent hand was removed, Stewarts, Ogilvys and Lindsays, Ruthvens, Humes and Hepburns instantly fell upon each other; Boyds, Livingstones and Crichtons had now, too, won through into the private-army income group, as who should move into the Jaguar belt, and laid on with a right good will. Even James Kennedy, the saintly and spirited Bishop of St Andrews and a grandson of King Robert II, wielding ex-communication like a powerful broadsword, was unable to sort them out; though he achieved a kind of posthumous success when the body of Lord Crawford, unshriven and unhouseled, lay out for a week because no one dared to bury him.

In 1439 Alexander Napier and others rescued the queen and her son from Stirling and he was later given a handsome piece of Perth-shire for his pains—'our beloved Alexander Nepare, for his constant and faithful services bestowed upon the late Queen, our most dear mother, and in recompense of grievous injuries and wounds . . . All and whole our lands of Philde'—on March 7th, 1449.

The lead-up to this had been the seizure, by Alexander Livingstone, Governor of Stirling Castle, of Queen Joanna's second husband, and of his brother William Stewart; after which, according to the terse description of the contemporary Boswell of Auchinleck MSS, the Livingstones 'put them in pittis and bollit them'. Alexander Napier, defending the queen from Livingstone attack, was lucky enough to escape this culinary fate, being only badly wounded. Upon his accession ten years later the young James II moved swiftly. Livingstone, now governor of Dumbarton Castle, was seized by James on September 23rd at Castle Doune and he and three other Livingstones and followers suffered an obscure fate. 'The principall trispassours', records the Auchinleck MSS, were 'put in the Blacknes and their gudes tane'.

Meanwhile during James II's minority the free for all had continued. It was, records Pitscottie, a time when 'the whole youth of Scotland began to rage in mischief and lust . . he was esteemed the greatest man of renown and fame that was the greatest brigand, thief, and murderer'. The breakdown of honour, order, and good faith seemed complete. Two boy Douglases, summoned to dinner in Edinburgh Castle by Crichton and Livingstone, were murdered at the meal. But things are rarely so bad that no one has the heart to write a rude verse about them:

> Edinburgh Castle, Toune and Towre
> God grant thou sinke for sinne,
> And that e'en for the black Dinoir
> Earl Douglas gat therein

wrote some stout citizen, probably of Glasgow, in 1439. The only ray of sunlight on this smoky scene was that the current Black Douglas, James, 7th Earl, was too fat to move.

As far as stirring up trouble went, the Black Douglases, who had done this successfully for a hundred years or so, had now more or less shot their bolt. In the fifteenth century, Gavin Douglas of the Red Douglases so far forgot himself as to translate the *Aeneid*, and even to write some moving poetry of his own. Black were being superseded by Red Douglases. Brave as these descendants of the good Sir James Douglas were, they were not above treachery, owned half Scotland between them, and intrigued with the English and with the Highlanders. King James II, who was birth-marked, was known as James of the Fiery Face, but the fire was not confined to his visage, and as soon as he was twenty-one, he invited the new Black Douglas to Stirling Castle (on a safe-conduct), and having failed in argument to persuade him to break up his conspiring alliances, lost his temper and stabbed him. Those about the king had no hesitation in finishing the task. It is not known whether Sir Alexander Napier was amongst those present; he was Comptroller of the Household to James II from 1449 to 1461, duties which may or may not have included giving the *coup de grace* to Black Douglases. Besides Merchiston, and other lands a few miles outside the walls of Edinburgh, he held a charter of the lands of Lindores and Kinloch in Fife, and James II's reward for services rendered in rescuing his mother, the lands of Philde or Filledy near Methven, a rich rolling country in central Perthshire, red-earthed and well-wooded between ranges of grey surrounding hills.

Sometime in the 1460s, on an outcrop of upper old red sandstone on the south-western approaches to Edinburgh, Sir Alexander built Merchiston Tower, of the same stone as the twelve feet deep bed of rock on which it rests, a strong L-shaped fortress five stone floors high. Built of very large stones with small pinnings of the same stones in its joints, the dressed work droved or dunted in a free manner with a very broad chisel, its wing was to the north; a bold unbroken south front faced all comers. The tower was strengthened by an outwork of barmkin wall, probably ten or twelve feet high, surrounding a courtyard; and entrance to it was by steps inside the barmkin connecting with a drawbridge lowered from the tower at its second floor, which contained the great hall, principal rooms and kitchen. Above were solar and sleeping rooms, below were store rooms, and a ground floor was for cattle at need; all floors being connected only by spiral staircases in the walls. In this the Napiers lived, on and off, till 1914. The rosy-grey rock has weathered so well, over its five centuries, that there is now little difference between the look of the outer stone and the interior.

In conception and execution it was totally a Scots building, but Scotland was beginning to be a little more outward looking, and the builder himself had travelled.

Alexander Napier was sent on an embassy to England in 1461 and signed a three-year truce, taking the opportunity to go on a pilgrimage to the shrine of St Thomas à Becket at Canterbury. Henry VI gave him a free and safe conduct for whenever he wanted to come into England, which must have been useful during those intervals when Henry was actually in possession of the throne. Alexander became 'Maister of Houshald' in 1461, Vice-Admiral of Scotland

3*

'For his lele and trewe service done of lang tyme to us and our progenitories of most noble mynd,' and Searcher of the port and haven of Leith, thus getting a grip on the customs dues for the infant James III, for the King of Scotland was by now once again a child. In the previous year James II of the Fiery Face, who had at length achieved a hold on his kingdom, burning the castles of the Black Douglases and driving them into England (where they remained a headache to both countries for some while to come), fell to a fatal accident. An enthusiast for new technology, and becoming too interested in one of his own guns when besieging the castle of Roxburgh, he had blown himself up and died at the age of thirty.

It would be interesting if Alexander Napier had recorded his impressions of abroad. Climate and terrain had made the Scots hard workers and frugal livers, qualities which would help Scots settlers to flourish in every corner of the globe: in general their comments upon more easy-living neighbours are sardonically descriptive. What did Alexander Napier, that cool customer, make of Burgundy, England, Denmark? Did he teach his children that there were interesting lands beyond the Tweed? Coming from a land whose only pictures as yet were wall-paintings, manuscripts, and church windows, did he gaze spell-bound at those early Flemish masterpieces in the Low Countries, in which, however sombre a catastrophe or how solemn an event fills the foreground, the distance reveals always a landscape bathed in bright and tender light?

Embassies for the infant King James III took Alexander Napier to Bruges, where Scotland had much trade, and Burgundy, to the court of Charles the Bold, that gorgeous and overbearing duke, whom the king addressed as 'his derrest coussing and confederat' and thanked for 'his hertly and tendre ressaving of his last ambaxate'; and again to King Henry in England, brushing his way through the sundry affrays of Lancaster and York. Far from being heartly and tender, Charles the Bold, a French prince of the blood, was possibly the most unashamed gangster of the age, and had openly admitted to setting his men on to murder Louis of Orleans, younger brother of the French king and his own first cousin, on no other grounds than personal dislike and envy. Burgundy's tenderness was perhaps for the pickled salmon which flowed into his dukedom from the rivers of Scotland. King James III's message, delivered by Alexander, was fairly crisp. What about the men-at-arms his dearest cousin and confederate had promised him if he kept the truce with England?

Burgundy had recently been at him demanding 'ane new abstinance of war', and James had sent 'his treue and famuliar knicht Schir Alexander Nepare' to say that this was all very well, but Scotland had both by sea and land 'sustenit great sketh and dampnage unredressut'. What about Burgundy's keeping his end of the truce and making England disgorge for all this scaith and damage? Would the duke now send 'autentic letters with personnis of fame and auctorite to the said King Edward [IV], to mak him redress incontinent the barge broken at Balmburgh'? A treaty is a treaty is a treaty. And would Burgundy call to mind his promise and his father's promise that the King of Scots' merchants had licence to set up their trading staples 'in ony toune of his cuntrie'?

With Andrew Stewart, Lord Chancellor, Alexander Napier went to Denmark to negotiate a royal marriage, maybe in rather smoother language. Andrew Stewart was the eldest natural son of James, Isabella of Lennox's second son who had fled to Ireland, and was an equivocal character. He became Lord Avandale, muscled in on the dispute over the Lennox inheritance where he made as much trouble as possible, took part in the murder of James III's favourites at Lauder Bridge. But this savage act was twenty years later; and in 1468 he and Alexander Napier brought back King Christian of Denmark's sixteen-year-old daughter to marry the seventeen-year-old King James III. This very pretty princess, dressed in a fashion which playing cards would presently immortalize, landed at Leith in July with a great train of Danish nobles, amidst large rejoicing crowds, and was received by James III 'with gallantry and ardour'. Great feasting and revelling accompanied the wedding, and there were splendid and various pageants and entertainments, for John Knox had not yet arrived to teach the Scots that fun is wrong. On this cheerful note Alexander Napier passed his last few years, being buried in St Giles about 1473 and succeeded at Merchiston by his son John, not to enjoy it for long.

For James III, in spite of his happy marriage, which in the end brought Orkney and Shetland into Scottish possession after centuries of Danish ownership, and in spite of having the burgesses of Edinburgh on his side, was looked on with suspicion by the Scots lords. He liked poetry, architecture, and of all things, music. Only an Edward I could get by with this kind of thing. Especially James III liked the lute; his great grand-daughter, Mary Queen of Scots, was to suffer from the same predilection. Unlike his younger brothers,

Albany and Mar, he was not good at jousting, and worse still, he
was bored by government and kept refusing to enforce punishments.
Six times successive Parliaments enjoined him to govern, and 'to
hold the law to his people'. Not content with simply employing them,
he appeared to enjoy the company of artists—'fiddlers and masons'
they were contemptuously referred to by the Scots lords. Only one
construction could be put upon all this: and it was duly put.

Here was a subject to unite Hamiltons, Grahams and Stewarts, to
join Douglases of every hue. Fond of musicians? He must be a prey
to unnatural vice. The favourites were accordingly strung up at
Lauder Bridge in 1482; and poor James became known as 'a man
that liked solitariness'. It occurred to no one that he could possibly
be simply a man who liked being somewhere where the Scots earls
were not; a man who had a renaissance feeling for colour and form,
for the light pouring through stained glass windows, for the refreshing sound of music through his bare and pillared halls, for the poetry
of Henryson, heard as he supped the wine from shapely silver goblets.
There is no evidence for perversion, though James III was certainly
an unsuccessful monarch, and jealous and capricious with his
disaffected brothers. While the Scots lords were busy hanging his
musicians and architects at Lauder Bridge, the English seized Berwick,
so lately recovered by the Scots, and have kept it ever since.

In the person of Alexander Stewart, Duke of Albany and second
son of James II by Mary of Gueldres, both Scots lords and ambitious
Stewarts reach their nadir. He rebels against his elder brother, James
III, escapes from the consequent imprisonment in Edinburgh Castle
with a rope supplied by the French envoy, carries his wounded page
on his back to Leith and wins to Paris, where he marries a French
heiress. (He had been suspected of practising witchcraft to dislodge
his elder brother, and his agents had been burnt as warlocks or
witches.) Albany allies with Edward IV of England, promises him
Scotland's southern fortresses if he will help him to his brother's
throne, crosses the Border without decisive success, and becomes
briefly reconciled with his brother, in token of which he rides through
Edinburgh from the castle to the Palace of Holyrood on the same
horse, and at Holyrood sleeps in the same bed. Subsequently he again
betrays both brother and country and is killed by a splinter from a
lance whilst watching a tournament in France, having as a final
gesture of brotherly defiance opened the gates of Dunbar to an
English army. Loving fine horses and brave men, this Alexander was,

says Pitscottie, "ane man of mid stature, braid scholderit, and weill proportionat in all his membris—braid-faced, red-nosed, great-eyed, and verie awful countenance when he pleased to show himself to his unfriends.' But *nil desperandum*: sainthood, like lightning, strikes where it pleases, and Albany's daughter marries Sir Patrick Hamilton of Kincavel, grandson of King James II, and becomes the mother of that mild martyr, Patrick Hamilton, burned at St. Andrews in 1528 for expressing some moderately Lutheran views.

Whatever his *penchant* for architects and musicians, James III had loved his wife, the Danish Princess Margaret, and when she died he tried to persuade the pope to canonize her. What with the plague and the poverty and the suborning and seizure of his sixteen-year-old son by the Douglases (Red), things went ill with James III, who was forced to give fight to rebels in 1488. A true Stewart, he rushed boldly into the battle before the vital reinforcements from the northern earls who supported him could arrive; beaten back, he was killed in flight from the battle. John Napier, who had succeeded his father Sir Alexander at Merchiston only fifteen years back, was killed fighting for the king, having taken the bizarre view that a fondness for music does not disqualify kings from being allowed to die a natural death.

This death by the Sauchieburn was fatal to the high ambitions of his family (if they had any). The Honor of Lennox would slip from John Napier's widow and young son. It was also unlucky for the royal house. Jameses II and III had had a hard struggle to keep Scotland from falling apart under the tugs of her great nobles: they built themselves a body of loyal families who were indispensable to their survival. The Lennoxes, until they tangled with the Albany Stewarts, had been such. Now that their male line was ended, their Napier kinsmen, with rather less of dangerous splendour, and fewer followers, took on from there. They stayed plain Napiers; luckily in view of the subsequent fate of Darnley, whose great grandfather had won the Lennox earldom.

The life and violent death of James III was clearly not as he would have had it be. A private gentleman, patchily avaricious, enjoying the arts, encouraging creation with his wealth and patronage, would life ever give room for such?

> Blessed be simple life withouten dread,
> Blessed be sober feast in quietie

James III's poet Henryson had written. But there was small chance of either while Douglases, Black or Red, were at large. The king who sat in Dunfermline town, drinking the blood-red wine, was fortunate if he saw old age, or even got through his meals, with any degree of quietie.

V

The happy epoch of Edinburgh's reconstruction was slowly drawing to an end; already the waves of England's civil agony had started to wash over Scotland's shore. After her defeat at Towton, Margaret of Anjou, Henry VI's queen, had taken refuge at the court of Scotland, having scooped up *en route* and brought with her her luckless husband who had been having a fine religious time celebrating Easter at York. On their behalf John Napier who later died at Sauchieburn had gone on an embassy to the newly crowned Edward IV in London, and for this, in the general lavishness by which Queen Margaret hoped to win the Scots to the Lancastrian cause, he was given a pension of 50 marks a year for life. Perhaps it was even paid for a year or two; beautiful Margaret, the she-wolf of Anjou, having at this time an extremely rich French general under her spell. Scotland had also been offered back Berwick, which was barely at that moment in Margaret's hands to give.

John Napier (of Merchiston and Rusky) had also been provost of Edinburgh, and one of the Lords of Council in a country beginning to prosper. His death at the battle of Sauchieburn in 1488 was unlucky for his family, and more than immediately: the Lennox inheritance was at stake, and all those involved started sharpening up their claim. The Napiers already had a bit of it, and just before his death Alexander, father of John, had been let off a sum of 250 marks due to the Crown as composition for part of the earldom of Lennox, on account of his 'lele and treue service done of lang tyme to us and our progenitours'.

Sauchieburn had been fought against James III's rebellious son (though perhaps more cat's-paw than rebel): the son winning, and becoming James IV, inaugurated a reign of mercy by which the heirs of those slain were, by special grace, admitted to their fathers' estates. Of these Archibald Napier, 4th of Merchiston, was one.

Like his father Alexander, John Napier had been Master of the King's Household, and he had married Elizabeth, elder daughter of Murdoch Menteith of Rusky (grandson of Duncan, 8th Earl of Lennox), Murdoch having held the earldom for his lifetime. Upon his death his family embarked on what John Napier's great great grandson Archie Napier was afterwards to describe as 'great strife and controversies for the title and honor of Lenox'. Had John Napier, who was in a powerful position, survived, they would probably have won. Haldane of Gleneagles who had married Elizabeth's younger sister was also a contestant, and so also was a character with the unfamiliar name of Derneley, who had one supreme argument: though descended from the youngest of old Duncan's three daughters, he was a Stewart; and so by this time, was the king. Elizabeth Napier contested on behalf of herself and her young son, who already bore 'the arms, surname and descent from the house of the Earls of Lennox', over and above his mother's senior and immediate rights. A merry time was had by the lawyers, for by this time several Scotsmen had hung up their swords and switched to the fierce pleasures of litigation.

Unaware that Columbus was sailing westward amongst the murmurs of his trembling crew, and that America was about to be discovered, the contestants spent 1492 wrestling on to a conclusion. Elizabeth Napier's weakness lay in her husband's ever-powerful family habits: he had stayed loyal to the reigning king. Her son, Archibald, was therefore in danger to his rebellious son, the new king, and could be thought to be lucky to hang on to even his Napier inheritance. Derneley was sitting pretty, having fought for the rebellious prince who was now king. He held on grimly, insisting that Agnes Haldane had been born out of wedlock. And it is doubtful if Elizabeth Napier fought very hard. In the event Napiers and Haldanes lost, and Derneley won. He became the first Stewart Earl of Lennox, took to spelling his name Darnley, and was rapidly swept up into the Euphemia Ross swoop towards the throne, his great great grandson marrying Margaret Tudor's daughter, thus qualifying their son as a suitable husband to Mary Queen of Scots, which caused this most tiresome and unlucky of Stewarts to get himself blown sky-high at Kirk o' Field in one of the more baffling of history's unsolved murders.

The Napiers accordingly remained plain Napiers, rightly or wrongly; and were probably none the worse for that. Although inclined to take a line of their own, they might hardly have been able as Earls of Lennox to keep out of the Euphemia Ross movement. The new Stewart Lord Lennox, already descended from James of the Fiery Face, instantly lined his family up at the starting gate for the throne race by marrying his son Matthew to Elizabeth Hamilton, a dangerous investment whose dividends were liable to be either throne or scaffold. None of the contestants for the Lennox inheritance came off empty handed. Still arguing about whose mum or whose grandmother had been the elder sister, they finally contented themselves with going shares in the land, Derneley getting half, plus the earldom of Lennox; Napiers and Haldanes a quarter each. 'The revenue was divided among them,' Sir Archibald Napier reported in 1625, 'and I hold some lands to this day in Lenox which came to my ancestors by the same division as also certain lands which did anciently belong to the said Menteith . . . the Lord Darnley was in the King's special favour and inclination which being known unto Napier of Merchistoun being then in the King's service, he relinquished his suit and it is said got Blairnivader for that cause. But I do find that he did give his part of the fishing of Leven and watermouth of Inch Taverock with the patronage of some churches for Blairnivader. And for further testimony for this affection of the said Napiers of Merchistoun, the Lord Darnley did in recompense of their relinquishing their claim to the dignity of Lenox tie himself and his heirs to support and maintain the said house of Napier and their heirs in all just occasions and engagements, as by ancient evidences is manifested and appeareth.' Elizabeth Napier was declared legal possessor of a quarter of the earldom. This *modus vivendi* was arrived at late in 1492, at about the same time as Columbus set foot on the Bahamas, hopefully convinced that they were India; an event that did not at first repercuss very strongly in Scotland.

Why did these apparently rational and level-headed persons keep on dying for kings, to their own endless detriment and loss? In his character and person James III was hardly a man for whom to sacrifice dear life. Was it all simply a self-interested gamble—*if we triumph I shall have*? But people, and still less medieval ones, are rarely as uncomplicatedly hard-headed as that. It was about now in England that the Duke of Norfolk, if we may believe Holinshed, uttered his famous reply when people asked him how he could bring himself to fight for such a man as Richard III. 'He was my crownèd king, and if Parliament put the crown upon the head of a stock . . .' For many it was as simple as that. The king was the established authority: to overthrow him was to call in chaos and civil strife. To romantics the monarch was hero or lodestar: to that unchanging element in every population which shrieks at pop-stars, he was an object at which to shriek. To sensible men like John Napier the king was law and order, a being not enslaved by the need to improve his status, and thus liable to be less swayed by personal ambition than his ministers. To religious people, and most were religious, the king's power was ordained by God. To people of all kinds the king had a sanction reaching far back into the perilous pagan beginnings of their race; an irrational knowledge in their bones told them that kingship was blessed and lucky and could extend these joys to other men. He was talisman and protection: without the king the hell of faction and disorder would break loose. Without the king the lonely villages were burned and armed men rode through the standing corn. Kings were like weather, they came in all sorts; one endured the bad and rejoiced in the good, for without them the seed would fail to quicken in the cold ground and the trees would never form their fruit; corn would not ripen, and the stock would wander barren on the hills. Every attempt to edge them out would bring a diminution of good fortune; with them some vital pulse would die. Kings answer that obscure pulse in the human soul that impels it to take giant teddy-bears to help win football matches. Deeper than reason, deeper even than selfishness, an archaic fidelity bound men to their king; a sure acknowledged king, drawn as it might be out of some celestial hat but inheriting through due law; a kind of divine insurance policy against a violent take-over. When Charles I's severed head was held aloft, so terrible a groan went up from the gathered crowds in Whitehall as listeners hoped never to hear again; a profound searching sigh of shock and horror and accepted guilt. Even now, one of the funnier sights on television news coverage is the expression on the faces of persons of advanced views trying not to be delighted at shaking hands with kings and queens. The other alternative is a sacred flag, a piece of canvas on a pole. Or Monsieur Chaban-Delmas; and how much active pleasure does anyone (except perhaps Madame Chaban-Delmas) derive from him?

*

North of the Tweed, they were now in for some royal luck: under the splendid and glamorous James IV the budding renaissance of Scotland burst into full flower. The Stewarts were by now fairly tightly established; Parliament had exonerated James II for stabbing the Black Douglas, on the grounds that he was a proven traitor; and the earls who had rebelled against James III were obliged to issue an 'apologetic declaration'. So secure did the Stewarts feel that the poet William Dunbar was allowed to publish some uncomplimentary references to King James IV's early love life. Edinburgh had long been a frontier fortress, but was now a capital city, law courts and all. Visitors from all over Europe came to see it, and found a land that had always been proud and was now prosperous, with poets and musicians and gay clothes, glittering tournaments in the field below the castle rock, and a new and brisk navy with two great ships— the *Margaret* and the *Michael*—and some smaller ones sailing up the Forth, and successfully defying the vessels of Henry VII. All this the foreign visitors noticed and recorded; the grandeur of the court, the richly dressed subjects, the stir and bustle in the streets. In 1498 the Spanish ambassador, de Ayala, told Ferdinand and Isabella that the Scots cultivated charming gardens.

There were annual plays, and Robin Hood revels every May, with processions and bands: all burgesses were commanded to be 'ready with their arrayment in green and yellow with bows and arrows' to be true foresters to Robin Hood. Now and at the feast of the Abbot of Unreason minstrels played before, and pageants were put on, as described by William Dunbar in *Blyth Aberdein*; though the Church, shortly before the Reformation, tried to suppress the plays on account of their sharp and mocking criticisms of clerical corruption. Through streets whose verges were still piled with midden and fish-offal and roamed through by dogs and swine, the colourful processions rollicked undeterred: (the Puritan obsession with cleanliness and soap were in reaction to the steamy reek endured for hundreds of years by town-dwellers.)

But even in terms of human life, not all was sweetness and light: the western crags still echoed to Campbell and Macdonald banging it out bravely; arrows of McLean, McLeod, and Mackinnon still twanged; from Lochaber, Badenoch, and all places east the thump of claymore on leather jerkin could yet be heard. The calm of Perthshire must have been ruffled when about now the Drummonds pursued a hundred and sixty Murrays into the parish kirk of Monivaird where their wives and families were already in refuge and put a match to the lot. (Not that this last is any different from the holocaust of French families incinerated by the Germans in 1944 at Oradour.) James hanged a considerable number of Drummonds at Stirling, and many more had to light out for Ireland.

Even the Highlanders, and notably the potent and unreachable Lord of the Isles, were brought under some sort of remote control. 'The King speaks the language of the savages who live in some parts of Scotland and on the islands' was Ayala's less than flattering reference to the Celtic fringe. All Scots had been obliged by James I to practise archery twice a week, so that they might no longer be outranged by the English; but they showed an un-cooperative tendency to prefer football, and were accordingly fined 4*d* a time for playing it. Education, too, raised its head: James IV passed a law by which the eldest sons at least of all noblemen and gentlemen were to be properly schooled, so that they could sensibly administer justice in their own areas. 'Of noble stature . . . and handsome . . . he is a very humane prince and much loved,' Ayala reported, and Erasmus wrote of his 'wonderful intellectual power and astonishing knowledge'.

Of this gay and stimulating royal household, Archibald, 4th of Merchiston, was one. Three times married, he had many sons, of whom his heir, Alexander, legally obliged to learn to read and write and study Latin and the arts, was knighted in 1507, and for whom, by a charter of 1512, James IV made Merchiston and the other Napier possessions into a free barony. (Security of tenure from reign to reign now seemed a not impossible dream.) This was an addition to one of several charters confirming his father Archibald in the lands of 'Merchamston near the burgh of Edinburgh, "cum turre et manere eundem" ' in 1494: in 1512 the charter incorporated Lennox and Rusky inheritances with the lands of Merchiston 'with castle, fortalice, manor place, yards, gardens and orchards in one free barony; the reddendo being one silver penny yearly'—nearly the most privileged form of land tenure, with jurisdiction over its inhabitants. For a sunny moment, the Napiers seemed settled folk in a settled land, with that pleasing licence to do what one liked with one's own which a free barony gave.

*

James IV had married Margaret Tudor, daughter of King Henry VII of England. 'London thow art the flowre of Cities all,' exclaimed the poet Dunbar, probably sent in the Scottish party who went to negotiate the marriage. A sound of happiness is heard:

> Now fair, fairest of every fair
> Princess most pleasant and preclare
> The lustiest one alive that been
> Welcome of Scotland to be Queen!

and through her all the post-Tudor kings and queens of a united kingdom were to descend. Back in Edinburgh, the Palace of Holyrood House was being built for her; and although Dunbar complained that this city contained far too many slow justices, scolding women, bad smells, and importunate beggars, the note of desperation heard in earlier centuries is gone. The dark, at this moment, fails to overshadow the bright: it is only in communities with a basis of security and contentment that such complaints are made. Was it possible that the horrors of the Scots wars of independence were truly over, and the issue of this marriage would unite two daggers-drawn countries, without diminishing the individuality of either? Dunbar's joy, though premature, rings true.

For alas, the new-risen sun of Scots prosperity was to have a spectacular setting. As an insurance policy, the auld alliance had to be kept warm. Needing to create a diversion for his ally France, wanting to have a crack at obstreperous Henry VIII, King James IV (known mockingly as the Knight Errant by the more sardonic among his subjects), disregarded the wisdom of his councillors and the prophecies of his soothsayers and crossed the Border, and there encountered the English under Norfolk on that terrible September 9th, 1513. Maybe Henry VIII, with the willing compliance which this unshakably popular man was always able to exact from his subjects, would have come at Scotland anyway: in any case the results were dire.

Intellectual he might be, but James IV, too, was a Stewart when it came to the crunch of battle. Alas for the difficult country, for the heady fumes of the witches brew! Fatally abandoning his strong position on the hill of Flodden, the king headed a romantic charge down into the plain, allowing the English to get between him and his retreat northwards, and here died fighting, and the flower of Scotland with him. Lord Home, a notably non-Stewart character, alone kept his head and covered the minute remnant who were able to retreat. The English troops, well-led and in a furious temper because their beer supplies had run out, fought with savage courage. Lennox was among the killed, and young Sir Alexander Napier; but his father, Archibald, now elderly, was one of the few survivors, and came back miserably to Merchiston, where he lived another few years, long enough to instil the family legend into Sir Alexander's three bereft little boys, Alexander, James and John.

When his father died at Flodden with the pride and glory of Scotland, the twelve-year-old Alexander who succeeded his grandfather at Merchiston in 1521 had been a child of four; all Edinburgh had been loud with weeping about his bewildered ears; the women ordered to the churches to pray, the men to the smithies to sharpen arms. The new king himself, James V, was only eighteen months old. Once again there was woe to the land whose king was a child; great lords contending for power, private armies marauding; the Scots involving themselves in what the English pithily described as 'rare broileries'. Alexander Napier was not robust and as a young man was sent to France for his health. The orphaned childhoods of Scotland at this time cannot have been gay. Flodden was so terrible a word that it was never written in the Scottish annals.

(Flodden looked different from the English side. 'To my thinking this batell hath bee to your Grace and al your Reame the grettest honor that could bee, and more than ye shuld wyn al the crown of Fraunce,' wrote Katherine of Aragon to her husband Henry VIII; and she was sending him 'a pece of the King of Scottes cote for your baner. I thought to send hymself unto you', she added with Spanish toughness, 'but our Englisshmene's hertes would not suffer it;' and Surrey wanted to know what Henry wanted done with the body?)

But Alexander grew up not so frail as to be unable to extricate himself from a marriage contract framed in his minority through 'sinistre mechinations and false informationes', although one of the signatories was Archibald Douglas (Red), and a son of old Bell-the-Cat Angus, not a family to be trifled with. James V, sadly in need of reliable support for many years after Flodden's great slaughter, whose effects lasted for generations, summoned Alexander back from France for Parliament: 'our weilbelovit freynd the Lard of March-aynston . . . cum hame within this our realm and compere in our said

Perliament.' Ill once more, Alexander was allowed to stop compèring and go back to France—'Our lovit Alexander Naper of Merchamstoun is vexit with infirmities and seikness, of the quhilkis he may nocht be curit and mendit within our realm.' In 1543 Alexander was off again—'We for the guid, trew and thankfull service done to us be our lovit bruthir Alexander Napar' allow him 'to pass furth of our realm be sey or be land for fulfilling of his pilgrimage at Sanct Johne of Ameis (Amiens?) in Fraunce.'

James V himself, a character genial to the poor but rough with his peers, had learnt in a tough school. For two years the Douglases held him prisoner, while they secured every good job, ecclesiastical or political, in the country. 'Nane durst stryve with ane Douglas,' Lindsay of Pitscottie gloomily recorded. The young Stewart Earl of Lennox was killed at Linlithgow while rescuing James from Douglas power: by 1526 the king was his own man, and instantly turned upon the Douglases and scuppered them. He was shrewd, active, and determined to rule: difficulty surrounded him. To the north and west Huntly and Argyll, and to the south Douglas and Home, were locally all powerful, still acting mainly in the interests of kin, still hanging on to the royal revenues they had exacted through his minority. James's mother did not simplify matters for him by her matrimonial activities; less spectacular than those of her brother Henry VIII, they were prosecuted with the same vigour. Early widowed from James IV, she had married a Douglas, Lord Angus, and thereafter spent much time and energy trying to swop him for Lord Methven, casting, *en route*, a meaningful glance in the direction of the Duke of Albany.

James sought a wife in France. His beautiful consumptive Valois princess, Madeleine, died at once; but his second attempt, the more stalwart Mary of Guise, prospered; bearing him two little boys with satisfactory speed. His dowry with Madeleine, he had told his cousin Albany, who was conducting the negotiations, must include cloth of gold, silver cups, and gunpowder. Living as like a renaissance prince as he could manage, James screwed as much money as he could from his country, recognizing wealth as the sinews of power. He appointed bishops for clan or other secular reasons, lived well, kept his gold hoarded in separate boxes scattered for safety in different places, and now that the Border was quieter, de-forested Ettrick and kept sheep there; a paying proposition but one which Henry VIII told him was beneath the dignity of a king. Having seen what happened to the Douglases, James's lords were less keen for near service under him: the king's enthusiasm for ruling, for law and order and for building up the finances of the Crown, seemed to pinch them both in purse and power. In 1530 he hanged Johnny Armstrong of Liddesdale on the Border for reiving—'I have asked for grace at a graceless face,' Armstrong laments in the ballad—would he butt in to the north and west as well? His peregrination in 1540 of the Highlands and Islands was an impressive demonstration, and the officials he planted there sent him in money; but his father's action against the potent Lord of the Isles had mainly resulted in making the other clans more uppish. And—alas for the future—Mary of Guise's two little boys died in 1541. By next year she was with child again, but with a little girl, Mary, born at a moment of high tragedy and destined to lead a life of the same.

From France King James had brought back tendencies of which the Scots bishops disapproved. Bishop Lesley commented unfavourably upon them in the 1530s: 'thair was mony new ingynis and devysis, alsweil of bigging of paleicis, abilymentis, as of banquating and of menis behaviour, first begun and used in Scotland at this tyme, aftir the fassine whilk thay had sene in France. Albeit,' the bishop continued sternly, 'it semit to be varray comlie and beautifull, yet it was moir superfluous and volipteous nor the substance of the realme of Scotland mycht beir furth or susteine; notheless, the same fassionis and custome of costlie abilyments indifferentlie used be all estatis, excessive banquating and sic like, remains yet to these days, to the greit hinder and povartie of the hole realme.' And what, as the bishops must certainly have pointed out, happened? When James V died the English came rampaging north in a war called 'the Rough Wooing', because Mary of Guise, Queen Mother, would not allow the infant Mary Queen of Scots to marry the little Edward VI and be brought up in England.

In spite of all the banqueting and the building of palaces [Falkland and Linlithgow] that were going on at home, Alexander Napier was still in France; he had thus missed the battle of Solway Moss in 1542, almost another Flodden; a muddled defeat after which James V fell ill with anger, 'speaking displeasant things against his Borderers'. He died of a broken heart, a kind of despair of the spirit; although he was only thirty and a healthy man; calling on his favourite Oliver

Sinclair who had been captured by the English at the critical moment, 'Oh fled Oliver!' James's baby daughter and heiress was three days old.

Alexander Napier also missed the burning of Edinburgh under Henry VIII's instructions two years later by Hertford (Edward Seymour, afterwards Duke of Somerset, whose great, etc. granddaughter was three or four hundred years later to marry Alexander's great etc. grandson); for Scotland's capital, with its flowers and its gaieties and its famous reek, had yet once more to go up in English smoke—the flaming timbers crashing on to the bright gardens, the scolding women scolding more than somewhat, and the poor left naked to the howling night—before it took its final, defensive, tall-housed form. Alexander Napier was however back from France in time to be killed fighting the English under this same Seymour in the battle of Pinkie near Musselburgh; the Scottish regent contending against them during the babyhood of Mary Queen of Scots. Alexander was thirty. Perhaps with his 'infirmities and seikness' he was not in any case destined for a long life.

But who was? Flodden had struck deep at the heart of Scottish joy; that unnameable battle and the long record of kingly tragedy, of civil war and early death. A poet, in the uncanny way that poets have, had recognized the bright sunshine of James IV's renaissance glory as being but a gleam between long storms. '*Timor mortis conturbat me*,' wrote William Dunbar, suffering from post-flu depression; he who had earlier rejoiced in the king's marriage with such lively cheer. Born in 1465 and dying seven years after Flodden, he was not the only one whom death troubled. Of what use was courage, learning, innocence, beauty, goodness of heart, when life was so inescapably and brutally short? Doubt had raised its smoky head: could one be sure of Heaven?

> He spares no lord for his puissance,
> Nor clerk for his intelligence;
> His awful stroke may no man flee—
> > *Timor mortis conturbat me.*

> He has done piteously devour
> The noble Chaucer, of poets flower,
> The Monk of Bury, and Gower, all three—
> > *Timor mortis conturbat me.*

Why be blameless? Death would take babes at the breast, lovely women safe in their bowers. What good was courage? Death would take captains close in their castles, champions triumphant on the field. Not even the goodhearted would escape. Death was everywhere; and the faith of the ages was getting frayed round the rim.

> He has ta'en Rowll of Aberdeen,
> And gentle Rowll of Corstophine;
> Two better fellows did no man see—
> *Timor mortis conturbat me.*

But such darkest hours generally produce a dawn, however slow, specially to such self-helping characters as the Scots; even if it is the unlikely dawn involved in sharing a king with the English. So, too, the ailing Alexander, whose first memory was the frantic wailing of bereaved Edinburgh, whose life can have known small joy, whose death was on a lost battlefield, lying 'cauld in the clay' while the English overran the Lothians, was to leave a powerful and healthy progeny behind him.

Archibald Napier, son of this luckless Alexander, was born in 1534, and was therefore thirteen when his father died at Pinkie; so naturally his Lennox inheritance at once fell a prey to cousin Haldane of Gleneagles who rapidly swiped Blairnavader and the Isle of Inchmurrin and rights of fishing over the whole of Loch Lomond. But not for long. In 1558 they were confirmed to Archibald Napier of Merchiston by Mary Queen of Scots, on the express grounds that, as well as his hereditary right to them, his father, grandfather, and great grandfather had all died fighting for her family. A live and intelligent character, Archibald wasted no time. Death reaped as swiftly as ever; but there was plenty a brisk man could do about that. A powerful will to live in the human race always impels it to reproduce lavishly in the teeth and tail of disaster. At the age of fourteen Archibald married Janet Bothwell, and became the father of three children before he was twenty. Left a widower a few years later, he married again and had three more sons and two more daughters. Some time earlier, perhaps after Pinkie, his father's two younger brothers, James and John, had drawn their own conclusions and set off for the south, taking with them their younger brother shares of the Napier and Lennox inheritances, where, with some perspicacity if they were out for a quiet life, they settled in Dorset. Go south, young man, was an urge not often felt in the Scotland of the sixteenth century; though possibly it was the first moment affording at least an even chance of crossing the Border without having one's throat slit. Injun country, still; but an adroit younger son could get through. And in the deep south and west what lands, what oaken hillsides dreaming under cloud, what sumptuous valleys thick with cattle and corn! What sleepy inhabitants, how easy for a tough Scot to buy out! Archibald's two younger brothers, Mungo and Sandy, seeing small chance of inheriting Merchiston, followed their uncles to England. They left a bright light behind them. It was Archibald's first son, born to a fifteen-year-old father at Merchiston in 1550, who came to be known to his contemporaries as Marvellous Merchiston, and to be later described by the Scottish historian and philosopher Hume as 'the person to whom the title of a great man is more justly due than any other whom his country ever produced;' John Napier, inventor of logarithms and of that handy and civilized little object, the decimal point, possibly also of the irrational letter e, later used both by Leibnitz and Newton, and an essential ingredient of Calculus.

Part III

Logarithms John

VI

In August 1560, Mary Queen of Scots, aged eighteen and widow of Francis, King of France, landed at Leith in a thick fog: 'Sorrow, darkness, dolour, and all impiety,' John Knox muttered. But Maitland was nearer the mark: 'The Queen my mistress is descended of the blood of England, and so of the race of the lion on both sides. I fear she would rather be content to hazard all than forego her right.' Sent to France as a five-year-old, what sort of world had she been reared in? By some accounts the ambience of the French court was all of charm and graciousness, fine clothes and good manners. Jeanne d'Albret, who came to the French court prospecting for a bride for her son (Henry of Navarre) and found one in Marguerite de Valois, the sister-in-law and contemporary of Mary of Scotland, described her future daughter-in-law as "*belle et bien avisée et de bonne grace, mais nourrie en la plus maudite et corrompue compagnie.*' Could the same have been said of Mary?

In this charming and courteous, or in this corrupt and cursed company, presided over by Catherine de Medici, Mary had grown up, loved and petted and very nearly forgetting her Scots tongue. If the genius of Clouet's portrait drawings tells truth, she was as luckless in her first husband, the sly, degenerate, young Valois king who died of an ear infection in his teens, as she was to be in Darnley and Bothwell. In Clouet's beautiful portrait of fifteen-year-old Mary, the artist seems to glimpse, through the bravery and charm of that sweet oval face, something sheeplike, some look of the destined victim, a hint of the father who with nothing physically wrong with him lay down at thirty years old to die, leaving his difficult country to a bossy widow and a week-old daughter, who would in her turn refuse the life and liberty she could have had through the simple expedient of resigning her claim to the English throne during Elizabeth's lifetime, and plump instead for life imprisonment and execution.

(The contemporaneous near-Clouet portrait of the Queen of Scots's cousin, Mary Tudor—after Antonio Moro—known to the bulk of her subjects in after years as Bloody Mary, shows her as being practically a man, with a stalwart, strong-featured face in sharp contrast to the exquisite femininity of the French court ladies. An Italian ambassador reported home from England that in spite of being loaded with jewels by Philip of Spain, Mary Tudor dressed '*comme un homme*'. Everyone mentions her deep voice. Poor Mary, caught up in dynastic necessities and clearly more of a duty than a pleasure to Philip of Spain! A few hundred years later she would have stayed single, cut her hair short, worn collar and tie, kept whippets, and martyred nothing except wasps and foxes.)

Mary Queen of Scots' rule began sensibly and mildly. She interfered with no one's religion. 'It is a sore thing to restrain the conscience,' Knox was told; and her Protestant brother, the illegitimate James Stewart, Earl of Moray, held the doors against the Edinburgh mob whilst on her first Sunday in Scotland Mary heard mass in peace. She turned a deaf ear to all papal suggestions that her life would be easier if a few of the more powerful Protestant lords were executed. All religious parties had to accept some kind of compromise, for Mary had as yet no heir to Scotland, except Arran the hope of the Hamiltons (whom she had declined to marry, and who, in his chagrin and sadness, was slowly going off his head) and his younger brother John, eventually 1st Marquis of Hamilton, both of whom were followed in the Scottish succession by Darnley and his brother. Mary and these four young men, besides a Lennox Stewart settled in France, were the sole surviving descendants of King James of the Fiery Face: rivalry betwixt Lennox and Hamilton was intense, and as usual, disruptive to the peace.

Four years after she stepped ashore Mary married Henry Stewart, Lord Darnley, son of the fourth Earl of Lennox and great grandson of the Lord Derneley who had defeated the Napiers in their claim to this earldom. In some ways this was not an attraction of opposites, but of similars. Mary and Darnley had the same brilliant fairness of complexion, the same tallness, the same vaulting ambition. Both alike aroused attraction, and felt it less easily themselves. Mary had a dash of the tomboy and loved riding, and Darnley excelled at all sports. He was also an accomplished lutist, and a fine dancer; two things which Mary also loved. Melville disparaged him to Queen Elizabeth as 'liker a woman than a man', but this perhaps described his temperament rather than his physique. Dancing a galliard with him at his first appearance in her court, Mary described him, 'the properest and best-proportioned long man that ever she had seen;' and it was clear to all that she had enjoyed the dance. Perhaps it was a refreshing rarity to the six-foot-tall queen to have a suitor not obliged to mount on a stool in order to kiss her.

Darnley was the son of the Stewart Earl of Lennox who had been declared traitor and forfeit for taking Henry VIII's part in his invasion of Scotland. He was a selfish, tricky boy brought up in exile by a selfish, tricky father, far from the duties and responsibilities of the Lennox countryside. He was vaunting, handsome, hollow as a shell; avid for power and devoid of responsibility. He and Queen Mary were first cousins, and both were Stewarts. It was not a marriage that boded well; but neither was it an incomprehensible one.

Darnley is inescapable, he is in everybody's pedigree; his grandchild, Queen Elizabeth of Bohemia, is the forbear of every crowned head in Europe as well as Great Britain. And one age-long fissure in Scotland's body politic at least was healed. For this Darnley who died by violence at Kirk o' Field from person or persons unknown had a mother who was a Red Douglas, as well as being half Tudor. The shade of virtuous Euphemia Ross could now rest in peace; her blood would triumph even though it had to pass through Darnley; her descendants from James VI and I onwards would indeed bear the orb and the sceptre and the tremendousness, be crowned at last above the sacred stone. There was a kind of justice about all this; the Grahams had disqualified themselves by murdering James I; Euphemia Leslie, an odds-on favourite, had given up the whole project some while back and become a nun; there had been something fishy about the marriages of one of the Black Douglases which made them virtually non-starters, though Sir James came into the running with Margaret Douglas, Darnley's mother; and the Hamiltons arrived through Elizabeth Hamilton's marriage to the second Stewart Lennox, though they did not see it that way, and harped on their nearer claim. All these would make the grade through detrimental Darnley, one of those rare characters for whom no single historian has a good word, although he must at least have had the charm to make Mary Queen of Scots fall madly enough in love with him to marry him. 'Cold, cold, cools the love that kindles o'er hot,' wrote a contemporary poet, though Mary's ruling passion was more for her hereditary rights, Tudor and Stewart.

4

This scalding preoccupation with being king or queen now seems rum. But to reign as a medieval or renaissance monarch was to enjoy the glamour of a film-star, the authority of a president of America; to spend life in an aura of infallibility and God-givenness like a pope or a dalai lama. It was a prospect to turn all but the strongest heads: the powerful element of risk seems to have deterred no one. The human race, it must be concluded, generally likes gambling. Even being an earl was fun; you could at worst insist on being hanged with a silken rope. The Duke of Hamilton went on being haunted by a prophecy that he would succeed King Charles I; when he succeeded him on the block instead of the throne it was all in the day's work. Supporters fought for their several candidates with all the vigour and fanaticism of a Manchester United fan with a team on the way to the Cup Final: it was all disturbing to order, and heavily primed with risk to life and limb; but goodness, exhilarating.

For some months before the fatal summer of 1567, Henry Darnley had been carrying on nohow, jealous of his wife Queen Mary, suspicious of the power of her brother Moray, even conspiring against her and murdering her secretary and lutist, David Rizzio. He had alienated everyone in Scotland, except his doting father, Lennox. Soon after the birth of his son, James VI of Scotland and in due course James I of England, Darnley had himself been murdered by a band of unknown conspirators, one of whom was certainly James Hepburn, Earl of Bothwell. And then Mary, willingly or unwillingly, had allowed herself to be carried off by this same Bothwell, had disgraced herself in the eyes of Europe by marrying him, had found that even Bothwell could not rally enough men to fight for her in that last sad attempt at Carberry, had miscarried of twins by him in her imprisonment on Loch Leven, and had escaped to a disaffected country, so that there seemed to be nothing for it but to fly to England and throw herself upon the mercy of Queen Elizabeth, which she might have obtained had she consented to sign away her claim to rule in England during Elizabeth's lifetime.

The family at Merchiston regarded Mary with loyalty rather than enthusiasm. The Napiers had indeed rallied to the queen in her final fight, and had gathered without much conviction to the lost cause in its crumpling effort at Carberry, when the citizens of Edinburgh were grimly shouting, 'Burn the hoor!' The attempt to reinstate her had folded up against opposition pressure, and after her escape from the castle in Loch Leven Mary had fled to England. Young James, a not so distant kinsman of theirs, would grow up and must succeed in time. That the Napiers, like thousands since, should feel sorrow for Mary, was likely enough; but of all prime ways of taking the gloss off a royal image, of turning luke-warm the stoutest of supporters, there is nothing to equal an immediate marriage with a character known to have just murdered your former husband.

That Scotland should stay Protestant had been virtually decided in the settlement of 1560: it hardly seemed vital whether one lot of nobles ruled the country in the name of the imprisoned Queen Mary in England, or another lot in the name of the infant James VI who was already proclaimed King, and whose succession was in any case secure as his mother's eldest son; whether Moray murdered the Hamiltons or the Hamiltons murdered Moray—this last was what in fact occurred. By the 1570s the Napiers had laid off war for the time being and settled for religious philosophy, mathematics, agricultural experiment, and physics.

Edinburgh was still held for the queen, but a certain absence of enthusiasm appears even amongst the active protagonists (except for the Hamiltons, who battled on in the west.) In May of 1572 Archibald Napier was called upon to render up his house and fortalice of Merchiston, since strategic points outside the town were important to the queen's garrison in Edinburgh, dependent on the countryside for food supplies. Her general drew towards Merchiston this month, but found it so strongly held that all the attackers could do was to spoil the buildings round about and attempt to smoke the holders out with fires; and a further attempt next month ended in deadlock when Regent Morton from Leith (king's man) and the queen's party from Edinburgh 'being within 1,000 foot of their enemies stayed an hour without any offer of skirmish to each other', after which everyone went home for supper. Kirkcaldy of Grange had however sent a culverin from Edinburgh which ineffectively banged a number of 26 lb shots into Merchiston Tower for three hours—'if they had bought a cannon they might in all likelihood have won it,' Sir William Drury concluded in his dispatch to Burleigh in London. (One culverin ball, slightly rusted, was discovered in the 1960s, still securely nesting in the east front just below the parapet wall.) Maitland and Kirkcaldy of Grange were holding out in

Edinburgh Castle, soon itself to be reduced by artillery, and all hope of Queen Mary's return to fall with it.

Culverins or not, Archibald stayed friends with Edinburgh, though he had given up hope of the fleeting queen who had once been the hope and the darling of her country. Why must they send her to France, to learn dancing and popery and all that dangerous charm? One must look in hope to her son. Meanwhile in March of 1584 the town council of Edinburgh gave Archibald a piece of the borough muir 'for the guid will and favor borne and schawn (shown) be him to the guid toun at all tymes . . . a littel piece of waist and un-proffitable roum . . . lyand contingue to his lands of Merchistoun for completing owt of the form and fassoun of his yaird in just propor-tion of the four nuiks thereof.' Besides the waste and unprofitable room for squaring off his nooks, Archibald now owned around Merchiston the lands of Tipperlin, Langhill, Myreflat, Myreside, and Gorgiemuir, as well as the original Over and Nether Merchiston, Pultrielands etc. (all now incorporated into Edinburgh).

Still making up for Flodden and all those disastrous battles, Sir Archibald had thirteen children; John, Francis, and Janet by Janet Bothwell (no relation of Queen Mary's Bothwell, whose family name was Hepburn); and Alexander, Archie, William, Helen, Elizabeth and four non-survivors by Elizabeth Mowbray. Knighted in 1565, aged thirty, he was a man of a thoughtful and speculative mind. Master of the Scottish Mint to James VI, with the additional duties of superintending the mines and minerals within the kingdom of Scotland, he believed, as most people then did, that the soil of Scotland was teeming with gold and other precious metals. The kingdom lacked enough currency to speed her rising trade, and he was often away prospecting for gold in the Pentland hills, and was once, during the king's and queen's civil war that swept to and fro across Edinburgh, hailed before the Council for failing to come back and take sides. (This was waged between supporters of imprisoned Queen Mary and the infant king James). There is no record that he found any gold, but he cleared his estate of encumbrance and redeemed—once again!—his lands of Gartness in Stirlingshire. In 1589 he was appointed to a commission for chasing Jesuits, but con-tinued to display more interest in mining than in this popular blood-sport. He was told to 'keep ward in Edinburgh' after his third son, Alexander (clever, but inclined to be a rake-hell), failed to appear before the Council after a serious assault.

When one starts the responsibilities of fatherhood at the age of fifteen as Sir Archibald had, they may grow rather tedious over the years; but, happily intent on his farming and mine-prospecting, he lived on to be seventy-four. In any case his eldest son, John, studious and a bit of a prodigy, took a lot of the weight. A member of Assembly, Sir Archibald was sent on a deputation to London, where, according to Sir James Balfour who went with him, to the great amazement of the English he carried his business with a great deal of dexterity and skill—'his witt and knawledge was wonderit at be the Englischmen,' still astonished to find that these qualities existed north of the Border. There is an extreme insularity about this: one look at the National Portrait Gallery in Edinburgh shows that Scotland was full of intelligence at this time—Buchanan, Regent Hamilton, with his look of weary surprise, the shrewdness of Moray; even James V, long-faced, saturnine, with an auburn fringe beard and a Henry VIII flat hat; and above all the careful, calm intelligence on the faces of Mark Kerr, Abbot of Newbattle, and of Helen Leslie, his wife. Mark Kerr renounced Roman Catholicism and married; but managed to stay Abbot of Newbattle: what could be more dexterous than that?

Sir Archibald was still only twenty-eight when his eldest son John Napier went at the age of thirteen and a half to St. Andrews University; which is young enough to have to cope with an undergraduate son. Fortunately John needed no coping with; his 'grave and sweet countenance' concealed a clear powerful intelligence. He could do everything in the world except spell. He was entered at St Salvator's College as Johannes Neaper. He himself spelt it Nepair, Naipper, Neper, Napper, Napeir, or Napare with perfect indifference; sometimes writing his Christian name Jhone. Henry VI of England had spelled it Naper, James II—'his lovit and familiar squyre, Alexander Napare of Merchamstoune,' James III—'our lovett familiar Knicht and maister of housshold Alexander Napar of Marchamstoun,' James IV—'our lovite familiar sqwiar John Nepar.' Robert Napier, knighted in London by James VI (I of England) spelled it Nappir, and half the Napiers in the west country spelled it Napper. The fifteenth and sixteenth centuries contained many headaches, religious or political, but spelling was not one.

At St Andrews John Napier studied Latin, Greek, and Hebrew,

as well as science and philosophy. The pros and cons of the Reformation were now being freely argued, and the students were exercised
once a week in theological debate. The bitterness and fanaticism of
later years had not yet crept in, and the young men were told 'not to
bite and devour one another like dogs, but to behave as men desirous
of mutal instruction, and as the servants of Christ, who ought not to
strive, but to be gentle to all'. Over this injunction to mildness the
Scottish temperament rapidly prevailed. 'In my tender years and
bairn age I contracted a loving familiarity with a certain gentleman
a papist,' John Napier later wrote; but listening to the sermons of
Maister Christopher Goodman on the Apocalypse he was 'moved in
admiration (wonder) against the blindness of papists', and 'not only
bursted I out in continuall reasoning against my said familiar, but also
from thenceforth I determined with myself by the assistance of God's
Spirit to employ my study and diligence to search out the remanent
mysteries of that holy book.'

John Napier was unfanatical, devotedly a scientist as well as a
theologian, and longing to get on with his mathematical probe; yet
no man of faith, heart and imagination could have held aloof from
the great religious stir of his day. He felt sorrow at the parting of the
ways. Surely a little calm discussion with the Catholics would put
things right? He rushed his *Playne Discoverie* out in English without
waiting to put it into Latin because 'it doth so pitie our harts seeing
them put more trust in Jesuits and seminarie priests than in the true
scriptures of God.' Their Church was very dear to the Scots. In the
terrible loneliness of their War of Independence when France had
turned away and the pope had excommunicated the king, the
bishops and priests of Scotland had staunchly supported her cause.
Judgment by race is shallow; yet in the main the Scots have more
religious spirit than the English. In its directness and depth of feeling
no contemporary poem addressed to God compares with the
anonymous fifteenth century 'All my love, leave me not' of Scotland.
Feeling as deeply as they did, they would be lucky to settle the
dispute without hatred and the spill of blood.

Through the fifteenth century the orchestra of faith had swelled and
diminished, echoed as ever by those sure sounding boards the poets.
The soothing harp of Henryson, writing in the lifetime of Isabella
and Margaret of Lennox and of the second Sir Alexander Napier,
summoned them to an unquestioning acceptance:

For God is in his power infinite
And mannes' soul is feeble and over-small,
Of understanding weak and unperfect
To comprehend him that contains all;
None should presume, by reason natural,
To search the secrets of the Trinity,
But trow firmly, and let all reason be.
Yet neverless we may have knowledging
Of God Almighty, by his creatures,
That he is good, fair, wise, and benign . . .

But fifty years later the violin voice of Walter Kennedy mourned:

For no reward except the joy of heaven
Would I be young into this world again;
The ship of faith tempestuous wind and rain
Drives in the sea of Lollardry that blows;
My youth is gone and I am glad and fane . . .

To be answered by the great trombone of William Dunbar in a triumphant fortissimo of affirmation:

Done is a battle on the dragon black
Our champion Christ confounded hath his force;
The gates of hell are broken with a crack
The sign triumphal raised is of the cross,
The devils tremulous with hideous voice;
The souls are bought and to the bliss can go,
Christ with his blood our ransome does endorse
    Surrexit Dominus de sepulchro!

No doubt there were, as in King James V's poem (sixteenth century), untoward doings 'At Chrystis kirk on the green', when quarrels broke out there, and 'The wyffis cast up one hideous yell . . . so rudely rang the Commune bell, while all the steeple rockit'; but a contemporary ballad perhaps came nearer the heart of the matter, in a command that all alike could still utter:

Go, hart, unto the lampe of light,
Go, hart, do service and honour,
Go, hart, and serve him day and night,
    Go, hart, unto thy Saviour.

Go, hart, to thy onlie remede
Descending from the hevinlie tour
Thee to delive from pain and dread,
Go, hart, unto thy Saviour.

Go, hart, with trew and whole intent,
To Christ thy help and whole succour;
Thee to redeem he was all rent,
Go, hart, unto thy Saviour.

Absorbed as he was by his cyphering and discoveries, a heart as feeling and a spirit as ardent as John Napier's must quicken to such voices, search itself in prayer, stand up to be counted on one side or the other.

Slowly and not at first violently the Reformation had taken hold in Scotland. James V in an acute state of poverty had acquired from the pope the sum of £10,000 a year from the Scottish Church revenues, on a promise to stay faithful to Rome. But though the Scots churchmen compounded with the king for a lesser sum, this drain on her resources had further weakened the Church; and by 1530 copies of Tyndale's translation of the New Testament were reaching Scotland. They unlocked a great desire for closer contact with 'the unsearchable riches of Christ'. Somewhere, lost and smothered under a long corruption and carelessness, lay, as the deeply religious Scots well knew, the beauty and truth of the Christian revelation. Belated attempts were made to reform the Catholic Church from within; in 1549 the Scottish churchmen, in their own provincial council, declared that the two main causes of heresy were 'the corruption of morals and profane lewdness of life in churchmen of almost all ranks, together with crass ignorance of literature and of all the liberal arts'. Statutes to remedy abuses and exactions were passed, and repeated in 1559—priests must at least read and write and be capable of expounding the faith (some of them could not even say the Lord's prayer). But these remained paper statutes: the vital impetus had gone. Even the friars had ceased to succour the poor and the distressed and seemed to their critics to live lives of slothful ease.

Chastity seemed to be getting more difficult; or perhaps the fear of hell was growing less intense. By now two-fifths of all the legitimizations of bastards were for the children of priests, but this may have been because priests took more trouble to have their children legitimized. James V had nine natural children, closely followed by Cardinal Beaton with eight; though these scores were low for the age: Philip the Good of Burgundy had a recorded twenty-six. This laxness jarred; and why should all the remote hangers-on of the Church have clerical status? Just by being able to write his name a man appeared able to get away with murder in the clerical courts. Straining after political power, terrified by new ideas, nervously killing heretics, was the Church whose light had burnt so steadily through the night of barbarism to fall apart in corruption and apathy? To the customary tidal dangers of feud and counter-feud, of ambition for money, place, and power in Scotland, would the rip-roaring cross-current of religious fanaticism now be added?

Three-quarters of the parish churches in Scotland belonged to monastic houses, or universities, who left them without regular priests. Visits were infrequent and seemed too exacting—'Nae penny, nae paternoster,' the poorer Scots cynically complained. In 1528 Patrick Hamilton, royal descent or not, was burned for heresy at St Andrews; he was followed by Wishart (partly a political murder), but the scene was not darkened by anything like the holocaust of three hundred burnings of Protestants in three years which in England stained the last years of poor Mary Tudor's reign. In Scotland the change-over was comparatively bloodless and fireless. But there were the usual consequences of martyrdom: 'the reek of Maister Patrick Hamilton infected all it blew upon:' burn the Patrick Hamiltons and you get John Knox. Hamilton had preached that God could be the friend of ordinary men, and that holiness of life alone gave a priest his spiritual authority. Difficult to say whether the Abbots of Kelso, Melrose and Holyrood, or the Priors of Coldingham and Perth fulfilled this condition, as they were all still in the cradle or the nursery, infant illegitimate sons of King James V. An element of jobs for the boys had crept in: once in a family, a bishopric was inclined to stay there for several generations. And Christendom had long been divided. Early on the Monophysites had sulked out, on what now seems a legal quibble (oh dear, the bossy Greeks); and in 1054 the Eastern Church had parted from Rome over papal supremacy and the procession of the Holy Ghost (oh dear, the bossy Italians).

4*

For some while the two variations of western Christianity peace-fully co-existed in Scotland. A passionate dislike of Henry VIII and English invasion had fortified the Scots in their allegiance to the old religion, but an equally passionate dislike of the Regent of Scotland, Mary of Guise, and of domination by her French officers pushed them the other way. (Oh dear, the bossy French.) The road was being prepared for John Knox, sweating as a slave in a French galley from 1547–9, and hardening his heart against the French and all their works and ways with every pull of the oar. In the same year as Wishart, Cardinal Beaton had been murdered at St Andrews, but that, too, was partly political: he was pro-French. The Auld Alliance was all very well, but the Scots had come to see that the French were really only interested in France.

Property, too, raised its insistent head: the steady absorption of land by the Church aroused unlovely thoughts in the hearts of the disinherited. All very well for Isabella Lennox to give three farms in pure and perpetual alms for the singing of masses for the soul of King William the Lion; or Sir Alexander Napier three more for masses for the souls of Robert the Bruce and Kings James I and II; after a while younger sons and nephews, watching these lush farms slipping from them, come to feel that the souls of long dead kings can shift for themselves: what about a living for the live? Resentment fastens on an institution which accepts so much; as lovers of their acres now resent a state which opens its mouth so wide in death duties; for no visible good they watch the carefully tended woods erased by speculators, the house roofless, the sealing concrete closing over more and more of the generous land like the blight of an eternal frost.

For many ages the Scots had loved their Church and their Church had loved Scotland. Defying the papal excommunication, the Scots bishops had stood by Robert the Bruce in his war for independence, declaring in 1310 their resolution 'to live and die with him as one possessing the right of blood and other cardinal virtues, fitted to rule and worthy of the name of King and the honour of the Kingdom, since by the grace of the Saviour he has by the sword restored the realm'. Nor was there a Henry VIII, desperate for a male heir, con-vinced that the death of eight sons by Katharine of Aragon must mean that his marriage was cursed, furious that the pope out of fear of the Emperor should refuse him the divorce he granted so many others upon dynastic grounds. The Scots reformation seemed rather to grow out of the nature of the Scots themselves, out of their stubborn belief that the faith of Christ had got itself into the wrong hands, was being manipulated by a bunch of worldly and cynical Italians for their own glorification and by un-Christian means.

As ever, there was a long time when the terrible new breach might have been avoided, and, as ever, the chance was missed. In 1552 a catechism by John Hamilton, Archbishop of St Andrews, was printed, 'ane common and catholik instructioun of the christin people in materis of our Catholik faith and religioun' revealing a spirit of compromise and a near agreement with the principle for which his cousin Patrick Hamilton had been burned. It was too late. Feelings now ran high; and politics bedevilled the issue. By 1555 Knox, hot from Geneva, was busy organizing a Calvinist group amongst the Scots lords, led by Argyll; these, increasing in numbers and power, became known as the Lords of the Congregation. In 1559 a mild request from the less militant reformers for services and mass in the vernacular was refused, and the Protestant pastors were summoned to Perth to answer for their preachings. They arrived with their unarmed supporters, prepared for reason. But iron-hearted John Knox was back from his galleys. At Perth, on May 11th, he preached an inflammatory sermon against idolatry, an excited boy threw a stone and broke the statue of a saint, riot broke loose, the friaries of Perth were sacked, and the long bloody scandal of Christian division had been clinched in Scotland as elsewhere.

In religious as in civil life, too long a disregard of reasonable aspirations, too long a connivance in corruption, too blind a determination to crush all requests for reform, had brought forth its Lenin and its Trotsky, its unstoppable Chairman Mao. Much good would in the end flow to Scotland from those generations of sincere and inspired preachers in their bare white-washed kirks, a popular education and an intellectual freedom above any known in Europe, a spiritual impulse that would carry them to the ends of the earth; but it was an impulse that could have worked with the old Christendom and not against. Something precious and holy would be lost, as would the lives of many brave and noble-minded men. 'Killing times' had been and would be, to leave a long bloody estrangement in which the slightest movement of rapprochement would be anathematised as treachery. The terror of old persecution strikes to the very marrow of the bones. Even amongst the less extreme English it would be believed for hundreds of years that to set so much as a cross, the very symbol of Christendom, on an altar, would be to find themselves dragooned out of their most dearly-held truths by a pack of hatchet-faced Dominicans from the stony places of Spain and made to worship idols; things and not spirit.

As in communist countries, a savage self-righteousness would grip the reformers: even Cromwell, much of their persuasion, was to write to the Covenanters: 'I beseech you, in the bowels of Christ, to think it possible you may be wrong.' They could not: all other views were of the devil. Edward I had uttered some extremely rude Norman-French words about the Scots four hundred years earlier; and so no doubt had their much raided neighbours over the Border, but visitors had always liked them up till now for their good cheer and their hospitality. In the seventeenth century this altered.

'There is' complained Samuel Pepys forty years after the Covenant, 'a rooted nastiness in the Scots,' and he was not the only one to think thus. Some charm, some kindliness, had been temporarily blighted out of them. The battering to death of the Czar's innocent children, the pushing down a dry mineshaft of other Romanoff boys to die of slow starvation, finds a parallel in the pursuit and slaughter of the Catholic Irish women and their children after the battle of Philiphaugh. Racial bitterness pales before bitterness of opinion. Communist China would echo the Puritan smashing of stained glass windows by the yet more nonsensical breaking of exquisite china, for the sole reason that it was made by craftsmen living under imperial rule. 'Burn it all down' the undergraduates scrawl in chalk on Oxford's most beautiful buildings; but behind the terrifying violence there is a blind but pure innocence—a belief that spiritual values are more sacred than the most lovely objects in the world, and that if we worship things, we can and do forget to love our neighbours. Perhaps, at long long last, something as much of value and virtue would come from Lenin to the world as flowed in time from those farouche kirk elders who howled behind John Knox.

Such spiritual tempests churned the minds and maybe clouded the studies of young men at universities in the sixteenth century then as now. (Scotland had three to England's two, and King James VI and I was about to found a fourth.) Sent off to travel without taking a degree—'Send John to the schools either to France or Flanders, for he can learn no good at home,' advised his uncle, Adam Bothwell, Bishop of Orkney—John Napier visited Italy and the Low Countries and learnt mathematics at the University of Paris from Petrus Ramus, a Protestant professor whose murder a few years later in the Massacre of St Bartholomew hardened John's heart against papists, although he kept sympathy for Mary Queen of Scots. Learned also in Greek, theology and science, he was back in Edinburgh by the time he was twenty, and seems to have settled at once upon his great works, scientific and religious. The times were unpropitious. Plague had swept Edinburgh in 1568 and continued intermittently to visit the city throughout his lifetime; and Edinburgh was stretching ever nearer to Merchiston. Commanding its southern approach, it was but a mile or so from the city, where civil war raged through the streets up till 1572. High in Merchiston's 'war and weather-beaten tower', he started work. At twenty-one he married Elizabeth, daughter of Sir James Stirling of Keir, and earlier in the same year, his father, still only thirty-six, had married again, a cousin, Elizabeth Mowbray. So that his second family were exact contemporaries of John's children and always addressed them as brothers; a practice confusing to historians. The fertility of Marvellous Merchiston was not confined to his brain and by two wives John Napier had Archibald, John, Robert, Alexander, William, Adam, Joan, Jane, Elizabeth, Anne, Helen and Margaret; mathematical precision prevailing here as elsewhere. At least the wars with England were at last over and anyone who could escape the pestilence and the street fighting had a fair chance of growing old: nearly all of these did.

The patter of these twenty-four feet did not stop John Napier from delving deep in his logarithms nor prevent him from publishing, in 1594, his *Playne Discoverie of the Whole Revelation of St John*; first indication of what his biographer Mark Napier calls 'that combination of power and simplicity which were the leading features of his mind'. Its preface is disarmingly un-dogmatic. '. . . our good intention and Godly purpose doth always proceed of a very tender and frail vessel, and that as all liquors, how precious soever, do take some taste of their vessels, so this holy work may in some things, though not espied of myself, taste of my imperfections. Therefore humbly I submit those imperfections whatsoever to the gentle correction of every wise and discreet person who in the motion of God's spirit judgeth uprightly, without envy or partiality, praying all good men to have me apardoned of whatever is amiss.' To King James VI, to whom the work is dedicated, he was rather crisper.

This was the earliest widely read Scottish work on the interpretation of the Scriptures; it caused a stir; more particularly on the continent, where they were astonished to find a scientific theologian appearing out of the northern mists. The fame of it spread round Europe, as also did the joke of Napier's punning name. 'A Scottish gentleman named Peerless' the German scientists and divines called him, and on the title page of the French translation he is called 'Jean Napeir (NOMPAREIL), Sieur de Merchiston'. His *De Arte Logistice* was also written now, a treatise on algebra which remained unpublished till 1839, by when it was a trifle out of date.

John Napier had also just invented the decimal point; a useful little device which he neglected to patent. He was a true scientist, intent on what his son called 'the publick good' and unsustained by any Nobel prizes. As a farmer and landowner he came into quite another category, fighting the least encroachment by law suit or sword, and neglected nothing in the management of estates which stretched from the shores of the Forth to the banks of the Teith and the islands of Loch Lomond. After his father's re-marriage for the most part he lived in the quiet of his house at Gartness, in a bend of the winding river below the Campsie fells, where a long green plain slopes westward to Loch Lomond, there to wrestle with his mathematics. Though free from the cheerful yells of twelve children it was not wholly safe from tribal affrays. In 1603 Peter Napier of Kilmahew, son of Patrick Napier by his wife Katherine Noble, had been slain by the Macgregors at the 'conflicte of Glenfruin', sometimes called 'the field of the Lennox', fought by Colquhoun of Luss and Napier of Kilmahew against the Macgregors as the result of many Macgregor raids on the Lennox (pushed on from behind by the Marquis of Argyll), ending, it is said, in the murder by the Campbells of eighty schoolboys from Dumbarton school who came out to see the fight.

The poor Macgregors, who had been legally outsmarted over their lands and were stooges to the acute Argyll who wished to destroy Colquhouns, Napiers and Macgregors themselves, were condemned as 'lawless limmers and villains', and their clan proscribed; even their name was to be abolished; any clergyman bestowing it even as a Christian name would be struck off the list; it remained unspeakable for over a hundred years. Rightly supposing that this arrangement might prove ineffective, John Napier made an agreement to guard the

peace of Gartness at least until he could get his central problem
worked out; compounding with Campbell of Lawers and the
Stirling brothers that 'if the Macgregors or other heiland broken
men should trouble his lands in Lennox or Menteith they should do
their utmost to punish them.' What with estate affairs, occasional
attacks upon his Merchiston Tower, the charge of his own twelve
children and more than half the charge of his unruly half-brothers,
and frequent demands upon his 'singular judgement' from the
General Assembly of the Church, he led a full life; and was in the
middle of a treatise on the Trinity—'the marvellous harmony and
accord in all points betwixt God and His holy Jerusalem'—when
a renewed international threat obliged him to switch off this happy
subject and invent tanks and submarines.

In 1596 came a fresh scare of Spanish invasion; another and bigger
Armada was on its way to completion. On June 7th a letter from John
Napier was despatched to Anthony Bacon in London, entitled
'Secret Inventions, profitable and necessary, in these days for the
defence of this Island, and withstanding strangers, enemies to God's
Truth and Religion'. Eight years earlier the Spanish Armada had
come and gone, with terrors and rumours, and tales of great galleons
battered to pieces on Scotland's west coast. 'He blew with his winds
and they were scattered,' the contemporary medal recorded; a
comment containing more humility and realism than some of the
later ones. Courage, intelligence, Drake's fireships, and above all,
luck, had prevented the finest army in Europe from being landed in
an England which had, as usual at times of mortal peril, a pint-sized
standing army backed by a number of zealous characters with bill-
hooks whose main skill lay in knowing when to harvest the hay.
Queen Elizabeth's wise Church compromise, though less spiritually
glamorous than either Rome's or Calvin's religious extremes, had
made it possible for most of the English to co-exist without anguish
of conscience, whilst Europe was to drench in a huge fanatical blood-
letting. The papal bull of 1570, excommunicating Elizabeth and calling on all good Catholics to dethrone her, and another of 1580
promising absolution to her assassins, had alerted the security forces
and generally put the cat back among the pigeons; causing the deaths
of a great many noble characters, martyrs more to papal intransige-
ance than to any wish of Elizabeth's to chop them up. When poor

Mary Queen of Scots was executed in 1587, comfortingly under the impression that she was being martyred for her faith, her death had been followed by that great crescent of Spanish galleons bearing up the Channel approaches, and both English and Scots had felt their nakedness and trembled. Spanish defeat allayed their fears only for a breathing space: cries of the tortured Netherlanders still echoed across the North Sea. Would God blow with his winds a second time?

In case not, John Napier, shutting his book on the Trinity and shelving his mathematical notes, bent his mind in the 1590s towards engines of war. Spanish cruelty and English and Scots stubbornness would have made of their forcible conversion a bloodiness to cloud the air for centuries to come: John would invent tanks and swing-guns to keep the dons out while passions cooled and reason and tolerance raised their presently drowned heads. Goodness in time might effect the great reconciliation; a change of heart to all but everything the reformers had asked in 1560. But force would not. By Catholic Europe the British were hugely outnumbered; they felt like an island Czechoslovakia shielded from a Russia only by a few wooden ships and the heaving sea: a mutual terror united England and Scotland more firmly than a mutual king. There were at this time four million English, and perhaps a million Scots: the entire annual revenue of England was about half a million pounds. Britain had only her marvellous site athwart the ocean passages, and her handful of skilled and dogged seamen. Spain in 1588 was the only world power; in 1580 she had added Portugal and her vast dominions to her own, which included half Italy, Burgundy, and the Nether-lands: she commanded a huge manpower and the illimitable gold of the New World. Elizabeth's defiance was as wildly improbable as if Cuba, without any Russia in the background, were now to take on the U.S.A.; her success almost equally unlikely. But when, seventeen years later, John Napier lay dying, peace had been made with Spain. The fear of suppression had passed: he said he would leave no design of any killing machine.

Not only Britain was threatened in the 1590s; Christendom itself was in danger and its ranks briefly closed, for everyone in Europe then believed the Nicene creed as implicitly as they now believe the multiplication table; though it is doubtful if they would defend this with quite the same verve. 'The Turc is entret Christendome with a potent armie,' John Napier wrote, and King James sent a messenger to the Emperor with Napier's 'Secrett Inventionis' on purpose 'to de-bell the Great Turc, the great ennemie to our Salviour Chryst'. One was a huge burning glass (copied perhaps from Archimedes at Syracuse), another a gun 'which shott passeth not linallie through the enemie, destroying onlie those that stand in the random therof, but ranging abrode within the whole appointed place'. The third was a tank—'a round chariot of mettle made of the proof of double muskett, which motion shall be by those that be within the same, more easie, more light, and more spedie by much than so manie armed men would be otherwise. The use hereof as well in moving serveth to breake the array of the enemies battle, and to make passage, as also in staying and abiding within the enemies battle. It serveth to destroy the environed enemy by continuall charge and shott of harquebush through small holes; the enemie in the mean-time being abased and altogether uncertaine what defence or pursuit to use against a moving mouth of mettle.'

'These inventions', he concluded optimistically, 'besides devises of sayling under the water, with divers other devises and strategems for harming of the enemys, by the grace of God and work of expert craftsmen I hope to perform.' There is some evidence that his tank went as far as a trial. Sir Thomas Urquhart of Cromarty describes it—'an almost incomprehensible device . . . an engine which moved by virtue of some secret springs, inward refforts, with other imple-ments enclosed within the bowels thereof . . . He would be able, with the help of this machine alone, to kill thirty-thousand Turks without the hazard of one Christian . . . On a wager he gave proof upon a large plain in Scotland to the destruction of a great many head of cattle and flocks of sheep.' Horrified by its powers, he is said to have ordered its breaking up, and the deep burial of the pieces. In his last illness John Napier was 'earnestly desired to reveal the manner of the contrivance of so ingenious a mystery'. His answer was 'that for the ruin and overthrow of man there were too many devices already framed, which if he could make to be fewer, he would with all his might endeavour to do . . . Seeing the malice and rancour rooted in the heart of mankind, he would not suffer their numbers to be diminished by any new conceit of his.' 'Divinely spoken truly' was Urquhart's comment.

In 1590 King James married Anne of Denmark, with whom he was as happy as he could be with any woman, taking with him on the nuptial trip his mathematical physician, Thomas Craig; and there, in between some festive Danish drinking bouts, king and doctor visited the famous Tycho Brahe in his observatory at Uraniberg: it is probable that it was Craig who made Napier known through Brahe to Kepler, the German astronomer and mystic, who reported to Cugerius in 1594 that a 'Scotus Baro' was revolutionizing calculation (and making astronomy that much easier). James was much taken up with Tycho Brahe and his discoveries in Denmark, causing John Napier a pang of jealousy which he did not hesitate to express: 'At Marchistoun the 29 day of Januar 1593. Let not your Majesty doubt but that there are within your realme (als well as in other countries) good and godly ingynes', (intellectuals, ingenious men?) 'versed and exercised in all manner of honest science and godly discipline, who, by your Majesty's instigation might yeelde foorth workes and fruites worthie of memory, which otherwise (lacking some mightie Maecenas to incourage them) may perchance be buried with eternal silence. Hoping, therefore, that your Highnes will be a protector of us . . .'

Against the day that the king might perhaps found a chair of mathematics at Edinburgh or Glasgow, or at Napier's own St. Andrews, he battled on with his figures in the small high room at Merchiston. Though jealous for royal help and patronage he was not covetous for himself, or desirous of making money from invention. Discoveries were for all (except perhaps Turcs). Both here and at Gartness people commented unfavourably upon John Napier's habit of walking around his fields at midnight accompanied only by a large dog, which was both dangerous and suspect; at Gartness he encouraged the local tendency to believe him a warlock, as it made for uninterrupted work. He was already forty-four, a long life span for the sixteenth century: it may be that the fear of never completing his discovery sometimes haunted him.

In the *Playne Discoverie* he had been in love with mathematics in their bearings on religious truth: now he was in love with mathematics for themselves. But whether this love would enjoy time to bring forth fruit was still a matter of chance.

Robert Napier, the philosopher's second and most scientific son, shared his conscience on inventions. (His son, Alexander Napier of Culcreuch, married Margaret Lennox, and in 1686 their descendants became head of the male line of the Napier family, the Napiers of Milliken and baronets of Merchiston.) Robert bequeathed a book on alchemy and hermetic philosophy to his son, with a firm condition. It was 'to be keipit secret among a few in all ages whose hearts are upright towards God and not given to worldly ambitione and covetousness, but secretly to do gud and help the poor and indigent of this world . . . Above all', he concluded, 'embrace God with your whole heart and purity of mind, for without his guidance all is vanity, and especially in this divine science.'

VII

The scare of invasion passed; but a more near anguish now distracted John Napier from his happy labours with figures amongst the silence and the green fields of Gartness, and it is in these letters about a family tragedy that the Napiers finally shake off the chain armour and the furred robes and stand as recognisable human beings, banging on in the eternal father-son argument. John's three younger half-brothers, Alexander, Archie and William, sons of his father Sir Archibald's second marriage, had long been a worry to their parents. Disconcerted by a lull in clan feuds, and no further wars with England, they refused to settle; spendthrift, light-hearted, and regrettably unserious. What was there to *do* in Scotland now the wars were done? They even talked of emigrating into England; as if there had not already been quite enough of that. Had not their cousins in Dorset made good? And there was Francis Mowbray, a cousin on their mother's side, who had got himself to the court of Queen Elizabeth. 'Alexander!' his father Archibald threatened, 'believe any of you to obtain in other countries such room and rent as ye have apperiance here to? . . . exposing yourselves to unnecessary dangers of lives, or at least to fall for lack of entertainment into miserable poverty, and then ye will say ye wish to God that ye had followed the council of your parents and friends rather than the wilfulness of yourselves . . . Be not as the forlorne son, lest your fathers may not relieve you of your calamities,' Sir Archibald continued, striking a yet more sombre note, and anticipating a row of prodigals, ragged and emaciate, trudging back at him from far countries. And then there was their extravagance!

'Ye write touching the providing of one body servant to every one of you! Ye cannot justly burden us with any strait dealing towards you, for we were content at all times that either of you should choose whom you best please a wife of honourable parentages, at which time we should extend our good will to you and her in such manner as justly neither you nor her friends should receive occasion to plaint ... but propone or do what we could, all for nought except we would have given greater rent and lands to you than our power might extend to, and that only to yourselves to play the ryot with, and not to be used as we have said before.' It was not as if they were not younger sons, all three of them. 'Alexander! Ye know that ye were nought provided by birth, neither to lands nor rent, and yet God of his mercy by the providence of me and your dolorous mother has obtained an reasonable living to you, if sufficience were contentment, which we could not have done if we had played the riot as ye would.'

It was no good. They were, as their parents complained, not to be advised, 'uncounsillabill'. Archie was the flashpoint, the Mercutio of the party. In vain had he married a pretty young wife, Alison Edmonstone, and had a baby daughter. Off he must go 'an inobedient contempter of father and mother, departing away at his own hand to the north to fight in ane ungodly cause', and on an August day in 1600, down to the Border, asking for trouble, where presently he met it.

A horse of his had been stolen, and sweeping south for news of it he encountered Scott of Bowhill, to whom he described the horse. Bowhill, whether in a bad mood, whether regarding the territory as his preserve, or whether because Archie was a young twenty-year-old with a swagger that riled him, decided that he himself was being accused of stealing the horse. He told Archie to defend or die, but the young man was so rash as to laugh at him and go his way. Like the baddie in a Western, Scott of Bowhill lay in wait for him all day and in the late afternoon met him and attacked him 'in the strait of the gate, betwixt low dykes (deep ditches),' and here Archie Napier fought with him and killed him. It was a straight fight, in self-defence, and Archie Napier may have thought it was all in the day's work, as he cleaned his sword on the wayside grass and repaired back to Merchiston. Here he told his brothers what had happened, and they decided that he should make himself scarce for a few months.

He returned to Merchiston in November. But the Scotts were ready for him and a few days later they laid in wait and fell on him as he rode home; 'hard by the Palace, under cloud of night, in outright felony, by the number of seven, armed with sword, spear and pistolets, with which all he was slain being a young man not yet twenty-two years for no more cause but that he defended himself against their brother.' His brother Alexander's rage bites into the paper. Seven Scotts to kill one Napier; for it was from many wounds that Archie's quick blood flowed over the grey cobblestones below the Holyrood walls. This was the kind of crime that incited King James to frenzy, for murder within the royal precincts was accounted murder twice over. Approached by the young man's father he swore to him that 'as soon would he remit the treason of the brother of Gowrie as that felonious murder', which 'his Majesty detesting when it was acted did agree even out of his own considering that it was done in time of his highness' Parliament.'

Alexander and William, Archie's two bereft brothers, were beside themselves; wanting to kill all Scotts from Buccleuch downwards. His parents and elder brother John counselled them to wait for justice, which to the young men seemed an interminable and doubtful process. If nothing happened soon and they were not allowed to kill any Scotts they would leave the country rather than live with the shame of it. 'Ye lament your brother's death', their parents wrote, 'but we lament both his death and your follies, and the more that he was in his time uncounsellable, so ye appear to follow the same course. God make ye end better . . . Judgement, wit, and experience craves reasoning in matters of great importance before conclusions.' Why demand what could not be done? 'It behoves to reason and oppose against unpossibility, not leaving off the meantime such possible preparations as time and occasion offer.' Why, the father asked, make 'such pretexts to colour your inobedience?'—Alexander and William were talking again of going off south—'your old foolish intention . . . your folliful deeds . . . your uncomely and dishonourable doing?' On and on they went, as parents will, rarely content with saying the thing once; as if common-sense could by re-iteration sink through into the hot brain of youth. 'What shall it be said but for fear and feebleness you have left the country, fearing to fall in the hands of your enemies? . . . Leave off, in God's name, such vain enterprises and apply yourselves to wise counsel . . . embrace our wise counsel towards you both for your honour and weal . . . return to us your loving parents and be nought ashamed . . .'

The handwriting of philosopher John joins in, too, in support of his father. 'Is that small delay any argument that we mind to overpass the matter with silence, and not rather to provide with diligence, conform to the common consent and conclusion of kin and friends?

Ye take in mind deeply the revenge of the said murder, and no marvel, for so do we all, but why neglect ye the original part of the tragedy, forgetting how your erstwhile brother became an inobedient contemptor of father and mother . . . We set before you life and death, blessing and cursing, therefore choose life, that both you and your seed may live in the land. And so praying the Almighty to inspire your hearts with a more quiet and obedient spirit, we remit and commit ye both to Him and his protection. At Merchistoun this last day of November 1600.'

Alexander and William were left still darkly brooding. The hopeless patience, stuffiness and law-abidingness of parents and older brothers! Was Scotland, glad land of vengeance and the free-for-all, to sink into a slough of lawfulness and civilization just because of their parents' pedantic belief in the King's writ? Must the flame of kinsman feeling be dowsed for good, because of brother John's incredible notion that the King's peace was something worshipful before which personal rage and rancour must be sacrificed? Not if Alexander and William could help it. Who to try next?

The Scotts had the bold Buccleuch behind them; he who had recently captured Carlisle in order to rescue the imprisoned Kinmont Willie, and been forgiven even by the great Queen Elizabeth herself, for putting so brave a face on it before her. Where was the Napiers' natural protector and advocate, Lennox, who had sworn as price of the earldom 'to support and maintain the said house of Napier and their heirs in all just occasions and engagement'? The old Earl of Lennox was dead, and his son Darnley who would have been no support to anyone, had married Mary Queen of Scots and been done away with. And who was Darnley's son? King James VI himself; it is a bleak moment when one's chief protagonist is metamorphosed into the referee. For the sensible, civilizing king was anti-tribal: he would not take sides.

James had set his face like a stone against clan rows. Only fifty years back a brawl between Angus and Arran had ended in an affray known by the cynical citizenry of Edinburgh as 'Cleanse the Causeway', in which no fewer than eighty Hamiltons had been hauled off the streets feet first and more Douglases than anyone had time to count. In his capital James had hung an invisible sign saying No Montagues here, no Capulets.

He had yearned for peace and friendship, and found little. In 1579 another Lennox, Esmé Stewart, Lord of Aubigny in France and first cousin of James's father, Darnley, arrived at the young king's court. He was perhaps the first charming man the twelve-year-old boy had ever met. Intelligent, harassed, and frequently beaten by his tutor, George Buchanan, James fell in love with Esmé at once, thereby very likely setting his emotional compass for life. The Stewart Lennoxes had proved a poor lot in the end. After his capture at Solway Moss, James Stewart, Earl of Lennox, had been kept in English captivity, where his son, Matthew, Darnley's father, had also, to his detriment, been brought up. 'Lusty, beardless, and lady-faced', Matthew was forfeited for treason to Scotland in 1545, and died in the King's and Queen's Wars, in which naturally he had been fighting for his baby grandson, James VI. His successor, Charles, Earl of Lennox, Darnley's younger brother, had no son and was a nonentity. His Lennox earldom was inherited by Esmé Stewart, whom the infatuated king made Duke of Lennox. Esmé Lennox, though a Catholic, was at least a religious tolerator; but the air was full of papal bulls and consequent popish plots which made moderation in Scotland difficult, and when James was captured by the extreme Protestant Gowries in 1582 and kept prisoner for ten months in Ruthven Castle, the new Duke of Lennox gave up the Catholic struggle to convert James, announced that he himself had become Protestant, and went thankfully back to the vines and the mellow valleys of Aubigny, from which he never more emerged. (His son married a daughter of Buckingham's, settled in the home counties, and declined ever to come north, leaving the men of the Lennox leaderless.) James, now seventeen and rescued from Ruthven Castle, was on his own again.

With the hopeful idealism of youth, James in his twentieth year had caused the nobles attending the Committee of Estates in Edinburgh to walk two by two through the streets to a kind of open air cocktail party at the Mercat Cross; an evening drinking of wine and sweetmeats. Hand in hand they had had to go, sworn enemy clasping sworn enemy, and ended in an obligatory drinking to each other and to peace and friendship. Shocked and horrified at first by the murder of Archie Napier, and vowing justice against the killers to his brothers, James in calmer moments had decided that one Scott had died and one Napier, and that was that.

At this point the dangerous and threatening Alexander Napier was approached by a peace emissary. 'The brother of Bowhill has stirred up the Lord Baccleuch to suit agreement betwixt us and them.' Buccleuch sent a mediator. 'Lord Sanquhar', Alexander wrote, furiously spelling the name in five different ways on the same page, 'in their name came to me with a paper containing certain offers the which to look at I altogether did refuse; yet afterhand I received knowledge of the contents, to wit, they should give us a thousand pound and in all time coming be as brothers!' Alexander elaborates on the theme of his 'great disdain' of this low plan. He told Sanquhar to go to his father and see what answer he would get there. The patient Sanquhar went and returned, saying that Alexander's father had at least admitted to once paying £1,000 himself to settle a blood debt. Why would not Alexander consult Archibald his contemporary nephew, already at court, and the future head of the family, Sanquhar asked? 'The which to do I promised,' Alexander wrote, 'but so I must do it as Regulus, who being a Roman captived at Carthage was sent to Rome to treat . . . and forbade the Roman Senate to exchange the captives at Rome with himself . . . So must I say, though it be my duty as being nearest to the front of the feud, to take hold of offered peace. Yet, loving brother,' Alexander continued, speaking with the very voice of Scotland, 'never embrace dishonourable agreement.'

All, in Alexander's view, was dishonourable agreement where there was not 'eie for eie and tuith for tuith'; (this sentiment, when first uttered by Moses, was remarkably humane and progressive but was beginning to seem less so); yet he was calming down. 'And as I think, God willing, nothing shall divert me from the same, yea, not the thing Lord Sanchar said . . . The fear I have they deal by the Council or by his Majesty frays me,' Alexander admitted frankly, 'yet it must not divert me from the duty of a loving brother, of a mindful man . . . Seek justice . . . go to his Majesty earnestly asking promise of him neither to give respect for long or short time nor remission, which I assure me he will never deny to you if you put his highness in mind of what he swore to my father . . . beseech him at least to give no remission to the murderers of our brother, and to make means to get the Council forbidden from meddling with the same, because it was so detestable and hynus a wrong. I have written to my Lord Dingwall for the same cause . . .'

*

Nothing is more remarkable, during a century of our history, than the ability of all those citizens who could write at all to drop without difficulty into matchless prose. From 1530 till about 1660 they could hardly go wrong; the English language basked in a fadeless spring; one of those exquisite beginnings that break from time to time upon the world. It was Imhotep's stone masonry, it was the Attic smile, Fra Angelico's frescoes; it was Dutch domestic art, the first rain-washed English landscapes, the early French impressionists. Not surprising perhaps that the poets Surrey and Wyatt should write prose as they did, or highly educated Queen Elizabeth, or King James's learned panel of bishops translating the Bible, or the fierce genius of imprisoned Raleigh. But Howard writing a despatch to Walsingham after the Armada has the same sinewy simplicity— 'God send us to see such a company again when need is'—instead of 'Let us hope that an equally adequate personnel will be available in the event of a comparable contingency'. Strafford, a busy first minister, writing to King Charles from the Tower to absolve him from his promise to stand by him, uses an unforgettable turn of phrase; and even a young rakehell like Alexander, under the in-fluence of a powerful emotion, could do as well. 'So I do pray you,' he goes on to his same-age nephew, 'both for your own and my honour, but chiefly for the remembrance of him whose courageous love would never have lain so long idle in either your errand or mine.' He spells it 'curaguis luve', but the words still bite all the same. 'And let me be advised by some sure means, not by the packet, nor no common messenger. I need not entreat for this at your hand, and tell you that I am yours in any thing that I can, for thereof ye never need doubt, so God me sain, to whom I pray for you—Alexander Napier.'

On January 22nd, 1601, Walter Scott, James Scott, and William Scott, brothers to Robert Scott of Bowhill, and John Scott and John of Boynton, were all summoned to appear before the High Court of Justiciary. Archie Napier's widow and his father had obtained letters from the king denouncing these Scotts as outlaws; they were obliged to occupy the place of penitence in church for half a year, and expressed themselves unfeignedly penitent, but where was the satisfaction in that, specially for those who did not live in the same parish? Their minister, Patrick Shaw, of Selkirk, was directed to deal with them; but over every transaction loomed the potent figure of the bold Buccleuch, and nothing further happened. Perhaps the £1,000 had found its way into King James's pocket towards the cost of a royal pardon for the Scotts. James walked a tightrope. Hang five Scotts, and who knew what Buccleuch might do? Between these raging clan lords with their private armies of relations, he felt his life and throne still shaky. Before now, at the age of sixteen, he had been swept off by a bunch of them and held for ten months in Ruthven Castle. 'Nobleness and gentleness ought to be aided by nobles and gentles,' Froissart had firmly pointed out in his fourteenth century best-seller; but the message could not be said to have universally sunk in.

King James VI and I has been discredited in the eyes of posterity by the accounts which Sir Anthony Weldon gave of him in his besotted old age. (To condemn James on the word of waspish Weldon is like allowing Lytton Strachey the final word on Queen Victoria.) He was as 'pleasant and fellow-like' in theological discourse, thought John Hacket, as he was in the hunting field. There is no doubt that he was also very sentimental about his only surviving son, about other young men, about presents, about hounds, about horses. What is truly remarkable about this timorous, literate, learned man is that he alone of all his predecessors came to master and subdue those egregiously wild and arrogant characters, the lords of Scotland. James I had come near it, but he was aided by the fact that so many of the more vigorous spirits had gone off to fight the English in France, and that he was able to send the rest as hostages for his ransom to England (and was under suspicion of giving a good party with the ransom money whenever it was collected, so that the return of the hostages might be postponed). Orphaned, nervous, James VI and I succeeded by sheer intelligence, application and will-power where many a doughtier king had failed. His childhood was a blue-print for the production of a delinquent—a murdered father, an absent and finally executed mother persistently vilified by the tutor who beat James hard and often. Yet he survived, both sane and able.

James had inherited a distressful kingdom, not made easier by his long minority. The tribes, large or small, Highland or Lowland, seemed never at rest with one another: 'They bang it out bravely, he and all his kin against him and all his,' James told his son. What with the 'Wolves and Wilde Boares' of the Highlands and Islands, and the Borderers 'even from their cradells bredd and brought up in theft, spoyle and bloode'; what with the Catholic earls to the north intriguing with the Continent and the far more sinister Protestant Earl of Bothwell to the south intriguing with the devil in unsavoury forms of witchcraft that at once excited James and made his hair stand on end; what with the craftsmen who 'if they in anie thing be controlled' started waving banners and disrupting the peace; and Edinburgh itself, in Chancellor Binning's dramatic words 'being the ordinarie place of butcherlie revenge, and daylie fightis', what with 'the powerful and violent in the in-countrie domineering over the lyves and goodes of their weak neighbours . . . burnings, thefts, reivinges, hocking of oxen, breaking of mills, destroying of growand cornes, and barbarities of all sortes . . . the paroch churches being more frequented upon the Saunday for advantages of neighbourlie malice and mischief nor for Godis service; nobilmen, barons, gentilmen, and people of all sortes being slaughtered, as it wer, in publict and uncontrollable hostilities; merchandis robbed and left for dead in daylight . . . ministers being dirked in Stirling, buried quick in Cliddisdaill and murthoured in Galloway . . .' the difficult country was at its least easy. Maybe it was this contemporary Scotland that Shakespeare makes Ross deplore in *Macbeth*.

These things, by a marvellous exercise of intelligence and will on the part of James VI and soon to be I, had by the 1590s largely ended. Civil peace was what mattered most to James, born as he had been between one murder and the next, and loving hunting and intellectual argument more than steely encounters in the name of clan justice. Not for one young man would he put at risk the peace of his capital city. He temporized over the murder of Archie Napier; and in the spring of the next year a more spectacularly horrible event riveted the attention of the Napiers and all Edinburgh with them.

With so many conflicting and violently held religious opinions about, it was certain that occasional springs of conspiracy must break the surface of uniformity. The threat of kidnapping and assassination had rightly haunted James since he was a child of five. In the Gowrie conspiracy he had had to listen to the ancient hated taunt 'Come down, the son of Seignieur Davie!' that impugned his birth. He had been brought up in a tough Calvinism, and admirably educated in all save affection. Somehow he had managed to grow up preaching and loving the theory of toleration. Yet the wisest fool in Christendom had so little practical sense of it that in England he turned out three hundred parsons from their livings on grounds which the Church itself considered 'inessentials': He believed that if

Catholicism were tolerated the pope might be brought to acknowledge his right to reign and the sanctity of oaths of allegiance to him.
This vain dream made Puritanism more ranting, and disappointed
Catholicism more prone to violence. The majority of English
Catholics were loyal enough and only asking to be allowed to
worship in peace, but were teased into fanaticism by men like the
Jesuit Parsons, the John Knox of the Counter Reformation, who
believed any means justified, including assassination, if it led to the
forcible re-conversion of England, and had full plans for press
censorship and an English Inquisition. For the government it was
impossible to distinguish between dangerous and peaceful Catholics,
and the rank and file suffered from the excesses of the few. If it came
to the crunch would they join in with Spain? James alternately
repressed and tolerated, baffling and enraging the Catholics and
scaring their opponents stiff.

Francis Mowbray, the rash cousin whom Alexander, Archie and
William Napier had so much admired, was accused before Queen
Elizabeth, at whose court he was, of plotting high treason against
King James. His accuser was called Daniele, an Italian fencing-
master. Elizabeth sent them both up to King James, to stand their
trial in Edinburgh. Francis Mowbray was a violent young man, but
in this instance he was almost certainly innocent. He had been with
Buccleuch at the capture of Carlisle and next day, carried away by
the whole thing, he had stabbed a man in a fight and been outlawed.
There was little doubt that he had in his time been involved in popish
plots. These things went against him, but at the Edinburgh trial not a
shred of reputable evidence could be produced by his prosecutors.
Francis himself loudly declared his innocence.

'If ever I thought evil, or intended evil against my prince, God, that
marketh the secrets of all hearts, make me to fall at my enemies' feet!
make me a spectacle to all Edinburgh and cast my soul in hell for
ever.' He challenged Daniele to a duel to prove his innocence; which
seemed to many a proof of clear conscience, since Daniele's skill as a
swordsman was notorious. The time and place were appointed, but
on the morning of the day James postponed the trial; he had more
witnesses whose evidence must be heard, though these proved no
more convincing than earlier ones had been. That night Francis
Mowbray was moved to a different room in Edinburgh Castle, one

immediately below the room which held Daniele; and in the morning his strangled body was found at the foot of the Castle Rock. By attempting to evade the king's justice he had indeed committed treason; his body was dragged to the Mercat Cross and hung up to be drawn and quartered; his head was stuck on the cross and his quarters hung upon every several gate of Edinburgh, a warning to all who could allow treasonable thoughts to pass through their mind.

'His friends, for he was well born and a proper young gentleman, gave out that he had been strangled and his body thrown down at the window, but this carried no appearance and was believed of few,' Archbishop Spottiswoode smugly wrote. But it did carry a great appearance, since people do not often strangle themselves before jumping out of a window in an attempt to escape. Whether James devised it or not, he was certainly privy to this scheme to make it appear that God had taken Francis Mowbray at his word. ('His heinus' Alexander Napier had once called him, spelling better than he meant.) Mowbray had indeed fallen dead at his enemy's feet and been made a spectacle before all Edinburgh.

This repellently sanctimonious crime wrenched John Napier out of his logarithms. His 1594 dedication had directed at King James some more than crisp advice. 'Let it be your Majesty's continuall study to reform the universall enormities of your country, and first to begin at your Majesty's own house, familie, and court, and purge the same of all suspicion of Papists and Atheists and Newtrals, whereof the Revelation telleth that the number shall greatly increase in these latter daies . . . For what by Atheists, Papists, and cold professors, the religion of God is mocked in all estates . . . For partialitie, prolixitie, dearth, and deceitfulness of laws, the poore perish, the proud triumphe, and justice is no where to be found.' Two years after the Mowbray murder Queen Elizabeth died and James inherited the throne of England, leaving Scotland with a sigh of relief audible all round Europe; to reign in England where five successive Tudors had schooled the English not to address their princes in that tone of voice.

What particular horror of the 1590s it took to shock John Napier into such an utterance we know not: it was not a way of speech he habitually used. The preface to the second edition of the *Playne Discoverie* is far more characteristic. 'As we are commanded by the Spirit of God to separate ourselves from all disputers, contentiously by strife of words, so are we bound and commanded with gentleness and meekness to instruct all that are doubtful minded, that they may know the truth.' His own father-in-law, Chisholm, was a leader in one of the popish plots, and all the Mowbrays were Roman Catholics; John Napier was a convinced but not a fanatical or a persecuting Protestant.

Possibly Alexander and William were shaken by all this into choosing life and not death, and settling down. Certain it is that Alexander grew old, disputed wills, became Sir Alexander and a Lord of Session, inherited land through his mother, Lauriston from his father, and built Lauriston Castle—there is nothing like the inheritance of a sizable piece of land for reconciling a young man to the cruelty and injustice of the world. But it is to be doubted if he ever forgot Archie, or was on terms with any Scotts.

At quiet but threatened Gartness, or in his high room in Merchiston Tower John Napier, his serious half-brother, worked on and on; though in between the Trinity, the decimal point, and the arrangements for the marriage of his youngest sister to Lord Ogilvy of Airlie, he was not above a little speculative adventure in some extremely low company. In 1594 he contracted with Restalrig and Francis Hepburn, Earl of Bothwell (and nephew of Queen Mary's Bothwell), of whom the first was a noted robber and outlaw and the second a rebel and suspected necromancer, to divine gold which they hoped was concealed in the fortress of Fastcastle, an impregnable stronghold overlooking the sea, to which Bothwell sometimes resorted. They made a contract by which John Napier by the grace of God should do his utter and exact diligence 'to serche and sik out, and be al crafte and ingyne that he know, to tempte, try and find out' some treasure that was thought to be buried there, in consideration of a third of the loot and a safe return, all 'Trawell and paines' to be paid for if they found no gold.

Nor was he above a tease. He had a tame black cock of which he was very fond; to this deeply superstitious age, in any one less respected it would have seemed dangerously like a familiar. One of the servants at Merchiston was known to be stealing. He told them all that the cock would crow if touched by a guilty person, and before summoning them into his room one by one, he sprinkled its black back with soot. They were all told to stroke its back; the one with clean hands was of course the thief.

Life goes on, in spite of the Sunday papers, in spite of eager journalists and television commentators, magnifying disaster, aggrandizing petty transgressions. While philosopher John grappled with the Revelation of St John the Divine, or laid his mind round those recalcitrant mathematical figures, his son Archibald was also preparing a volume, for publication in 1598. His father Archibald had too been 'careful of stock, and curious in cultivation: the 'apparent' of Merchiston summed up their experience.

'After the corns are win, and put into the barnyard, the piece land tilled, and the wheat seed ended, you shall till down the land whereon you intend to sow down your bear (barley) seed; and if the same be clay, or reasonable stiff, and not sandy land, you shall sow on every acre red land thereof one boll of common salt, and if it be sandy ground, one half boll will suffice . . .

'Let every man cause bigg (build) ten or twelve parks, upon two or three year old ley land at the least, of hwat bounds he pleases, from the middle of the month of March till the eight of April, and that the dykes therof be strong and thick . . . and in the first or second day of the said March let the foresaid whole parks be sown with common salt . . .

'The said parks should be hained, and not pastured upon till Whitsunday thereafter, that they may be once exceeding good grass, and so will last the longer good . . .

'The first day that you enter and eat the first park, you shall let the cattle feed and pasture themselves untill eleven o'clock, that you give them water to drink and therafter put them into a common fold till two afternoon to dung the same as use is . . . put them again into the said first park to pasture until eight o'clock at night; then take them forth to drink, and thereafter all night put them to dung in the common fold, and let them never tarry over night in the said parks . . .

'Every night as a good servant' the cowherd was to clean the parks and spread the dung. 'One acre used this way will feed twice as many cattle as otherwise; and the kine fed thereon will yield twice as much milk as they that are fed on unsalted grass. Every year thereafter, there will be more corn and bear grow than may, in a manner, stand thereupon. Let the dykes stand notwithstanding the tilling thereof . . .' Dunging the parks, building the dykes, human advances move in unobtrusive steady trickles, over against those bloody hiccups whereby, like a car left in gear and then switched on, they leap forward to disaster or to dead stop.

Mary Queen of Scots
by Clouet. *Bibliothèque
Nationale, France*.

Francis II of France
the first husband of
Mary by Clouet.
*Bibliothèque Nationale,
France*.

Mary with her second husband, Henry Stewart, Lord Darnley.
National Trust, Hardwick Hall.

Mary's third husband, James Hepburn, 4th Earl of Bothwell.
Scottish National Portrait Gallery.

By 1614 the great work of philosopher John's lifetime was nearing completion. The nature of the logarithms is explained by reference to the motion of points in a straight line, and the principle upon which they are based is that of the correspondence of a geometrical and an arithmetical series of numbers. He was 'near spente with sikness,' or, he said, he would have taken more trouble over the writing out of the theoretical part: he always deplored his inability to express himself in Latin in a good literary style. 'Make use of this treatise', he urged posterity, when launching his logarithms, 'and give thanks to God the only inventor,' a piece of advice of which the first part has been more universally taken than the second. He dedicated it to Prince Charles, in terms depressing to the non-mathematical: 'Most Noble Prince, Seeing there is neither study nor any kind of learning that doth more activate and stir up generous and heroical wits to excellent and eminent affairs, and contrariwise that doth more defect and keep down sottish and dull minds than the mathematics; it is no marvel that learned and magnanimous princes in all former ages have taken great delight in them, and unskilful and slothful men have always pursued them with most cruel hatred, as utter enemies to their ignorance and sluggishness . . .' But here, for fear of the 'partialitie' which John Napier so deplored, let a finer pen than mine take up the tale.

'In 1614', writes Eric Linklater, in his *Edinburgh*, 'Napier published his *Mirifici Logarithmorum Canonis Descriptio*, and the world received the first announcement of a discovery that has been placed second only to Newton's *Principia*; perused the first table of logarithms; and heard for the first time that word which Napier had invented. As a contribution to science in that age it stands alone; there is no one but Napier, of British origin, who may be compared with Kepler or Galileo or Tycho Brahe. In a country where savagery and superstition were still the commonplace of life, it is remarkable indeed to come upon a man who deliberately, and in a solitude far removed from the assistance of any congenial mind, sets himself the apparently insoluble problem of simplifying the processes of multiplication and division; and by the use of arithmetic and geometry alone, finds the one simplification that could be found.'

John Napier's studies abroad made him believe that the Indians had invented numerals at their College of Madura. Certainly the Indians, Persians and Arabs are known to have had systems of multiplication, but they were involved, rarely used and unreliable:

5

division on any scale was thought to be possible only with the aid of necromancy. The English translation of the *Admirable Canon of Logarithms* declares the book's purpose—'Seeing there is nothing (right well beloved students of Mathematics) nor is so troublesome to mathematical practice, that doth molest and hinder calculations more than the multiplications, divisions, square and cubical extractions of great numbers, which besides the tedious expense of time are for the most part subject to many slipping errors, I began therefore to consider in my mind by what certain and ready art I might remove those hindrances. And having thought upon many things to this purpose, I found at length some excellent brief rules . . . Which secret invention being (as all other good things are) so much the better as it shall be the more common, I thought good therefore to set forth in Latin for the public use of mathematicians . . .'

The book's success was immediate, at least among the mathematical. Kepler, who had first referred to its author as 'a Scottish nobleman whose name escapes me' came to think him the greatest man of the age. He dedicated his next work to John Napier; and Briggs, professor of mathematics at Gresham College in London, wrote to Archbishop Ussher, 'Napper, lord of Markinston, hathe set my head and hands at work with his new and admirable logarithms, I never saw book which pleased me better, or made me more wonder. I purpose to discourse with him concerning eclipses, for what is there that we may not hope for at his hands?' His countrymen were less excited, and he is mildly described by a contemporary, Sir John Skene, as 'a gentleman of singular judgement and learning expecially in the mathematique sciences'. John Marr, another mathematician, describes a meeting between Briggs and Napier in Edinburgh, 'where almost one quarter of an hour was spent, each beholding the other almost with admiration, before one word was spoke. At last Mr Briggs began 'My lord I have undertaken this long journey purposely to see your person and to know by what engine of wit or ingenuity you came first to think of this most excellent help to Astronomy, viz. the logarithms; but my lord, being by you found out, I wonder nobody else found it out before, when now known it is so easy.' He was nobly entertained by the Lord Napier for a month, and every summer after that, during the Lord's being alive, this venerable man Mr Briggs went purposely to Scotland to visit him.' Napier's

Canon Mirificus was written in Latin; it was translated into English by Edward Wright, another mathematician. *Rabdologia*, another simplification of multiplication which came to be known as Napier's Bones, was published after his death. In an appendix to this he explains another invention 'the most expeditious of all', for multiplying and dividing by means of metal plates arranged in a box, a forerunner of the electronic calculating machine.

His portrait was painted by Jamesone. It is a noble face, full of intelligence and thought, but a concerned one. Well it might be. Rapine and lawlessness still stalked his land, though less uniformly than it had in his childhood: a sudden tumult any moonlit night, a successful Campbell or Macgregor swoop upon Gartness, might yet prevent his work from being completed. The Lowlanders still murdered, the Highlanders still clanged, the dolour of the poor and the weak still sounded in his ears. What with 'atheists, newtrals and cold professors', where was faith moving to? Not, he devoutly hoped, back into the rigid dogmas by which medieval popes had herded the Church of Christ so far away from its origins and from its early fathers, not back to the heritage of imperial Rome forever seeking aggrandizement and imposing uniformity—his *Playne Discoverie of the Whole Revelation* was written for 'Preventing the apparent danger of Papistry arising within this Island', and he roundly declared in it that the pope was Anti-Christ, which indeed with the pope's recent warm encouragement of political assassination was not wholly illogical.

Perhaps, too, that long puzzling over his mathematical tables deepened the lines around his eyes. His discovery was unique, 'a pure invention in the fullest sense and meaning of the word', its significance 'all the more remarkable from the fact that it was not connected with analogies or coincidences which might have led him up to it, but was the result of unassisted reason and pure science, and was arrived at by a slow systematic progress from gradual evolution of truth. It was the persistent effort of a great mind to perform a task it had deliberately set itself, and which step by step it pursued to the end.'*

'His very name is sufficient Elogium, and will be such as long as the world lasteth,' declared Dr George Mackenzie in the early eighteenth century; but endless many-volumed histories of Scotland never mention it. Later in that century Gibbon allows him 'a heart to

* W. Brownlie Hendry, 'John Napier of Merchiston', *History Today*, April 1967.

resolve, a head to contrive, and a hand to execute': in 1857 his great
etc. grandson, Francis, 10th Lord Napier, British Minister in
Washington, in an address at Harvard University, paid a just
tribute to John Napier for blazing the trail from mathematics as a
slightly sinister form of magic to mathematics as scientific truth—
'My ancestor lived on the border-line of fable and truth when
numbers were still enslaved by necromancy, and when the orb of
science was seen darkly through the clouded glass of magical superstition.'

W. R. Thomas, writing in 1935 in the *Mathematical Gazette*,*
suggests that Napier—a Greek scholar—derived the word logarithms from Archimedes' *Arenarius*, an edition of which was produced
at Basle in 1544; and that his ideas for a hydraulic screw and a
revolving axle may have come from Apollonius and Hero of
Alexandria. From Archimedes, too, perhaps came the idea of his
anti-Spanish burning glass—'the invention, proofe, and perfect
demonstration, geometricall and algebricall, of a burning mirrour,
which receving the dispersed beames of the sonne, doth reflex the
same beames altogether united and concurring priselie in ane
mathematicall point, in the which point most necessarilie it en-
gendreth fire . . . The use of invention serveth for burning of the
enemies shipps at whatsoever appointed distance.' But Mr Thomas
notes that both Moulton and Napoleon's professor of mathematics
at the Ecole Buonaparte, Peyrard, together with the great Lagrange
and Delambre, give Napier sole credit for his mathematical discovery.

Celebrating in 1914 the Tercentenary of his *Descriptio*'s publifica-
tion, 'Nothing had foreshadowed it or heralded its arrival,' Lord
Moulton declared, 'It stands isolated, breaking in upon human
thought abruptly, without borrowing from the work of other intellects
or following known lines of mathematical thought.' On this same
occasion Professor George Gibson wrote that in originality of
conception and depth of insight Napier was one of the small band of
mathematical thinkers represented by Archimedes in antiquity and
by Newton in recent times, whose genius consolidated the labours of
their predecessors and laid down the lines of future advance. His
lustre increases rather than dims over the years. Rosalind Mitchison,
writing in 1970, calls him a shining light, adding that 'in the first half
of the seventeenth century only one intellectual discoverer in
Scotland makes the world class, Napier of Merchiston.'

* Vol. XIX, no. 234.

In the spring of 1617 the old philosopher was failing. He died on April 4th, aged sixty-eight, calm and fully *compos mentis*, providing in his will for 'all my haille bairns', he signed it three days before his death—'Johne Naippere of Merchistoun being sick in body at the plesour of God, but haill in mynd and spereit.' He was buried at St Cuthbert's, the parish church of Merchiston. 'I have not done perfectly as I would, but zealously as I could,' he had humbly written. Like patriotism, science and mathematics were not enough. 'In vaine', he had once told the king, 'are all earthly conjunctions, unless we be heires together and of one body, and fellow partakers of the promises of God in Christ.'

Part IV

Montrose and Two Archies

VIII

Peace at last over Scotland; or so it seemed. Defence against England, the major concern, had ceased to preoccupy. A Scots king reigned in Whitehall, and the Border, if not mouse quiet, at least was not reverberant. Argyll was young, and still being educated abroad: the Macgregors brooded silently in their marsh: no clang of swords echoed round Loch Lomond. As well as the swords hung on the walls of Merchiston, there were golf-clubs in the corner, and piles of unwarlike fishing tackle. There were pipes as well as tankards on the table. The great Raleigh, now languishing in the Tower ('only my father', Prince Henry of Wales said of James VI and I, 'would keep such a bird in a cage'), had brought back tobacco from America, a substance of which the king disapproved; and also the potato, an import to which even the sternest of Puritans had been unable to object. The menace of Spain was easing; France had too many troubles of her own to look for more outside. The mutterings of constitutional upheaval from Westminster, though continuous, did not seem likely to boil over into any major dust-up. The Gunpowder Plot had misfired and at the other extreme a lot of the more excessive Puritans seemed about to take off for North America, there to drown their witches and till the starvecrow soil of New England without government interference, and good luck to them. The British have been much blamed by Americans for sending minor criminals and indentured servants as settlers, all relatively harmless: curiously no one has yet lodged a protest against the projection of those far more lethal rockets, the Pilgrim Fathers.

The philosopher's son Archie Napier, he to whom Alexander (an uncle of his own age) had addressed his impassioned appeal for vengeance on the Scotts, had given his own young brother-in-law James Graham, Earl of Montrose, his first sword; but it seemed possible that he would never have to use it against anyone except

5*

footpads. On June 1st, 1625—the larks perhaps high in an unclouded sky, the sun bright on the Pentland hills—'To my entirely beloved kinsmen,' Archie wrote, 'Sir Robert Napier of Luton Hoo Knt and Bart, Sir Nathaniel Napier of Middlemarsh Knt and Bart, Thomas Napier of Tintinhull Esq, John and Robert Napier of Puncknowle . . . kinsmen of my blood and branched from my house', sending their birth brieve—'to bear my arms, supporters and crest with their due difference as their lawful right and ancient inheritance . . .' There was time now to settle and list his clan: '. . . James Napier of Baglake in the County of Dorset, Edward Napier of Hollywell . . .' With arched eyebrows above round well-apart eyes, beaked nose, and a pointed beard below curving full lips, his long chin bent into his ruff as he wrote the birth brieves. 'William Napier of Puncknowle had issue John and Robert now living . . .' On he went, the long intelligent face concentrated above the slashed doublet—'. . . out of the natural affection and love which I bear to my loving cousins . . .'—the necessary establisher, level-headed and worldy wise. From the garden below came the cheerful zizz of bees; the shouts of his children, John, Archie, Lilias and Margaret, of his brother Robert's sons, William, John and Alexander. In the mirage of a June day none could foresee the fierce exactions which loyalty would compel from him, or feel the rising tide of violent opinion that would swirl the Napiers out of Merchiston for ever, that would wash Scotland far from her King Alysandyrs dream of loving and le, of wine and wax and gaming and glee, on to the stern coasts of an age-long Sabbath day.

On King James's accession to the throne of England, Archie Napier had gone south with him, in order to observe the English in their native habitat, for he, too, was scientific. But he was also shrewd. Perhaps he had noted that the lifelong labours of his father's magnificent brain had brought him in nothing (though in 1596 John Napier was awarded a monopoly for his hydraulic screw and revolving axle for pumping water out of coal mines.) After Archie left Glasgow University he brought out his agricultural treatise— 'The new order of gooding and manuring of all sorts of field land with common salts, whereby the same may bring forth in more abundance, both of grass and corn of all sorts, and far cheaper than the common way of dunging used heretofore in Scotland: set forth by Archibald Napier, the apparent of Merchiston,' for which he claimed and got a royal patent for twenty-one years. His youth was not blameless. In June 1601 he was brought before the Privy Council for an assault on a servant of the Lord Treasurer on the stairhead of the Tolbooth: case dismissed through lack of evidence.

Staying at home and salting the cherished fields of Scotland was not enough: Archie was ambitious. To serve the king faithfully 'would doe me (I thought) and my house good'. 'After I had left the Schooles I addressed myself to the service of King James of blessed memory and was graciously received by him,' until 'His Ma was pleased to cast the Earl of Somerset out of his favour and take in his place George Viliers afterwards Duke of Buckinghame, a powerful Favorite and no good Friend of myne.' His father (logarithms John), near death, had summoned him home. Riding north along the muddy track which is now A1, the indignant phrases formed in Archie's mind. After there had been 'large promises of friendship and fair blossomes of protestations and complements which never bore fruit' from Buckingham, 'the affaires of Court which are never long stable took another ply.' There were woods everywhere over the countryside, but by law they had to be cleared for twenty yards each side of the road to prevent ambush. The dark red of the fields of Rutland succeeded the orange plough of Northamptonshire, while Archie brooded the pitfalls of public life. At Newark the castle was black against the sunset; next day on the long rolling plains of Yorkshire the burnt sienna of the south would give way to the brownish pink of the North Riding. On the fourth afternoon the distant horizon began to swell, here was the beginning of the hill country, the green turbulence of home; the local speech was ruffling into the familiar tongue of his childhood and youth. The Border hills rose up; skirting them, he took the route by Berwick and the sea. Soon he was back at Merchiston, free within its thick and battered walls to write and speak his mind, to listen to the so different speech of Scotland, to ride the hills of home. Settling the considerable affairs of his father's estate, in 1619 he married the daughter of John, 4th Earl of Montrose, Lady Margaret Graham, fair complexioned, red-haired, religious, and to him supremely beautiful. In the early sixteen-twenties King James appointed him Deputy Treasurer of Scotland.

'This act of the Kings without my knowledge, without my sute, or any friends of myne, and in my absence, being singular (for although no living man had the art to know men more perfectly than hee, yet still importunity prevailed with him against his owne choyse) made me enter into serious consideration of the mater, and to set downe to myself rules and resolutions of honest proceeding in the dischairge of that place. First, because wee are commanded to serve our Masters faithfully, and for conscience sake, Next, because in my nature I hate the imputation of dishonesty, avarice and injustice. Thirdly, not to make his Ma: ashamed of his choyce, which was only his owne. And lastly, I thought it no safe way for me who was born to ane estate, by base scraping, purloyning, and bribery to endanger it: what I got by his Ma: bounty, upon consideration of good service, would doe me (I thought) and my house good. Armed with this resolution I entered that service, and my behaviour therein was according thereto, whereby his Ma: was well satisfyed, and if it had pleased God to grant him a longer lyfe, I had not (in all probability) been disapoynted of my hopes, for of his good opinion and purpose toward me there are yet living witnesses: and a little before his Death he recommended me (I being then in Scotland) to his Sonne King Charles, as his Ma: himselfe was pleased to tell me, than which a greater testimony of a gratious Masters favour to ane absent Servant at such tyme could not bee exprest.'

The fact that the Treasurer Principal, Mar, backed by 'the Duk of Buckinghame,' was one 'who could not well brooke a College', was a slight setback; but on finding that Archie Napier was the colleague he had to brook 'we served together in that service with reasonable correspondence as long as King James lived.' The king told Mar that Archibald Napier was 'free of partialities or any factious humor', and Mar agreed that he was known to be both judicious and honest. 'But he (the king) being dead, and his sonne King Charles succeeding him in his kingdome, and to his vertues too, although with some want of experience, which is only got with tyme, all the turbulent and discontented humors of the former tyme were up (as is usual in these great transitions) and plyed his Ma: incessantly with accusations, personal aspersions, new projects, and informations of abuses. And truely there wanted not matter, and there endeavors had deserved praise if splene to the persons of men, and there own privat interest had not given lyfe and motion to there proceedings, rather than service of the King and the good of the state . . . And no dreams or fantasy of innovation came in any bodies head, but presently he durst vent it to the King, and still the most ignorant were boldest.' Archie's apprehension glooms through his loyalty; could any honest man get into communciation with such an aloof and uncomprehending young king?

Archie I had been knighted on the king's visit to Edinburgh in 1617, and on August 20th of that year he was sworn of the Privy Council. By letters dated at Royston, October 21st, 1622, he had been appointed Treasure Depute for Scotland: he had occupied King James's last years in the development of Scotland's glass making industry, her coal-workings, and reports on the copper coinage, serving on Privy Council committees about the freighting of merchant ships, dealing with the feud between Buchanans and Macfarlanes, and enquiring into the state of Orkney and Shetland. He was undoubtedly a man of parts, with a passion for abstract argument: defending as a young man in 1603 the proposition: 'Suppose this man guyltie of the cryme that he is chairged with, yet it is nether for the kingis honor nor profeit to destroy him:' whether he pursued this anti-capital punishment line as a Lord of Session, which he became in 1623, is not known. In 1610 he wrote a letter to James Galloway, later Lord Dunkeld, about developing in Scotland 'a gallant and gentlemanlyk' stile of writing. In March 1626 he was a member of the Commission of Exchequer, and the same month sworn into the Council of War for Scotland. It all has a modern, political ring, unlike the recent times of dinging and banging around the walls of Merchiston, and the putting into pits and boiling of barely a couple of hundred years back. In 1627 Archie I was made a baronet of Nova Scotia, which meant that he forked out for a few hundred acres around New Brunswick that he was too busy to take up; and later in the same year he became 1st Lord Napier, an honour in some sense retrospective—'to Archibald Lord Nepare of Merchingstoun . . . considering the very many services over a long time by the predecessors of our faithful and loved councillor Sir Archibald Nepare of Merchingstoune Knight, in our kingdom of Scotland in peace and war, to our illustrious forefathers of happy memory, and bearing in mind the very many outstanding services of the aforesaid diligent and devoted Sir Archibald Nepare to our late renowned father of illustrious memory . . . and also to us, to our honour and benefit and to that of all our subjects . . .'

Fair enough; but as Archie had already noted, Charles was not

James; and the late king's eldest son, the brilliant and gifted Prince Henry, with a will and decision entirely his own—'only one religion shall lie on my pillow' he had declared at seventeen when pressed to marry a Spanish princess—had died or possibly been murdered some years before his father's death. For Archie the days of prosperity were numbered: the Scots lords, free of the shrewd eyes of King James, were back to their old games. The first whiff of cold wind came in 1629, a February letter from Robert Napier to his brother Archie in London, warning him that a letter from the king prejudicial to Archie's honour and estate has been handed to the Lords of the Exchequer on the twelfth of the month. Robert was presenting a bill to stay the registration of the letter until Archie could get home to answer for himself; he is certain the letter had been tampered with *en route*, but since it is 'thocht muche of' in Scotland, he advises Archie to put himself right with the king before coming home.

Urgently, Robert wrote again next day, to say that in spite of his bill the king's (tampered with) letter had been registered—Archibald Campbell has promised to get a copy for Archie to show the king to compare with his original draft. Robert had also heard that some instructions and papers from the king have been witheld by the Lords of the Exchequer. Those of them present were Lords Mar, Haddington and Erskine, the Advocate, Sir John Elphinstone, Sir John Scott and Sir James Bailizie—'how many friends ze have of this number ze knawe,' Robert commented cynically. He again urged his brother to deal only with the king and to trust no one else.

In July Archie in London wrote to the king protesting his innocence of any desire other than to surrender his lease of Orkney, which intention he had intimated by the hand of Sir William Balfour. He feared that his 'unfriends' were trying to prevent his re-instatement in the king's favour by representing him as fighting against surrendering the lease—they have sent him terms so 'unjust and unreasonable'. He petitioned the king to grant him a hearing and accept his absolute surrendering of the lease. He had been told to raise money for paying and victualling Scotland's three warships; for this purpose he had been granted the lease of Orkney for 42,000 merks annually and had sub-let it to William Dick for 54,000, thereby raising a storm, but how otherwise victual the ships or pay the seamen? with French privateers whipping in and out of Leith Roads?

Orkney, since its absorption into Scotland as part of the dowry of

James III's Danish wife, had had a bad deal. One of the terms of its cession had been that it should never be handed over to any king's son not of lawful bed, on the principle that bastards will be bastards; but this stipulation had been broken in favour of one such, of James V's unlawful bed, and a vicious and oppressive Robert Stewart, Earl of Orkney, and his son Patrick had bullied and squeezed the Orcadians over the last fifty years. 'The first thing I intended after my admission' (as Treasurer) 'was the fewing of Orkney and Zetland to the inhabitants,' Archie wrote, 'that the people might be freed from the cruell exactions and pittiful oppression of Leassies, who thought it lawfull for them to make there best advantage paying the rent of there Lease, neither wanted they power, for they were Sherifs; and they had not only set to them the rents and casualties of the Countrey; but forfeitures and unlaws of courts, whereof they were the sole judges. His Ma gave me commission with that effect;' but King James, although his 'just displeasure was kindled against Sir John Buchanan the present Leassy' had not wanted to break the lease and turn him out if things could be managed without going to this extreme, 'such was his justice and goodness;' and then James had died and Mar had been against going on with the scheme, and so . . .

It was a new reign. 'Then wes there nothing but factions and, factious consultations of the one, to hold that place and power they possest before; of the other, to wrest it out of there hands, and to invest themselves . . . Neither wanted there some honest and wysemen, who gave there advyse out of mere affection to his Ma: and the Publique, but wanting that bold forwardnes and factious assistance which the others had in prosecution of there privat ends, no great hold wes taken of them,' Archie added, perhaps giving an unconscious pen portrait of himself.

'The Thesaurer wes not free from this storme, but was charged home by his enemies with some abuses . . . There wes a Gentleman direct to me, desyring me to give them intelligence upon what poynts my Lord Mar might bee charged . . . This I flatly refused, as ane office unworthy of a Gentleman, and told him that I disdained any honor that should be acquyred by so dishonorable meanes against a man that wes in termes of outward friendship toward me . . .'

Then there were the tithes, called teinds, by which the people of Scotland were most grievously oppressed; no one could get in their harvest without a previous down payment, and barely could they milk their cows. The lords who had enriched themselves on dissolved abbeys were so avaricious in their 'teind-gathering' that people looked back with regret to the milder abbots who had sometimes let payment from a hard-pressed man go by default. The kings had genuinely wished to reform this abuse—'the bussines of Tythes, amongst others, wes most constantly presecuted by his Ma: a purpose of his Fathers, or his owne, who finding the heavy oppression of teynd-masters, and the servitude of the people, did earnestly endeavour to remed it. But in this, as in other matters, what truly might be said to be his (which were his intentions only) wes most just and princely: but the meanes (which were other mens inventions), were most unfit to compasse his ends, but fit enough to serve there turnes that found there privat prejudice, to render the bussines intricat, longsome, and difficult, upon hope his Ma: would relinquish the same.'

Charles appointed a royal commission to look into the tithes 'of the Commission of the teinds I had the honor to be one, and according to my duety and power did advance his Ma: just and gratious purpose.' This inspection and his lease of Orkney 'did so much offend the chiefe Statesmen, who were the greatest teynd-masters also, and (be a great incongruity) members of this commission, that in there privat meetings they concluded my overthrow,' Archie reported. The arguings and uncertainties about tithes and the grave loss when they were remitted by the king, so incensed the great lords that it was not only Archie's overthrow that was concluded; in some measure King Charles's was as well.

In view of all the jiggery pokery that prevailed it is not surprising to find Archie Napier advising the king to set up an intelligence service in Scotland and find out what really went on. But he is getting a bit cannier—in the same year he wrote to the king to ask that his warrant to prepare for the king's coming to Scotland should be altered to show the Earl of Mar as chief officer in the enterprise with himself as deputy, the earl being already far advanced with preparations for the repair of the royal houses in Scotland. He did not want to make more enemies than he could help. The king had been under the impression that Archie had refused to cede his lease of Orkney upon royal request, and to Sir William Balfour 'exprest his anger against me in great measure. When I came up I found his countenance altered, and therefore desyred the Marquess of Hamilton to procure me access and hearinge.' In this interview King Charles expressed himself satisfied, declaring that he did not now believe the calumnies against Archie. 'I desired no more but impartial hearing, and protection if my cause wer honest,' he insisted.

But the calumnies went on, and the king again sent for Archie. ('In the mean tyme all the terrors of the world were gevin me: that the King would send me home to be tryed, where my enemies were to be my judges; that I should not only want my fees pension and place, but the King's favor and myne owne honor also, and as a delinquent and criminal be warded in the castle of Edinburgh, and deeply fyned.') Next day 'when he wes going from dinner, he beckoned to me, and I followed him in to his bed-chamber; and being alone with him, Sir, said I . . . humbly thanks to your Ma: for giving me a choyce to stand to my justification, or submit myself to your Ma: I will not, Sir, absolutely justify myselfe before God, nor before you: your Ma; might have had a servant of more eminent abilities, never a faithfuller, nor more diligent, nor better affected. And as for submitting myselfe to your Ma: if my lyfe or estate were in quaestion, I could lay them both doune at your feet, but this is my honour dearer to me than they both, which loses by submitting, and cannot be repared by your Ma; nor any King in the world.'

'The wordes at first seeming sharpe and bruske, he mused a little, then burst out with these:

' "Begod, my Lord, you have reason!" and withall he told me some of there informationes.'

This gave occasion for another fine burst of rhetoric from Archie. The lords' complaints, he assured the king, were all based on Archie's refusal to comply with them in their base designs. . ' "I desyre no more than the most regorest and exactest tryall can be desyred, so it be just and your Ma: my Judge, and that I be not remitted to Scotland where my Enemies are to be my judges, and where (if I were as innocent as Jesus Chryst) I should be condemned. For the more exact the tryall bee, the more shall my faithfulness and integrity appeare to your Ma: and I will not only answere for my owne actions, but if my wyfe, friend, or servant (who by corrupt Officiars usually are set out to be Baudes to there bryberie) have done wrong, I am content it be imputed to me. If I had cousaned your Ma: and opprest your people, and then made some men sharers in the prey, your Ma: had not been troubled now, nor I persecuted, but had been delivered to your Ma: for a good and faithful servant." '

'And then his Ma: promised that he would heare all himself; which wes a poynt I desyred much to gaine, and did serve me after-wards to good purpose.' Archie had pressed King Charles to get a written and signed statement from his accusers. 'For the space of eight days thereafter I was free of their pursuit, so long as the King remained in Hampton Court (for the command to set down the wreat under there hands did much amaze them.)' Eventually they produced the accusations, but written right down to the end of the page, so that no one could sign it. Archie had no difficulty in refuting them: in one he was accused of having cooked the books on the king's visit to Scotland—'I confess I never bought to myselfe, nor to any other, housshold provisions, and have no skill in Catery or Butcherie, and if I had failed in that way, it is want of skill, not honesty.' No one questioned his answers, but the calumnies went on, and Archie would not depart for Scotland without a written warrant from Charles that if the matter came up again he and his accusers were to be sent to be judged by the king, and meanwhile he was to go on in the job of Deputy Treasurer. When he got back to Scotland, the chancellor 'whose manner wes to interrupt all men when he was disposed to speake, and the King too', had put the articles of accusa-tion 'in the publick register, without any warrand from the King or Councell, and would not by any meanes registrate my answeres to them, there to remaine for a dishonour and staine to me, my house, and posterity to after-ages, who should not know that they were shamefully disavowed to by the informers themselves, nor answered by me; ane Act of superlative malice,' Archie furiously recorded.

Lord Mar died, and Lord Morton succeeded him as treasurer, with Traquair as his deputy; and Archie had to be content with resigning Orkney, and his office of Treasurer Depute, for which he got £4,000 sterling, and a letter of approbation or quietus, under the Great Seal, on March 6th, 1631. He had lost out; but at least enjoyed the pleasure of justification and of the last word, which he had in Council, late in 1630. A document had been produced there, pretending to be a commission dated from Whitehall on June 28th, 1630, reducing Archie in his deputy treasureship to a mere cypher. At the meeting of the Exchequer at Edinburgh he questioned the authenticity of the document.

'This was done by the King's direction, and we will answer it,' Morton had said; and Lord Menteith, not unreasonably, had burst out, 'My Lord Napier, you are so passionate in your own particular,

that you will not forbear to question what the King commanded!
For his Majsety stood by while it was done, and we will answer it.'

'If it had been the King's direction,' Archie countered, 'why
would you not bestow upon him a clean sheet of paper, and ingrossed
these marginal notes of yours in the body of the signature, rather
than made use of this old torne thing? Then needed not the signature,
with the King's hand at it, receve validity from yours upon the margin.
Monteith maintained that the king stood by till he saw them sub-
scribe, and that it was his direction.

'My Lord,' Archie persisted, 'I marvel that you are not ashamed
to say so. Let the Lord look the date with a blacker ink than the rest,
"at White Hall the 28th June 1630"; then you were there you say
with the King? Your lordship hath ridden fast; for you were here,
and presided in Council, the 29th of June 1630; to verify which I
desire that the clerk of the Council's book of *sederunt* may be
looked on; and my Lord Morton, your lordship set out of London
before him!'

Archie noted with delight that Menteith could only mutter, at the
disclosure of this untruth, that the lords were all silent, and that even
the chancellor sat mute. He had survived round one, by the skin of
his teeth, with both honour and property intact.

IX

At long last, seven years late, King Charles I arrived in Scotland for his coronation. Every effort had been made by the still not very rich Scots to do justice to the event. All Edinburgh's town soldiers had been rigged up as a royal bodyguard, in white satin doublets and silk stockings and black velvet breeches; even their pikes were gilded. William Drummond of Hawthornden had written a masque called *Endymion*; and the loyal townsfolk had scraped up a golden bowl full of a thousand gold pieces. King Charles, for his part, had kept vigil all the night before in the church of Holyrood House. But the procession had started half an hour late owing to a furious argument between the aged Lord Kinnoull, Lord Chancellor (who died of rage a few days later), and the Archbishop of St Andrews, about who should walk first. Kinnoull sent a message by Sir James Balfour, Lord Lyon King of Arms, who was in charge of the ceremony— 'Never a stoled priest in Scotland should set a foot before him, so long as his blood was hot!' To which Charles sensibly replied, 'Weel, Lyon, let's go to business; I will not meddle further with that old cankered gouty man, at whose hands there is nothing to be gained but sour words.'

After that was settled, the waiting provost and baillie had given the king the golden bowl full of money: 'The King', wrote Archie Napier to his brother-in-law Montrose, who was away in Italy pursuing an erring sister,* 'looked gladly upon speech and gift, but

* Earlier this year Sir John Colquhoun of Luss, first baronet, married to Montrose's eldest sister, had seduced his young sister-in-law, Lady Katherine Graham, supposedly with the aid of his German manservant, Carlippis, a necromancer and sorcerer, and fled with them both to Italy. He was summonsed to Edinburgh to answer charges of incest and necromancy, but as these were both capital, he prudently remained in Italy. He returned alone fourteen years later, made peace (at a considerable cash price) with the Covenanter regime, married a new young wife, and for all we know lived happily ever afterwards. What became of Katherine Graham has never been known.

the Marquis of Hamilton, Master of His Majesty's Horse, hard beside him, meddled with the gift as due to *him* by virtue of his office.' The townsfolk, not unnaturally, were irritated by this piece of poaching; and still more by Archbishop Laud, whom they suspected of being about to whip out a cardinal's hat from under his robe at any minute. Never noted for tact, Laud had referred to the English Parliament as 'that noise,' and expressed the view that the Scots had no religion. Archie Napier had a good view of the coronation proceedings as he had held one end of the canopy over the king's head: its splendour and ritual caused many a boot face among the severer Scots.

Other events went better. King Charles was a consummate rider; his air on horseback had been much admired as he rode through the principal towns of Scotland. In Edinburgh the city had given a fine banquet to the king and the five hundred English nobles he had brought with him, as well as to all the Scots nobles, and afterwards they had all appeared with no hats on, and held hands and danced down the High Street 'with music and much merriment'. The king had opened the Scots Parliament wearing James IV's royal robe of purple velvet, furred and laced with gold, and then had wrecked the affair by making an extremely tactless speech. It seemed to Archie that there was no future in threatening the Scots' people with treason for not using a prayer book which had not yet even been printed. Charles for his part was deeply shocked by the Scots' refusal to kneel when receiving communion; what could you do with a people who were so determined not to kneel to a priest or a sacrament that they would not even kneel before the altar of God? Charles was unaware that no one in his kingdom had knelt for communion before the thirteenth century, and that the Scots were only harking back. A slight sensation of dancing on a volcano undermined the music and the merriment, as they twirled down the cobble-stones, very slightly high, and splendid in their silked and ribboned clothes.

Charles I's attempt to impose a new Church liturgy upon the Scots was one of those well-intentioned but fatal errors which clang on down the ages, promoting the death and destruction of hundreds not yet born; since once the Scots had made up their minds to address the Almighty in their own spontaneous words no potentate on earth could change them. In its power to engender strife it is like that fatal papal bull of the 1150s, by which Pope Adrian IV empowered King Henry II of England to conquer Ireland, then fallen from its earlier holiness and civilization into a state of anarchy and self-destruction—'Subdue and rule,' the pope commanded (he was English); and it is the one papal pronouncement which for eight hundred years was regarded as perfectly infallible by the whole English and Scots race, with results for which they and the Irish all still bleed. Even Charles's imposition caused fewer heads to roll, and for a shorter span, but then no one much except himself thought Charles infallible: as it was it was lethal enough. It was Charles's quarrel with the Scots that in the end brought half England out in arms against him.

A shadow of sadness comes over Archie's writings after the king had departed for England; as if he now knew that civil war must come. The gallant and gentlemanlyk style that he had striven after in his youthful writing is soberer, more measured. He was fifty-nine now; and could feel Scotland, the beloved country, heaving under his feet. Surely some compromise about the bishops could have been arrived at, if the king could listen, if Laud had let him listen: 'It is the humour of some of great trust and credit about Princes, to slight and cry down any motion, though never so good, which doth not proceed immediately or mediately of themselves, and will rather give bad informatione, and worse advyce, than give way to others, or seem incapable, in any way, themselves.' Could loyalty to the king, and loyalty to Scots religious freedom, still be made compatible? Certainly his young brother-in-law, Montrose, thought so; was it all the illusion of his youth and fire?

The thought of those accusations lodged unanswered in the State Register still rankled, and Archie was writing his 'Defence'. On he goes, fighting his way he hopes with honour and certainly with a ready pen, through the jungle of accusation. '. . . it was drawn by the Secretary, with words derogatory as he alleadged to his honor, of set purpose to put us together by the eares . . . Archibald Primrose, knowing I must have a hand in taxation wes loathe I should looke into that which he wes Clerke. These and such lyke business increast there splene against me, who still upon all occasions continued my wonted freedome to give advyse without respect of anything els but the publick good.' Archie had no worries about sounding self-righteous: this was not a fear that troubled the seventeenth century. 'The most part of my enemies being present at Court fell a consulting and plotting my overthrow, which from this tyme foorth they so eagerly prosecuted as they forgot conscience, honor, there owne qualities,

and the places they possess; and in this way they went to work . . .
James Douglas, a man religious and honest but too too simple . . .
wes perswaded to take there fault upon him, and thereby lost his
place . . .' He plunged on into the complicated business of the tithes,
over-exacted and unpopular in Scotland. 'I answered that there were
some Omissions which were not altogether my Lord Thesaurers
fault nor myne, but partly theres who served before us and that we
intended in tyme to bring them in; neither wes ther such perfection
among men as to omit nothing,' he grumbled.

There is something rich and velvet about seventeenth century indignation; flowing out in an uninhibited fountain like clear water over
moss. Archie Napier, in trouble over Orkney, and unpopular with
his fellow lords over the tithes, well knew how to employ the noble
rage. 'Neither my Lords doe I refuse tryall, for nothing can prove
more honorable to me nor more contrare to my advseraries desires.
For this I dare affirm without vanting, that never any officier hath
served the King with more honesty and integrity, with better affection
or les regard to my owne profit. I have not builded up a fortune upon
hill or hope by cozning the King, or wronging his Subjects, I have
bought no land since I was Thesaurer Deput, I have not builded fair
houses, nor married daughters, nor have I sowmes going out upon
intrest, but am as farre in debt as when I entred this service, and that
I have been no prodigal all men know that know me . . . I know none
of your Lordships so great nor so good as can plead exemption from
the malice of detractors, but may come in the same predicament that
I am in now, who of late thought my selfe as farre out of the compasse of it as another.' In the roll and swell of Archie's fine periods
it is hard to fathom clearly what substance swims beneath. A sense
of having been out-smarted, of not quite making the political grade,
a certain thankfulness at having so failed? Did he still hope for a
come-back in less tangled times?

For years he would have liked to give up the job. 'There wes
nothing I more desyred in my secretest thoughts then to be fairly
rid of that place long before my troubles: for after my wife dyed, a
woman religious chast and beautifull, and my cheife joy in this
world, I had no pleasure to remaine, having had experience of the
cheefe of Counsell and Session and of there maners, to which I
could never fashion myselfe, and considering the place I held could
never be profitable to a man that had resolved faire and direct dealing.'

Though King Charles, haltingly, had stood by him; and the case been quashed, Archie had copied out a Latin quotation into a book he was beginning to write—'How often is it to the interest of four or five ministers to join together to deceive their sovereign.' His view of King James, though coloured by that feeling for the sanctity of kingly office which was a current article of faith, had been shrewd— 'It was his manner to give way to strong opposition, or his Favorites intreaties, yet never to give over his purpose, but at another tyme to work it by the meanes of a contrary faction, to free and discharge himselfe of the others discontent upon the faction.' But Charles, as he was coming to find, was another thing, and without his father's skill in knowing men: 'his just and gracious inclination abused by misinformations, his eares blocked up and so straitly beleaguered as truth could not approach them . . .' King Charles, for his part, well understood Archie's main fault—'He said he could not but acknow-ledge my good service, my honesty, and integrity, but he was in-formed that the principall Officirs and I could not agree, whereby his service was hindered.' Archie would have none of this. 'Then desryred I his Ma: to try whose fault it was, theres who went about maters prejudiciall to him and the countrey, or myne who opposed them out of duety to God and to him.' 'Your Ma: (said I) may doe what you please; and if you joyne twenty Collegs to me I will serve just as I did before, when my owne conscience wes my colleg.' Upright, individual, unable to yield or to bide his time, he was no politician; though by the time he died the historian Wishart called him the wisest head in Scotland.

It was vital to establish 'honor, which I preferre before my profit'; though once honour was satisfied he was not reluctant to collect what was due to him. The whole thing rankled; and coming down the stairs from the Council behind the lame old dot-and-carry-one Lord Mar, he had heard the mocking courtiers saying loud enough for him to hear—'this is like Lord Napier, who is going down by degrees.' It might be so; or he might go down the whole flight in one act and land with a crash at the bottom. His days of prosperity were numbered. For him and for many the time was coming to stand up and be counted.

King Charles was living in a dream of total religious unity. In 1637 he imposed what felt to them to be a 'papistical' prayer book on the

Scots and had it smartly returned into his end of the court in its first service at St Giles. The legendary Jenny Geddes was not alone in this outbreak of Women's Lib. An unfortunate gentleman who said Amen at the appropriate place found the girl who sat in front of him crying out, 'What! dost thou say mass at my lug?' (ear), and giving him a great bash in the face with her Bible. The maidservants of Edinburgh, who were keeping places for their mistresses, 'rose in a tumultuous way, and having prefaced awhile with despightful exclamations, threw the stools they sat on at the preachers, and thereafter invaded them more nearly and strove to pull them from their pulpits, whereby they had much ado to escape their hands, and retire to their houses. And for the bishop (against whom their wrath was most bent), the magistrates found difficulty enough to rescue him,' the Bishop of Dunkeld, Guthrie, reported.

The Commons of England, glancing round Europe with some apprehension, deeply feared not only the religious menace but the rise of absolute monarchs backed by that new thing, a standing army. This cause and the religious cause became overlapping and confused. Discredited by the military fiascos of his favourite, Buckingham, and by his passion for his prerogative, Charles had parted company with his recalcitrant Parliament in 1629 and had ruled for eleven tranquil years by an absolute but not despotic or intolerant government, forwarded by the exceptional competence, especially in Ireland, of his great minister Strafford. It was his archbishop, Laud, who was the catalyst, fatally entering political life and irritating even the calmer English by instituting a religious bossiness which affected the daily life of everyone and aroused the Scots to the point of a war that would engulf both kingdoms.

In the unhappy situation following the introduction of the prayer book, Charles did not ease matters by gradually setting up what appeared to the Scots to be a Council packed with bishops to rule Scotland, and Archie wrote in protest—'That Churchmen have competency is agreeable to the law of God and man; but to invest them into great estate and principal offices of the State, is neither convenient for the Church, for the King, nor for the State. Histories witness what troubles have been raised in all places where Churchmen were great. Our reformed churches, having reduced religion to the ancient primitive truth and simplicity, ought to beware that corruption enter not into their church in the same gate.' On these grounds also he mistrusted the Covenant and refused to sign it; for on the last day of February 1638—'the great marriage day of this nation with God,' announced its protagonists—this famous document had been read from the pulpit of the Greyfriars Kirk, and a queue long enough for a lying-in-state had filed up to sign it. At last they were back to John Knox and the stringent simplicities of Calvinist Melville, and there had been a lifting of 'the spiritual plague of Aegyptian darkness covering the light of the gospel', claimed Warriston, eloquent but more than slightly daft. King Charles had sown the wind; and would reap a whirlwind of rage against a popery he had no notion of introducing.

Archie's brother-in-law, Montrose, who was much younger than him and considerably more carried away by passion for Scots religious independence, at first supported the Covenanters; but Archie feared that the Kirk elders were about to become as tyrannical as any priests, and he was right. A compromise settlement was not easy. Edinburgh had seethed with rebellion over the new prayer book, though some attention to Scots susceptibilities had been paid in its compilation. The Bishop of Brechin could only get through the new service by taking it with a brace of pistols conspicuously placed on his desk. Through Edinburgh at least there was a general chivvying and harrying of those who did not sign the Covenant, which did in fact promise loyalty to the king, as well as its insistence on the right of Scots to choose their own form of worship. In the lonely places men looked to their weapons, and the clansmen sharpened their swords. Well-trained Scots who had fought for the Protestant cause all over Europe began to hasten back to fight for it at home.

A confused few years followed. Hamilton, complaining to the king that he hated Scotland 'next to hell', was sent north to treat. His properties in Scotland were large and he hedged his bets. Acting ostensibly for Charles, he privately assured the Covenanter Committee that they had only to stand firm and they would get all they wanted. The Crown conceded: the Covenanters demanded more. Bishops were removed from civil office and at length their spiritual usefulness also came under question. In November 1638 the General Assembly crowded into Glasgow Cathedral, Hamilton protesting against the streams of laymen who were also admitted. Even the Reverend Robert Baillie, an extreme Covenanter, complained of the pandemonium: his brethren, he wrote, 'might learn from Canterbury or the Pope, or even from Turks or pagans'. Such was the din that if the assembled company had 'used the like behaviour in his chamber he would not be content till they were down the stairs'.

Baillie had meant to hate Hamilton but was unable to manage it. 'My thoughts of the man were hard and base: But a day or two's audience wrought on my mind a great change towards him, which yet remains . . . a man of a sharp, ready, solid, clear, wit; of a brave and masterly expression . . . if the King have many such men then he is a well-served prince.' At Berwick next year he complained that Hamilton was ambiguous, as indeed he was, but 'his absolute power with the King was oft there clearly seen.'

Hamilton at Glasgow made a mixed impression but the young Earl of Montrose made a bad one. He had argued in public with his father-in-law, Lord Southesk, and had clearly been in the wrong: he was thought to be a brash and thrusting idealist, throwing his weight about amongst the older and wiser. He was not forgiven; this and his subsequent bringing down of the cruel and hated Highlanders in force into the Lowlands, where they were seen as Bengalis see Punjabis, formed in too many quarters a suspicion of his motives. Montrose had high words with the moderator, who gave as good as he got. Hamilton stood on the king's prerogative and declared the assembly was illegal; after which everybody became very cross and noisy indeed. Hamilton tried to dissolve the assembly, which refused to dissolve: he departed gloomily and garrisoned Edinburgh Castle on his way south. One clever and determined man stood out— Argyll, who in an interminable but weighty speech fully aligned himself with the extreme and ever more powerful Covenanters. The bishops were abolished, many were excommunicated, and war was all but declared. Hamilton had come north to make peace: the Assembly's refusal to disband was to Charles the vital act of rebellion.

Montrose did not mind about bishops but he minded very much that sovereignty should not hang on a packed house of fanatics under the sway of one unscrupulous and ambitious man; as Argyll was revealing himself to be. Yet Montrose still believed that the religious freedom of Scotland must be put on a surer basis. In the north-east the Catholic and temperamental Huntly boldly declared that he would stand or fall with the Stewarts; a promise he kept in fits and starts and when he was in the mood for it. Montrose, con-fronting him, persuaded him to stand by the king *and* by Scots religious freedom, and offered him alliance on those terms. In April of 1639 Huntly went with him to Edinburgh, where Montrose, still in his twenties, was overruled by the sterner Covenanters, who insisted on full acceptance of the Covenant and put Huntly in Edinburgh Castle when he refused. Huntly was soon out, but he never forgave Montrose, and the king himself long remembered that Montrose had once been with the Covenanters.

No shot had yet been fired, but on May 1st Hamilton arrived in the Forth with all flags flying upon nineteen of the King's men of war, and five thousand soldiers on board; to find Edinburgh's approaches fortified against him. His mother, the terrible dowager, a Presbyterian to end Presbyterians, a kind of Barbara Castle, Ian Paisley, and Lady Astor rolled into one, arrived from Clydesdale with pistols in her belt and announced her intention of shooting her son if he set foot ashore. Whether she, or Archie Napier, deputed by the Council to persuade Hamilton not to start a war, had most effect we do not know; but with a Scots Covenanting army 20,000 strong on the Border, Hamilton played it coolly, though up north the impetuous Gordons, Huntly's sons, had already started one. Montrose won a battle against them, and on June 18th the Pacification of Berwick was signed: the crunch had been warded off for a while, in which either common sense or fanaticism might prevail. In that while the Covenant would change its character and Montrose his mind. By the end of 1639 Scotland was virtually independent and Charles felt bound to fight. To do this he must have money: he summoned Parliament: a Scots army, unresisted, occupied Northumberland and Durham.

Well on, now, in his sixties, Archie Napier had tried throughout to calm the storm. In August of 1637, with other members of Council, he sent a letter to Charles explaining the difficulty that the government would have in enforcing the use of the new service book; but Charles had set his heart on it. In September of 1638 Archie was one of those who subscribed to the King's Confession at Holyrood; but this, to the extreme party, did not seem to say much more than the king's determination not to reintroduce Catholicism into his realm, which, as they said, they knew already and took for granted. In the Council lists the name of Lord Napier begins to have DUBITO after it: he had never signed the Covenant, was he that terrible thing, that lukewarm anathema to the Kirk ministers, a religious tolerator?

As brother-in-law and one time guardian to Montrose he was doubly suspect.

In 1640, headed by Montrose, a party of the more moderate lords signed the Bond of Cumbernauld, a statement reaffirming loyalty both to the Crown and to religious freedom for the Scots; two things they still believed to be compatible, and in the main directed against the rising power of Argyll, as that shrewd character instantly perceived—'how that, by the particular and indirect practising of a few, the country and cause does so much suffer.' For before the year of the Berwick Pacification was out the king and his Scots Parliament had been at loggerheads again; Traquair, now Treasurer, had been mobbed in the streets of Edinburgh and feelings were running higher, acts becoming ever more lawless. Charles had summoned the Covenanter leaders to Berwick, but few of them went. Montrose, who did, was impressed. 'His Majesty', wrote Covenanter Robert Baillie, his enemy, 'was ever the longer and better loved of all that heard him, as one of the most just, reasonable, sweet persons they ever had seen.' Here perhaps, Montrose fell under Charles's charm, or recognized a good man. At any rate here he heard the king's case for the first time at first hand, and became convinced that Charles was now pledged to constitutional monarchy and had no further designs upon the Scots Kirk. He had yielded over Scotland's main argument; was it not now time Scotland supported his authority?

Montrose was always open in his actions. The Covenanters, who had deplored his merciful treatment of Royalists in the north, and his 'over-discretion' in not sacking Aberdeen, now became certain he was unsound. In Edinburgh the new Parliament reformed itself in such a way that royal influence was eliminated—the new master was Argyll, who presently conducted a particularly bloody clan raid against the Ogilvy family, and the Macdonalds of Lochaber, killing many; and tricking Atholl into captivity, sent him prisoner to Edinburgh; Parliament giving him an indemnity for, amongst other burnings and violent deeds, 'putting whatsoever person or persons to torture, or of putting any person or persons to death'. Flushed by all this, Argyll presently made a secret approach to Montrose, suggesting the setting up of a dictatorship in Scotland, with himself and two complete cyphers at its head. It was after this that Montrose drew up the Bond of Cumbernauld.

A solid party for moderation was with him—the Lords Marischal, Wigton, Kinghorn, Home, Atholl, Mar, Perth, Boyd, Galloway,

Stormont, Seaforth, Erskine, Kirkcudbright, Amond, Drummond, Johnston, Lour, Carnegie, as well as his usual faithful band of Ogilvys and Napiers, and the infinitely dashing and infinitely incalculable Gordons. All dreaded and disliked Argyll, already referred to by his soldiers as King Campbell—'Are you,' they would demand of all comers, 'for King Campbell or King Stewart?' But Montrose was a better soldier than a statesman. When it came to politics Argyll would always make rings round him. Montrose was fatally open: discretion was no part of his valour.

Clarendon, who knew and detested Argyll, admits that he wanted only courage and honesty to be a very great man. Hamilton had roundly told King Charles that Argyll was the most dangerous man in Scotland; and Argyll's own father had declared with passion that his son 'could love no man'. 'If he finds it in his power to do you mischief he will do it,' old Argyll had assured the king. Charles was becoming increasingly at odds with his English people, mainly Puritan in feeling and terrified that the Roman Catholics would win outright in the Thirty Years War against Protestants now raging on the Continent, leaving them hopelessly exposed. Nothing seems more foolish, in retrospect, than the fears that are not realized. We know, but the Puritans and Covenanters did not, that Protestantism will survive, that three hundred years later Protestant Britain and Protestant America will confront and subdue Nazi Germany, the most potent evil to threaten the world since the days of Attila the Hun, while Catholic Poland is overwhelmed, Catholic Austria and Italy play along, Catholic Spain and Ireland opt out, and Catholic France collapses like a pack of cards.

But the issue was still in doubt, and the Protestants becoming ever more fanatical with terror. This fanaticism the king was deeply concerned to hold in check: to deal with it in England he needed the help of the Scots lords, and fatally conceded power to the most fanatical among them.

Though small and cast-eyed and nervous, Argyll was a mastermind. At home in Dalriada he had put paid to the maraudings of the Macgregors, those dwellers in inaccessible marsh, and to the piratings of the Macdonalds; he had encouraged trade in his western ports and organized a fishing fleet which had made him the richest man in Scotland. Neither the handsome and charming Montrose, with all the gifts for a popular leader, nor level-headed Archie Napier, could begin to be a match for Argyll in political wits; he had a genuinely popular religious movement behind him and knew how to harness it: when the moment came he would pounce.

It came in 1640, when Montrose, a chivalrous character, parted company with Argyll over that Campbell raid on the Bonny House of Airlie. Argyll had taken advantage of Ogilvy's absence to burn it to the ground and turn young Lady Ogilvy out into the open just when she was going to have a baby:

> He hath taken her by the middle so small,
> And O but she grat sairly!
> And laid her down by the bonnie burn-side
> Till they plundered the castle of Airlie.

The Cumbernauld Bond had emphasized the original Covenant's insistence that there should be no diminution of 'the King's greatness and authority'; now it appeared clear to Montrose and Archie that Argyll backed by the Council was aiming to become dictator of Scotland. Back to the old clan wars again: against this the king's authority was the only safeguard.

The original Covenant had been proclaimed 'that religion and righteousness may flourish in the land, to the glory of God, the honour of the King, and the peace and comfort of us all': it had had pure and simple religious overtones that had induced men like Montrose to sign and fight for it. Now, by a process confirmed by the Solemn League and Covenant to be signed at Westminster in 1643, it had become the cover for an absolute religious dictatorship, seeking to impose Presbyterianism over all England and Ireland as well as Scotland, and backed by a selfish oligarchy of lords whose violent misdeeds it was prepared to absolve because they were done in the name of its own exclusively owned Lord of Hosts.

Sometime at the end of 1640 or beginning of 1641, Montrose, Napier, Stirling of Keir, who was a son-in-law of Napier's, and Sir Archibald Stewart of Blackhall, met together, perhaps at Merchiston, and wrote a letter to the king, beseeching him to come at once to Scotland and save his kingdom, not by arms but by discussion. 'Having occasion to meet often, we did then deplore the hard estate the country was in,' Montrose wrote: 'our religion not secured, and with

it our liberties being in danger: laws silenced, justice and the course
of judicatories obstructed: noblemen and gentlemen put to excessive
charges above their abilities, and distracted from their private
affairs: the course of traffic interrupted to the undoing of merchants
and tradesmen: moneyed men paid with failzies and suspensions.

'And besides these present evils fearing worse to follow, the King's
authority being much shaken by the late troubles; knowing well that
the necessary consequences and effects of a weak Sovereign power
are anarchy and confusion; the tyranny of subjects, the most insatiable and insupportable tyranny of the world, without hope of
redress from the Prince, curbed and restrained from the lawful use
of his power; factions and distractions within, opportunity to
enemies abroad, and to ill-affected subjects at home, to kindle a fire
in the state which hardly can be quenched without the ruin of King
People and State.

'These sensible evils begot in them thoughts of remede. The best,
they thought, was, that if his Majesty would be pleased to come to
Scotland in person, and give his people satisfaction in point of
Religion, and just Liberties, he should therby settle his own authority,
and cure all the distempers and distractions among his subjects . . .'
This account, in Napier's handwriting, corrected by Montrose, was
written to deny the charges of their having made a treasonable plot;
for as Montrose pointed out, the King could not come to Scotland
without the agreement of the Kirk's Commissioners in London
because the Scots army stood in the way—'if they did agree, the army
should be the King's army, and they would all lay down their arms
at his feet: there is no man so far from the duty of a good subject,
or so void of common sense, as to quarrel this matter.' Treachery did
not enter in.

Unfortunately Montrose had talked of his letter to the king with
an old friend, the minister of Methven, who had called in the
minister of Auchterarder, who had called in Mr John Robertson,
a minister at Perth, who in his turn had confided in Mr George
Drummond. Montrose had, he himself thought, simply been airing
his grievance over the official burning of the Bond of Cumbernauld
with a local friend: he did not realize how completely the Kirk
ministers were now in Argyll's pocket. The glad news of Montrose's
suspect doings sped to Edinburgh. Argyll moved swiftly, accusing
Montrose to the Council of corresponding with the king (as indeed
he had, and at once admitted to having done), and of being a traitor

'A woman religious, chast, and beautiful, and my chiefest joye in this worlde.' Lady Margaret Graham, red-haired sister of Montrose and wife of the 1st Lord Napier, by George Jamesone. *By kind permission of Lord Napier and Ettrick.*

Archibald, 1st Lord Napier, Deputy Treasurer of Scotland, guardian and brother-in-law of Montrose, reputed 'the wisest head in Scotland'. From an engraving after the painting by George Jamesone. *By kind permission of Lord Napier and Ettrick.*

James VI of Scotland
aged twenty-nine and
about to become also
James I of England.
*Scottish National
Portrait Gallery.*

James VI and I's
younger luckless son,
Charles I as a boy of
twelve. *By kind
permission of Lord
Elibank.*

to the Covenant. He had cleverly got his blow in first. Montrose and Archie Napier, together with Sir George Stirling of Keir and Stewart of Blackhall, were seized and imprisoned. On a bright day in the first week of June 1641 they trod up the steep cobblestones of the Castle Hill in Edinburgh, and the gates clanged behind them.

Round Two to Argyll.

X

Kept in ward in Edinburgh Castle from June to November without trial, Montrose, Stewart, Archie Napier and Stirling of Keir awaited the coming of the king as their best hope of escaping the vengeance of Argyll and the Covenanters, now in supreme power in Scotland. The English Royalists, too, were building on this. Nicholas, the king's secretary, hoped much of the visit. 'If the king shall settle and establish a perfect quietness with the Scots, it will open a way for a happy and good conclusion of all differences here;' but he overlooked the deep clefts and loyalties of the Scottish tribal system, and the extreme nature of a religion which insisted that daily life—as well as political life—was to be lived by the fierce precepts of 500 B.C. Israel. To be tolerant was, in the Kirk view, to be abject. They chopped sentences from the Bible at will, used them out of context, and proclaimed that here only was the word of God. Even Torquemada could have given them few lessons in bigotry and sadism.

The fatal letter to the king is in Napier's writing; probably it was drawn up jointly by all four friends. 'Sir, Your antient and native kingdom of Scotland is in a mighty distemper,' it begins crisply. 'The disease is contagious and may infect the rest of your Majesty's dominions. It is the falling sickness, for they are like to fall from you, and from the obedience due to you, if by removing the cause, and application of wholesome remedies, it be not speedily prevented. The cause is a fear and apprehension, not without some reason, of changes in religion, and that superstitious worship shall be brought in upon it, and therewith all their laws infringed, and their liberties invaded.

'Free them, Sir, from this fear, as you are free from any such thoughts; and undoubtedly you shall settle that State in a firm obedience to your Majesty in all time coming. They have no other end but to preserve their Religion in purity, and their Liberties entire. That they intend the overthrow of monarchial government is a calumny. They are capable of no other, for many and great reasons; and ere they will admit another than your Majesty, and after you, your son, and nearest of your posterity, to sit upon that throne, many thousands of them will shed their dearest blood.

'You are not like a tree lately planted, which oweth a fall to the first wind. Your ancestors have governed here, without interruption of race, two thousand years, or thereabout, and taken such root as it can never be plucked up by any but yourselves . . .

'The remedy of this dangerous disease consisteth only in your Majesty's presence for a space in that Kingdom. It is easy to you in person to settle these troubles, and to disperse these mists of apprehension and mistaking—impossible to any other . . . The success of your Majesty's affairs, the security of your authority, the peace and happiness of your subjects, depend upon your personal presence . . . Now is the proper time, and the critical days.

'For the people love change, and expect from it much good—a new heaven and a new earth—but being disappointed, are as desirous of a re-change to the former estate. Satisfy them, Sir, in point of Religion and Liberties, when you come there, in a loving and free manner; that they may see your Majesty had never any other purpose, and doth not intend the least prejudice to either. For religious subjects, and such as enjoy their lawful liberties, obey better, and love more, than the godless and servile; who do all out of base fear, which begets hate.

'Any difference that may arise upon the acts passed in the last Parliament, your Majesty's presence, and the advice and endeavours of your faithful servants, will easily accommodate. Let your Majesty be pleased to express your favour, and care for your subject's weal, by giving way to any just motions of theirs for relief of the burdens these late troubles have laid upon them, or by granting what else may tend to their good; which your Majesty may do with assurance that therein is included your own.

'Suffer them not to meddle or dispute of your power. It is an instrument never subjects yet handled well. Let not your authority receive any diminution of that which the law of God and nature, and the fundamental laws of the country alloweth: For then it shall grow contemptible; and weak and miserable is that people whose prince hath not power sufficient to punish oppressors, and to maintain peace and justice.

'On the other side, aim not at absoluteness: It endangers your estate, and stirs up troubles: The people of the western parts of the world could never endure it any long time, and they of Scotland less than any.

'Practise, Sir, the temperate government. It fitteth the humour and disposition of the nation best. It is most strong, most powerful, and most durable of any. It gladdeth the heart of your subjects, and then they erect a throne there for you to reign. Let your last act there be the settling the Offices of State upon men of known integrity and sufficiency. Take them not upon credit, and other men's recommendations . . . neither at hazard, but upon your own knowledge, which fully reacheth to a great many more than will fill those few places . . .

'So shall your Majesty secure your authority for the present, and settle it for the future time; Your journey shall be prosperous, your return glorious; You shall be followed with the blessings of your people, and with the contentment which a virtuous deed reflecteth upon the mind of the doer. And more true and solid shall your glory be than if you had conquered nations, and subdued a people.'

How much of this is Napier, and how much Montrose? As the two known to be good at getting things down on paper, it seems likely that they drew it up and that Stirling of Keir and Stewart of Blackhall signed. Montrose of course was the leading spirit, but Napier had been his guardian since he was a fatherless twelve-year-old, and doubtless a bit of that relationship still clung. 'Aim not at absoluteness. Practise, Sir, the temperate government,' sounds rather more like Archie Napier than like the man who wrote:

> Like Alexander I will rule
> And I will rule alone

except that nobody really knows whether the heroine of Montrose's poem is his wife, Magdalen Carnegie, or the kingdom of Scotland. (Magdalen Carnegie, from the very little that is known of her, seems to have been a bit of a Lady Nelson—Oh do stop, darling, my nerves really can't stand any more of your jumping on to French quarter-decks—but if so, how far less lethal than the come-back-with-your-shield-or-on-it school of thought.)

It is not certain whether the king ever received this sensible letter, although plenty of other people did. Yet his own to Montrose of May 22nd from Whitehall seems an answer to it, though nothing is said as to the pros and cons of practising a temperate government.

'Montrose:— I conceive that nothing can conduce more to a firm and solid peace, and giving full contentment and satisfaction to my people, than that I should be present at the next ensuing session of Parliament. This being the reason of my journey, and having a perfect intention to satisfy my people in their religion and just liberties, I do expect from them that retribution of thankfulness, as becomes grateful and devoteful subjects. Which being a business wherein not only my service but likewise the good of the whole kingdom is so much concerned, I cannot but expect that your particular endeavours will be herein concurring. In confidence of which, I rest your assured friend, Charles R.'

So away from Whitehall, and leisurely up the great north road again in the summer weather, with the corn turning yellow in the level Midland fields, and the heaths of Yorkshire beginning to flower. But by the time Charles clanked and jingled into Holyrood House the writers of the letter were under lock and key.

Merchiston was searched, and all Montrose's houses. 'The Lord Sinclair was commissioned to go to Old Montrose, the earl's chief dwelling-house, and search what he could find there to militate against him. At his coming he [Sinclair] broke open his [Montrose's] cabinets but found nothing therein belonging to public affairs, only instead thereof he found some letters from ladies to Montrose in his younger years, flowered with Arcadian compliments, which, being divulged would possibly have met with a favourable construction, had it not been that the hatred carried to Montrose made them to be interpreted in the worse sense. Sinclair . . . was much blamed by men of honour and gallantry for publishing those letters,' Guthrie concluded, 'but the rigid sort had him in greater esteem for it.'

The rigid sort were growing stronger and they had their way.

On July 1st Archie petitioned the Estates 'that nothing might be read which might give the House a bad information of them, until that first they were allowed to clear themselves'. When audience was granted, they pleaded that not only had nothing been done by them contrary to law, but that their main motive had been 'a regard to the honor of the nation'. No decision was arrived at: they were commited once more to the castle: all waited upon the king's arrival.

When he came Montrose and Napier were refused trial. Too much might come out; Argyll was not yet ready for an open break with the king. There was nothing simple and straightforward about this Campbell chieftain. He had been thoroughly educated; he spoke Gaelic and insisted that his sons should also learn it. At Inverary his own ships brought him silks and velvets and delicious wines direct from France: he held his less worldly western clansmen in the hollow of his hand. Convinced that the interests of the Deity and his own were identical, and controlling most of the country as he did, the pedigree-haunted and extremely able Argyll was wont to point out to his cronies after supper that he was only eighth in descent from Robert the Bruce, so? It was as well not to run the risk of exposing these thoughts and other machinations against the king by having Montrose and Napier brought to open trial before him. And against the combination of Hamilton, still brooding his jealousy over this Lennox elevation to the throne, and Argyll and the Kirk, the king was powerless or unwilling to insist on the trial, in spite of Montrose's bold demands.

'What I have done is known to a great many and what I have done amiss is unknown to myself,' he had declared to the Estates. 'As truth does not seek corners, it needeth no favour . . . My resolution is to carry along fidelity and honour to the grave.' But even Montrose's charm and eloquence failed: all that happened was that he was imprisoned apart from his friends. His elderly brother-in-law, Napier, seems to have been rather more flippant. On June 23rd, this *eminence*, now probably extremely *grise*, had been examined by Craighall, who had 'some interrogatories to pose me on. To which I answered, he need not interrogate; for as I told the Lord Balmerino and the rest that were with them, I had deponed all I knew, freely and ingenuously.' Their letter to the king had received additions *en route*, some of which took the form of a code. 'Then they read in their paper of one 'Signior Puritano': I demanded who that was? They told me it was my Lord Seaforth; whereupon I fell a laughing, and said he was slandered; and they fell in a great laughter.' By the time the king arrived the laughter had faded out.

On August 20th the four prisoners were brought before the Council and pleaded that they had thought they were doing good service to the king, the Estates, and subjects of the kingdom, in writing their letter.

Charles was in the middle of a slightly chilly honeymoon with the Covenanters, hopefully supposing he could win them later on. Nor could he, perhaps, have withheld consent to a verdict against Montrose and Archie Napier. Strafford's farcical trial had ended fatally in the spring, for all Charles's promise of safe-conduct. The Kirk had stretched its long arm south to London to press the doom of the king's great minister and was unlikely to be less potent on its home ground.

'I desired', Archie wrote, 'to have the liberty to speak . . . as that which I had to say was very short and would not trouble them. The King, as I believe bade voice it, but it was granted and not voiced.' Archie then raised his voice: 'God be thanked I see his Majesty there; I am confident we shall find the gracious effects of his presence; and, truly if we have failed either in matter or manner, maybe, but I never yet could conceive it; and yet we have received punishment that bears proportion with very great crimes, we have been eleven weeks in the Castle, which we do not think very much of, but by that means there lies a heavy imputation against us; and suspicion of the people, as if we had committed some heinous crime, and thereby we are barred from sitting here' (in the Council) 'as we ought, and are forced to hear libels, and summons with the most opprobrious and reproachful words which ever were used to innocent or guilty men. So my humble desire to his Majesty and the House is, that they will be pleased to take our cause and suffering to their consideration.

'His Majesty nodded to me, and seemed to be well pleased. So we took our leave.'

Nodding and smiling kindly were now almost as much as Charles could do in Edinburgh. 'There was never King so much insulted over,' wrote Sir Patrick Weymss, who was in attendance. 'It would pity any man's heart to see how he looks.' Montrose, Archie Napier, and the others left 'the stage appointed for delinquents' where they had been placed in Parliament, and were returned in the king's coaches to Edinburgh Castle. 'For the Lord Montrose and the rest,' the King's Secretary Sir Edward Nicholas wrote from the south on October 5th, 'some here that pretend to understand the condition of their case are of opinion that their innocence is such as they will not fare the worse for your Majesty's leaving them to the ordinary course of justice there.' Charles, who knew rather better what the justice practised under Argyll and the Kirk was like, wrote in the margin: 'This may be true what you say, but I am sure that I miss somewhat in point of honour if they all be not relieved before I go hence.' As nothing could be proved against them, they were let out in November, 'on condition that from henceforth they carry themselves soberly and discreetly,' Archie still arguing every inch of the way. He was in his late sixties by now, and wilier than Montrose: they signed a declaration that 'no wrinkle or the least shadow of blemish remain upon us in this behalf.' The Committee, who were Argyll's creatures, had spent two hours trying to persuade Archie to go quietly, but he had insisted that he and Montrose must first be declared innocent; knowing well that the whole thing could be raised again on a more favourable occasion at the drop of a hat. They were to appear before the Council in January.

Argyll and Hamilton now staged a dramatic night flight from Edinburgh, making out that there had been a plot by the king to assassinate them. They returned to cheering crowds; their stock rose ever higher; and terrible trouble in Ireland—the Maguire massacres of Protestants by Catholics—sent the king back to London. Nothing had been cleared up or settled: in vain had Charles sat listening to those long melancholy sermons in St Giles; his shrewd Presbyterian subjects were not deceived. The king had been revealed as powerless. But a promise was extracted from him never to employ Montrose or Napier again, and the two brothers-in-law were now thoroughly discredited for their complicity with a king who seemed to Scotland to be a near-papist. Although at any moment they might whip out a Book of Common Prayer, suspect as a hand grenade, they could be safely turned out of Edinburgh Castle, though not without the imposition of heavy fines from the ever-righteous Kirk.

The king rode south under the happy impression that he had settled the whole thing, placating the Covenanters and winning them to his side. He had made Loudoun, Argyll's kinsman, Lord Chancellor, Argyll himself a principal commissioner and a marquis, and General Leslie, Earl of Leven. He had promoted to the Council Lords Balmerino, Cassilis, and Maitland; and on November 17th he adjourned the Estates, gave a splendid feast at Holyrood to all these, his most implacable foes, and bade farewell entrusting his government in Scotland exclusively to them. He believed in Scots staunchness: if it came to the crunch these men would support him against any trouble from the English.

Montrose and Archie Napier celebrated Christmas together with their families, and this in itself was a legal offence. The Kirk had recently clamped down a censorship on all books, and had run up a new list of criminal offences; which included picking gooseberries in sermon time, sitting up drinking in company, indulging in 'promiscuous dancing', or in minstrelsy, 'which tends to great deboshry'. Greeting each other on Christmas Day, or walking up and down talking on that festival, as if it were a holiday, were also now punishable by law. Of the family gathered round that Christmas table in 1641, not prepared to support kirk tyranny, most were doomed to exile or to early death. There were the sixteen-year-old Master of Napier, young Archie, and his equally young wife, Lady Elizabeth Erskine; his two sisters, Lilias and Margaret, his cousins John and Jamie Napier, and Montrose's three little boys; few of them would ever meet again.

In summer the Civil War broke out in England. 'You are one whom I have found most faithful and in whom I repose greatest trust,' the king wrote to Montrose, 'your loving Friend Charles R.' Montrose had earlier been discredited in Charles's eyes by his youthful Covenanting activities: as ever, the king had discovered his truly loving friends, like Strafford, when it was too late for them to save him. It was a year before the king could possibly believe that anyone with as perfect a taste in pictures as Hamilton had could possibly be hedging his bets; not till seven years later, in 1648, did Hamilton lead a Scots army south to try and rescue the by then imprisoned king. Placatingly, affectionately, Charles had made him a duke and kept him in power, delaying for the vital year in which Montrose could have raised half Scotland for him. By the time Montrose was sent his mission was foredoomed.

In the winter of 1644 the king had at last made up his mind. Montrose, finally empowered to act for him, rode north from Oxford in the spring; being made a marquis by the king and excommunicated by the Kirk on the same day.

> He either fears his fate too much
> Or his deserts are small
> That dares not put it to the touch
> To win or lose it all.

wrote Montrose, and handsomely lived up to it. Before him lay a year of triumphant victories. 'I doubt not', he wrote from the Highlands in February, 'before the end of summer I shall be able to come to

6*

your Majesty's assistance with a brave army, which backed with the justice of your Majesty's cause, will make the rebels in England as well as in Scotland, feel the just rewards of rebellion.' Compromise and peace had everywhere lost out. Political passions, and above all, religious ones, were too powerful to be stayed.

Making for his native area of Strathearn, Montrose crossed the Border in disguise. He was joined by Alastair Macdonald from Colonsay, a gigantic young chieftain known as Colkitto (the nickname and the name of his left-handed father), who had come ashore at Ardnamurchan with 1,000 soldiers and followers. He was a king's man and a Catholic, and delighted to have a bash at the Campbells in either capacity. Montrose walked into Blair Atholl to head them and the Grahams and other men of his own Strathearn. Here was a first-class general, and bearer of the king's commission; the Royalists took heart; though Archie Napier and all his family were kept in close ward in their rooms in Holyrood House, able only for the moment to send messages and cheer from a distance. He was by now in his seventies: his eldest son, John had died as a child, but his younger, Master of Napier, was now seventeen and biding his time for a daring escape. 'Montrose himself, with the immediate group round him, presents a standard of honesty, generosity and decent dealing which is conspicuously absent otherwise in seventeenth century Scottish politics' (Rosalind Mitchison.) The Reverend Robert Baillie, Principal of Glasgow University, thought otherwise. From him Scotland had 'the greatest hurt our poore land gott these fourscore years'; and he particularly objected to Montrose's army— 'fifteen hundred naked Scots Irishes.' Of arms they were certainly naked; the victory at Tippermuir was partly won by men who had only bows and arrows. At Perth it triumphed again with some Royalists fighting only with sticks and stones.

As Montrose's victories mounted Archie Napier was once again rushed under lock and key by the Covenanter government into Edinburgh Castle, this time with his family, though all were kept separate. From close confinement at Holyrood his son, young Archie, had escaped to join Montrose and fight, with the wild Ulstermen and Highlanders, for the king; an event which caused the Covenanters to fine his father ten thousand pounds, a sum the present day equivalent of about seventy thousand. Also in solitary imprisonment in the castle was Montrose's second son James, a stalwart twelve-year-old who refused to be exchanged into freedom with someone else more immediately valuable to the Royalist cause, and who may have been the author of the when-did-you-last-see-your-father movement. In the spring of a harsh winter, his older brother, fourteen-year-old John Graham, died from the snows and the forced marches of his father's winter campaign against Argyll. Lilias and Margaret Napier (now Lady Stirling) were closely interrogated by their gaolers for their treasonable action in wearing mourning for this young first cousin.

Kept apart from each other and allowed no communication with their father, they were permitted to take the air twice a day on the battlements, as nobody wanted them to do anything awkward like dying. From the still unfilled loch that lay below the castle, the morning mists came floating up; Lilias and Margaret could gaze out at the wide gleam of the Forth with the ships lying in Leith roads, the great sleeping dragon of King Arthur's Seat, the afternoon sun behind the Pentland Hills. Friendly noises of free people going about their business in the town below echoed faintly to them, the jolly sounds of rude life; cheerful couples passing in the streets and chatting each other up, shawled babies with high peremptory yells, and housewives hurling back-chat with vigour from the wynds. To the south-west was Merchiston Tower, the stalwart walls and the warm roofs of home. Unlike the uncompromising dark grey of Edinburgh's rock and her houses, Merchiston had the faint reddish glow, like old brick, of the sandstone layer on which it was built; a look as if the ruby earth of the Lothians had mixed into its iron-grey stone, as the warmth of tolerance had mixed into the steely Presbyterianism of its owners. Were the Covenanters in the house now? Who was feeding the dogs? Would things ever be happy and settled again? An east wind would bring up the evil smells of the town, and now in the spring of 1645 a more perilous waft—the plague had come to Edinburgh.

Less lucky Royalists were imprisoned in the Tolbooth, and bore the marks of rats' teeth to their dying day, if they were fortunate enough to escape the plague.

> My wife will dance and I will sing
> For sure it is the very best thing
> To drive the Plague away

a hopeful English cavalier had written; but the Covenanters had made these two activities criminal offences, and could only thunder gloomy Old Testament denunciations about the rewards of sin. They were kind enough, however, to allow old Lord Napier and his family to be imprisoned at Linlithgow, further away from the plague. From here his family were delivered in 1645 by Archie Napier and Nat Gordon after Montrose's resounding victory at Kilsyth. These two young men then proceeded to Edinburgh with all possible cavalier panache; riding up with trumpet and drum and a bare two hundred horse; the worthy burghers hastily sent their humble submission to Montrose, whose Highlanders they had good reason to fear, and released Lord Ogilvy and Lord Crawford from the Tolbooth, who unwound their anti-rat bandages and hastened back with Napier and Gordon to join Montrose.

That bright meteor had all but run his course. 'All this work of Montrose is above what can be attributed to mankind,' Secretary Digby wrote at Oxford; and feeling that God could be left to complete the business single-handed, he neglected to send Montrose the long-promised 1,500 horse that he so vitally needed against the swelling Covenanters' army. But Home and Roxburgh promised support, and even the Douglas, a sophisticated traveller and less Black than of yore, came to bring with him his ever-powerful legend of Bruce's heart, and a number of recruits from Clydesdale, all of whom folded up in the hour of need at Philiphaugh, though Douglas himself did not.

Montrose was riding south in hope of saving the king, roundly defeated earlier in the summer at Naseby. Although now seventy-three-years-old, old Archie, Lord Napier, had joined his son with the army, belting on what was by now a very unfashionable sword. His level head and his advice were much needed. Most of the Highlanders, disappointed at not being allowed by Montrose to sack and pillage Glasgow, sloped back now into their hills to reap their narrow fields of oats. The gay Gordons, all but Nathaniel who stayed to fight and be captured and executed by the Covenanters, prisoner of war or no, had fallen into a sulk and took their vital cavalry away into their home country. And up from the south was coming Leslie, a fine general who had learnt his job with Gustavus Adolphus of Sweden and hurried home to sign the Covenant on the chance of a good whang-dang at the near-Papist English. At his back were the 6,000 seasoned men who had recently routed the Royalists at Naseby.

On the approach of these, Lords Home and Roxburgh had rapidly changed their minds about supporting Montrose and the king. Fair enough: but less fair was Traquair, a Stewart and an alleged friend to Montrose, who graciously offered to send his own men to relieve Montrose's tired troops by keeping watch for them, meanwhile passing a message to Leslie to tell him exactly where Montrose was. At dawn Leslie attacked the unwarned Montrose, who had a bare 600 troops and was one of those honest men too slow to suspect treachery in others.

Philiphaugh, fought where the Yarrow and the Ettrick rivers join, was more of a surprise and a massacre than a battle. Again and again Montrose and his few friends led desperate charges against Leslie's seasoned veterans. Soon most of Montrose's 400 Irishmen were killed, the rest surrendered on promise of quarter. All these, with their 300 women and children, were subsequently done to death in the name of the Lord by the powers that now ruled in Edinburgh. The conquering soldiers themselves pleaded for mercy for the captives after the battle; but the civilians, so often more cruel, insisted on their execution. Two hundred cook boys and horse boys and all captured officers were also butchered. 'The work gangs bonnily on,' triumphed Mr David Dickson, Kirk elder, as an Irish captain swung from the battlements of Edinburgh Castle. Covenanting troopers and other keen helpers rode down the Irish women and their children over hills still known as Dead Man's Lee, hacking them down with total confidence. Had not the Irish Catholics recently butchered 40,000 hapless Protestants, living unsuspectingly if starchily in their midst, killing man, woman and child, not driving off their cattle but hacking the beasts into mincemeat or leaving them wounded in the fields for the crime of having Protestant owners, settled on tribal lands?* And as they chased the poor Irish women over the hills of southern Scotland and put them to the sword, the Calvinist troopers, and the pastors who paid them and drove them

---

* Accounts of the numbers differ. Cornelius O'Mahoney, a Jesuit father, delightedly wrote in 1645 that 150,000 heretics had been killed up to that time by all admissions: he thought there were more. But this was a fisherman's tale. Petty, first to attempt a critical estimate, put the deaths of Protestants at 37,000 in the first year; Clarendon had said 40,000. Froude thinks 20,000 were killed in the first two months; for these figures he quotes an eye-witness. Lecky thought 8,000, as did Miss Hickson (*Ireland in the Seventeenth Century*) who examined all the depositions closely: these were either killed or starved to death. 'The number of the slain I looked not after', wrote Tichbourne, on the other side, after the re-capture of Dundalk, 'but there was little mercy shown in those times.'

on, consoled themselves with the certainty that these women had all openly broken the seventh commandment; how many of them had got proper marriage lines? An eye for an eye and a tooth for a tooth, and everlasting woe for the conquered.

'All extremes, naturally and infallibly, beget each other,' wrote David Hume. The Maguire massacres in Ireland have rightly been forgotten by the English: would to God that the atrocities of Cromwell, which followed on after them, could equally be forgotten by the Irish. 'No one can paint the rage and cruelty that was vented, far and wide over the land, upon the unarmed and defenceless by the Catholics,' wrote Ranke. 'The astonished English,' wrote Hume, 'living in profound peace and full security, were massacred by their nearest neighbours, with whom they had long upheld a continual intercourse of kindness and good offices. Death was the slightest punishment inflicted,' there were also 'all the tortures which wanton cruelty could devise, all the lingering pains of body, the anguish of mind.' Even the instigators of the massacre could not halt 'that contagion of example which transports men beyond all the usual motives of conduct and behaviour'.

The Scots in Ireland were spared, because the Irish had hopes of detaching them from the English. As Ulstermen they were to remember Maguire and to nurse bitterness for three hundred years. Starving Protestant survivors filtered through Dublin to England, and there spread tales of the atrocities suffered by their fellows, which fell with lethal emphasis upon English ears, placing the Irish Catholics beyond the pale where human pity operates or is received. From now on the indigenous Irish seemed to the English not to be fully paid up members of the human race, more savage than wild beasts tearing a living prey. After fifty years of English settlement Ireland, according to Hume, had begun to wear the appearance of a European country, with houses and cultivated fields instead of huts and wandering tribes; and now this had come of it. 'You think well of Ireland,' wrote that world-famous Irishman Edmund Burke to his friend O'Hara a hundred and twenty years after the Maguire massacre, 'but I think rightly of it, and know that their unmeaning Senseless Malice is insatiable . . . I wish your absurdity was less mischievous, and less bloody,' and condemned the 'miserable bigots' on both sides whose hatred of religion other than their own was greater than their love of the substance of religion. Now seen more as innocent victims, through the rosy spectacles of time and of ever-efficient Catholic propaganda, to their neighbours and contemporaries, and not only in England, the generality of the Irish were then seen as savage outcasts, beyond compassion: a dour and Puritan Commons in England passed a bill by which they were never to be given quarter when taken in battle or rebellion. Yet the Irish needed the English and would always need them. The same was true in reverse; but the activities of Maguire and Cromwell would set the matter back by hundreds of years.

Only in the light of all this is it possible to understand the appalling English indifference to the Irish famine of the 1840s, which, although partly the result of ignorance, stemmed also from a shuddering recollection of the events of 1641. At the time, the massacres hardened many hearts against the king whom the Irish were said to support.

Montrose, even though he little guessed what would be done to the prisoners, had wanted to stay and die fighting by their sides. His friends cut a way for him out of the ruined battle. 'As they disappeared into the green hills, with them disappeared the dream of a new and happier Scotland,' John Buchan thought. It did not seem so at the time. Surely no cause could be permanently lost with such a bonny fighter at its head? He would be back, though round three had emphatically gone to Argyll.

But the shock and grief of Philiphaugh and its aftermath were too much for the oldest protagonist, who had ridden away up the Yarrow with Montrose. 'About this time', the Royalist Bishop Wishart wrote, in the famous history that was hung round Montrose's neck at his execution, 'the Lord Napier of Merchiston departed this life in Athole; a man of a most innocent life and happy parts; a truly noble gentleman, and chief of an ancient family; one who equalled his father and grandfather Napiers—philosophers and mathematicians famous through all the world—in other things, but far excelled them in his dexterity in civil business; a man as faithful to, and as highly esteemed by King James as King Charles. Sometime he was Lord Treasurer, and was deservedly advanced to the rank of the higher nobility; and since those times, had evinced so much loyalty and love to the King, that he was a large partaker of the rewards which the rebels bestowed upon virtue—frequent imprisonment, sequestrations, and plunder. Montrose, when a boy, looked upon this man as a most tender father; when he was a youth, as a most sage admonitor; when he was a man, as a most faithful friend; and now that he died, was no otherwise affected by his death than as if it had been his own father's.'

For by summer's end old Archie, seventy-three and deathly tired, lay dying at Fincastle, on the edge of the Highlands, north-west from Dunkeld. Far down in the valley the infant river roared softly, flowing from Loch Tummel and south to mingle with the grander Tay. In the high hills behind the house the stags were beginning to shout sexual defiance to each other; a wild remote sound with its autumnal threat and promise of extinction and renewal. Beyond the hill was the pass of Killiecrankie, and the rock that had not yet been named the Soldier's Leap. Berries burned red on the rowan trees that frightened off the witches and made the blackcock drunk; the wind moved in leaves already singed by early frost; the time had come to go.

Hearing these sounds through the silence of crisp mornings, he lay and floated in the dream of life; remembering maybe most clearly the racings and chasings of his cheerful childhood with his many siblings and his young half-uncles. The hopes of early manhood had been bright; studies and nightlarks at Glasgow University, and the challenge of King James's perilous and silken court among the towers of Windsor or the warm brick of Whitehall. There had been fireside bliss at Merchiston with Margaret, his dear and red-haired wife; and then the long lonely middle age, with comfort trickling out of him like sand in the stress and failure of public life; the struggle to make clear his honest name, that had been like beating upon fog; the frustrated effort to make both sides see reason and save Scotland from civil strife; and in the end the homelessness and worldly ruin; imprisonment and flight and bloody war. But he was not dying alone on a cold hillside; loyal friends sheltered him, his children were by; Montrose, that near-son, had risked his life to linger with him now. At the last Archie had been left with all the riches there are.

Always vocal, he had written his valediction some time since, and did not now gainsay it. 'Whoever thou beest either of my posterity or others to whose hands these presents shall come, if thou fear God and trust in him, and frame the course of thy life according to justice, thou shalt never want the assistance of a powerfull and mercifull God: for although storms aryse, and persecutions rage, yet all shall prove for the best to him that feareth God, to whom be all praise, honor, and glory, for ever and ever. FINIS.'

Finis is the one word that never can be said in human affairs: the world had still a drop to squeeze out of the person of Archibald, 1st Lord Napier. His heart, that talismanic thing, was buried under an oak tree in the garden at Fincastle; but Montrose, at great risk to himself, paused on his flight to bury his brother-in-law's body in holy ground at the churchyard of Blair Atholl. From this shelter the Covenanters, once they had discovered where it was, proposed to dig Archie's body up and desecrate it, all in the name of the Lord of Hosts. To prevent these men from 'pronouncing a forfeiture upon his bones' cost his family a fine of 5,000 marks, about £25,000. He had been, as John Buchan says, 'an exponent of the unpopular doctrine of toleration' come hell or high water; and this is sometimes an expensive thing to be, more especially in that serrated paysage north of Tweed.

'Archibald Lord Napier,' Guthrie commemorated him, 'a nobleman for true worth and loyalty inferior to none in the land, in the year 1645 died in his Majesty's service at Fincastle in Athole.'

XI

An elder brother John, having died as a child, another Archie was now Lord Napier, and would have need of his father's exhortation. Why so many Archies? Was it after his father, 1st Lord, or philosopher John's father Archibald, whose dexterity and wit had so surprised the English, or were the Napiers haunted by the short life of that wild young man who had died under the walls of Holyrood with seven triumphant Scotts standing over his gashed body? This Archie's life was to be twelve years longer, but his end no less sad. After he was twenty he never saw his home again, nor his native country. His lands would be seized on by Argyll and other Covenanters, his moneys forfeit, his tenants bullied, squeezed, or driven out. That greatest friend and most admired leader, Montrose, his young uncle and the star of his life, would be publicly executed in Edinburgh with every circumstance of ignominy. Archie himself would never return to the strong tower of Merchiston, ride to Gartness in its green fields, or fish the waters of Linfren. As he lay dying at Delfshaven in Holland in 1658, two years before King Charles II's restoration, did it all seem to him worthwhile? He was thirty-two, and did not leave us his conclusions.

The beginning had held blaze enough—the happy cherished childhood, the daring escape from imprisonment under the noses of the Covenanter guards, the perils and intoxications of Montrose's whirlwind campaign and the share in his lightning victories. Archie, then Master of Napier, had fought through most of it. Montrose had led Argyll a fine dance through the Highlands; and when he had thought himself safe through the winter in his impregnable western kingdom, they had crossed the snowy hills and taken him by surprise at Inveraray. Argyll had had to skip away by sea and leave his Campbell clansmen (putting it about that he had a dislocated shoulder); and although not many were killed, they were obliged to stand by while Montrose's armies, Ulster and Highland, had a merry time working off the old scores of centuries by looting and burning the Campbell heartland with tireless satisfaction. Leaving the hated hills of Lorne, Montrose and his men soon appeared to be trapped between Argyll and Baillie's armies in the Great Glen, but through the snowstorms of a wild January they broke out and crossed the trackless Highlands to drub the Campbells once more at Inverlochy. With 700 men Montrose seized Dundee in order to replenish his supplies of food and ammunition, and, helped on and off by Huntly, almost as powerful as Argyll and much braver, in May beat the Covenanters at Auldearn near Nairn.

Auldearn was only a small battle, fought near Culloden, which followed it a hundred years later, as Bannockburn was followed by Flodden. But it was a kind of Celtic Thermopylae; and its hero Colkitto, that astonishing brigadier who without his general Montrose eventually dwindled into nothing, became for the Highlands and Islands a more legendary figure even than Montrose. As usual the Royalists had not nearly enough men, and were obliged to be clever with those they had. Drawing up his Highlanders in front of the village of Auldearn in the half light of a damp and misty dawn that followed a drenching night, Montrose gave Colkitto the royal standard in order to fox Hurry (at this point a Covenanting general), into thinking that his was the main force; though this was in fact just over the crown of the hill to the south of the village. A few scattered men in front of the cottages in the centre were told to keep up a continuous fire to sound like a larger body. Lord Gordon with his cavalry was also concealed to Montrose's left.

Colkitto, with only 500 Ulstermen and Islanders, confronted and held Sir John Hurry with 3,000, which included cavalry; and increased his own difficulties by rushing down from the dry ground where he had been posted, to attack the Covenanters in the bog. Here the kilted swearing clansmen fought with desperate courage, driven in and out the backyards of Auldearn village. With his great scything, decapitating sweeps, Colkitto broke two swords, repeatedly advancing to gather in his straggling clansmen who had fallen in the stubborn, step-by-step retreat. Ranald Mackinnon of Mull fought swordless, armed only with his shield against a dozen pikemen, and with an arrow sticking out of either cheek; and Hurry, sure now that he had Montrose, pressed on with deadly persistence, never looking sideways. But Montrose had now for the first time enough cavalry to employ shock tactics; he sent in Gordon with his horsemen on Hurry's right flank and at the same time swept down from his ridge to join and rescue Colkitto. 'The bravery of young Napier shone with signal lustre,' Wishart reported; and it was good company in which to shine.

The pursuit went on through the long May evening and the Covenanting army was almost annihilated. The Committee of Estates retaliated by putting under examination 'John Napier, his wife and boy taken with him.' This was John Napier of Easter Torrie, old Archie's fifth brother, caught passing messages for Montrose, 'against whom they mean to proceed in a seeming legal way,' Montrose said; 'which if they do, let them be assured I also use the like severity against some of their prisoners:' he had a Campbell of Crinan in his grip. In fact Montrose never killed a single prisoner, even when his dearest friends were being executed by the Covenanting side. But the threat worked, this time at any rate.

At Alford-on-Don in July Montrose again outwitted Baillie and totally defeated him, largely with the aid of Nathaniel Gordon and his horse; but the battle was made bitter for them all by the loss of Nat's eldest cousin, Lord Gordon, shot in the back just as he had almost captured Baillie, gripping him by the belt on his galloping horse. Gordon was the flower of his family, a true and splendid friend to Montrose; and by the waters of Don the Royalists all sat down and wept for his excellence and his early doom. In August Montrose crossed the Forth a mile or two above Stirling to triumph once again in a major battle at Kilsyth. Alastair and his Macdonalds had stravagued back once more to the fray, augmented by 700 Macleans from Mull under Lachlan of Duart and Murdoch of Lochbuie, and many others, making a total of 1,500. Old Lord Airlie arrived with 80 Ogilvys, and Aboyne, Huntly's eldest surviving son, with 200 horsemen. Montrose had heard that Lanark was coming up fast from Clydesdale with reinforcements to join General Baillie, and had decided to get between them. He established himself in the Campsie fells, and there, doubtless in a cloud of midges, the decisive battle was fought.

Here, in the dawn of a piping hot day, Baillie attacked him. Like Robert the Bruce before Bannockburn, Montrose asked his men whether they would rather retreat or fight: he was answered by a similar yell. Knowing that they would have to charge up hill, a feat of which as Highlanders they were well capable on the milder slopes of Campsie, Montrose made them take off their plaids, and they fought with the tails of their saffron shirts tied between their legs. Baillie's task was made more difficult by Major Haldane who, advancing without orders to seize a vital farmhouse, revealed the Covenanter line and invited a Highland charge which broke it clean in the middle. The horsemen on the hill were hard pressed, but Montrose knew exactly how to handle them, when to reinforce them. The defeat of the Covenanters was complete, and once again Argyll never stopped till he was safely at sea in the Forth. General Baillie fought with stubborn courage and some skill, badly hampered by religious commissars breathing down his neck with inept advice, culled from the Old Testament; and if there can be anything worse than a political commissar leaning on one in a battle it must surely be a religious commissar.

But all Montrose's skill and courage, all the dash of sixty-year-old Lord Airlie leading in his horsemen to where the Gordons were hard beset by Baillie's cavalry in an effort to deploy their superior numbers over the rough ground of the fells, all the valour of the shouting saffron-clad Highlanders was in vain. A few weeks before, amongst the mild pastures of Northamptonshire, Cromwell's Ironsides had broken Prince Rupert's cavalry, sent the king flying in retreat, and shipwrecked the Royalist hopes in England at the battle of Naseby.

Yet Montrose was now master of Scotland, and treated both Edinburgh and Glasgow with a total clemency which they were not to return to him. There seemed quite a hope that freedom of worship, kingly authority, and the rule of Parliament, might survive against these dour and dedicated men; whom Montrose described as 'the present perverse and infamous faction of desperate rebels'. Distressed though Archie sometimes was when he thought of his imprisoned family, for him all this was as young men often like it to be at twenty; a life of gallop and scramble, full of challenge and excitement and the glow of a just cause.

These hopes crumbled at the sad rout of Philiphaugh. After his father's death, Archie defended Montrose's castle at Kincardine, escaping with the garrison under cover of night when the water supply ran out after a fourteen days' siege. The king had ordered Montrose to leave Scotland for the while; there had been a sad parting near Blairgowrie with the faithful Highlanders and with 'Airlie and Ogilvy and young Napier who in good and evil report had been true to their salt'. Archie's only absence had been in the previous February when he had had to go temporarily to the relief of his beleagured tenants in Menteith and the Lennox. Soon he followed Montrose to France, and before leaving Scotland on July 28th of 1646 he wrote to King Charles from Cluny in the glowing hyperbole of his epoch: 'I have taken the boldness before my departure humbly to show your Majesty the passionate desire I have to do you service . . .' Not yet of age, he left behind a wife and five children.

On the Continent there was not much service for Archie to do, except, for the rest of his days, to eat that unattractive diet, the bread of exile. The arrival of Montrose in France presented Henrietta Maria, exiled Queen of England, with a difficulty. They were not at all each other's types. The Queen, half Navarrese, half Medici, and wholly French and Catholic, confronted without rapport this tall young general, at once Puritan and romantic, a dedicated supporter with no *sauve-qui-peut* anywhere about him, and doubtless a strong regional accent which Henrietta Maria did not find easy to follow.

Yet something, surely, should be done to ease the lot and reward the services of so genuine a royalist—'the eminent fidelity and generosity you have shown in my service,' Charles had written—and even Henrietta Maria was at last coming to sort out the men from the boys. Would the Marquis of Montrose like the queen to take his niece, Lilias Napier, as a lady-in-waiting? The words of Montrose's reply are not recorded; he had charming manners, even if they were not French ones. His impressions of the court in exile were not favourable: they were obliged, poor things, to suck up to the French royal family in order to get enough to live upon. It galled him to see the royal house of Scotland and of England so emphatically in the role of poor relation at the court of the young Louis XIV. 'There is neither Scots man or woman welcome that way,' he wrote; 'neither would any of honour or virtue, chiefly a woman, suffer themselves to live in so lewd and worthless a place.' He would see his niece further before he let her row in such a galley. Politely he declined the queen's offer for Lilias Napier.

Montrose himself was made much of in Paris. Cardinal de Retz welcomed him as a Roman hero, and Mazarin offered him honourable employment with the rank of a Marshal of France. But Montrose despaired of help for King Charles from this cousin's court. Recruiting in the Low Countries, he spent his time with the Queen of

Bohemia, Elizabeth, the Winter Queen, daughter of James VI and I, born a Stewart and raised in Scotland. She was aunt to King Charles, and now elderly, but as full of charm and life as ever. While he waited for his plans to mature they hunted together, and had archery bouts, with Archie Napier and Kinnoull in attendance. Elizabeth's opinion of her sister-in-law's entourage coincided with theirs. 'They are all mad or worse,' she wrote firmly. The undimmed 'Queen of Hearts' was still cheerful company, surrounded by pretty daughters, and from time to time, by dashing but slightly incalculable sons. Her former subjects, the Czechs of Bohemia, had by now been exactly halved by their conquerors, since their disaster under the White Mountain. Only fifty per cent of the population remained, mainly peasants, under their new German or Spanish overlords; the other fifty per cent, which contained most of the nobles, and burgesses, all priests, doctors, and learned men in general, having been compelled, under the supervision of the papal nuncio, to recant their Protestantism, which they almost unanimously refused to do, to die, or to go into permanent exile; with results to that country which are still apparent. Twenty years later in the Netherlands their Scots-English queen appeared to have recovered her spirits; the Winter Queen having, after all, only spent six months in their country as a girl in her teens. The British seem remarkably inept or luckless in their dealings with the Czechs; seemingly doomed to be swamped out of individuality by one totalitarianism or another.

After two hundred years Merchiston had had to go, the strong tower falling for the first time into other hands. In 1647 Archie II was sued by the Covenanter Parliament for the £10,000 fine imposed on his father through his own escape to join Montrose. He besought the Estates 'to consider that his condition is so hard that for payment onlie of a pairt of his debts he has engadged his lands of Merchistoun and his lands in the west cuntrie are ruined and ovirburdened with quarterings'—plea refused. The liabilities had included also the heavy sum he had had to pay to stop the authorities from digging up his father's body and desecrating it. The lands and barony of Merchiston were contracted to a Covenanting gentleman suitably named Cant, who sold it to the Lowises, owners for the next seventy years.

Meanwhile his friends had written to Archie to entreat his return—'upon this very nick of time depends the utter ruin or safety of yourself, of your house and estates, lady and children and posterity, your nearest friends and of all that by the link and tie of nature should be dearest to you, for certainly if you continue in that evil course your forfeiture will not long be delayed, your lady and children shall be reduced to extreme want whereof they already feel the beginnings, your whole estate being already cantoned, divided, and taken up ...'

Yes, but the decision was taken. He closed his mind against all thought of those ever-yielding fields which to many men all round the globe are far more loved than wife and child. 'My dearest heart,' Archie began from Brussels in June of 1648, in a long explanatory letter to Elizabeth his wife. Besides the French offer to make Montrose a Marshal of France, with 12,000 crowns a year of pension as well as the pay, there had been the offer to himself of a regiment in Spain with active service, perhaps in the Indies. Montrose was suspicious of where the French job might lead him. 'If he did engage with them he would be forced to connive and wink at his Prince's ruin,' Archie wrote. Montrose had decided that Germany would be a better place, 'where he would be honourably appointed. Which sudden resolution did extremely trouble and astonish me ... If he had once been in charge I am confident in a very short time he would have been one of the most considerable strangers in Europe. For believe it, they had a huge esteem of him ... He, seeing me a little ill satisfied with the course he was going to take ... convinced me so with reason that I rested content.'

It had been agreed between them that Archie Napier should stay in Paris, 'go often to Court, make visits and ever in public places, at comedies and such things, still letting the word go that my uncle was gone to the country for his health. Which was believed so long as they saw me. For it was ever said that Montrose and his nephew were like the Pope and the Church, who would be inseparable. Whereas if I had gone away with him his course would have been presently discovered ... and if he had been taken going to any of the House of Austria who were their enemies, you may think they would have staid him, which might have been dangerous both to his person, credit and fortune ... The first letter I received from him was dated from Geneva. So when I perceived he was out of French ground, I resolved to come here to Flanders, where I might have freedom of correspondence with him; as also liberty to go to him when it pleased him to send for me, which I could not do conveniently in France. For I was afraid how soon his course should chance to be discovered, that they might seek assurance of me and others not to engage with their enemy, which is ordinary in such cases. Yet would I never have given them any, but thought best to prevent it. And besides, I had been at so great a charge, for month after his way-going, with staying at Court and keeping of a coach there, which I hired, and coming back to Paris, and living at a greater rate than I did formerly (all which was his desire, yet did I consume much moneys) . . .' Archie and several of his friends decided to be in a handier place and to eat the rather cheaper bread of exile available in the Low Countries, and took ship for Middleburgh from Havre-de-Grace and thence to Brussels, 'where we are daily expecting Montrose's commands. which, how soon I receive them you shall be advertised by him who entreats you to believe that he shall study most carefully to conserve the quality he hath hitherto inviolably kept of continuing my dearest life, only yours, Napier.'

It does not all sound so very glum, in spite of the expense of the coach and the comedies and the strain of keeping himself inviolably hers. Let us hope that some of the exiles, some of the time, had fun (like banished Russians junketting in S.W.7); and indeed, with Elizabeth of Bohemia about, it is probable that they did, however short of food and cash. 'Ere I be very troublesome to you,' he added in a postscript, 'I shall live upon one meal a day. I have been most civilly used in this town by many of good quality; and was the last day invited by the Jesuits to their college, where I received handsome entertainment. After long discourse, they told me that, if I liked, the king of Spain should maintain me. But I showed them that I would not live by any King of Christendom's charity. They said it was no charity, for many of eminent places received allowance from him. I told them, if I did him service, what he bestowed upon me then, I might justly take; but to be a burden to him otherwise, I would never do it. But I know their main end was to try if they could persuade me to turn Catholic. But I shall, God willing, resist all their assaults, as well as their fellows who plied me so hard in Paris . . .

'If it had not been for waiting on Montrose, I might before this time have settled somewhere. For just before my parting from Paris, I received letters from some friends at Madrid in Spain, that if I pleased I should have a commission for a regiment, and ten pistoles of levy-moneys for every man. Which was a good condition . . .

The reason why I am so impatient to engage, is to have your company
. . . I would go six times as far, through all dangers imaginable, only
to see you. I confess I have satisfaction in nothing whilst we live at
such a distance. For though I should enjoy all those things which
others do esteem felicities, yet if I do not enjoy your company, they
are rather crosses than pleasures to me; and I should be more
contented to live with you meanly, in the deserts of Arabia, than
without you in the most fruitful place in the world, and with all the
delights it could afford. You may possibly think these *compliments*,
as you showed me once before, when I wrote kindly to you. But
God knows, they flow from a real and ingenuous heart . . .'

Love is a wonderful thing: whatever the delights of Elizabeth
Erskine's company, her face is as plain as a pikestaff, she had a fine
complexion but her nose did that unseducing thing which is to go
on forever, practically hanging down over her mouth. Yet this letter
ends with begging her, 'Be pleased, dear Heart, to let me have one
thing which I did almost forget—your picture, in the breadth of a
sixpence—and I will wear it upon a ribbon under my doublet,
so long as I, or it, lasts. The other is so big as I cannot wear it about
me.' She must have been a very very nice woman, and extremely
good company, for him to love so dearly, beyond the outward
semblance. He was around twenty-four at the time.

At the imperial court the Emperor Ferdinand made Montrose a
Marshal of the Empire; and told him to raise what troops he could
from his domains, the Netherlands being the most advisable and
nearest place. At the Hague Archie found the young Prince Charles
intriguing with another Scots clique, but approaching Montrose
secretly. 'If your Highness shall but vouchsafe a little faith unto your
loyal servants, and stand at guard with others, your affairs can still
be whole,' Montrose pointed out to him on January 28th. Two days
later King Charles I was beheaded in Whitehall. Whatever else could
still be whole he at least could not.

The effect of Charles's beheading was appalling. All over Europe
monarchs shook and prelates prayed and anglophobes doubtless
pointed out that they had known all along just how barbarian the
islanders were; still basically painted blue. Montrose, very far from
being either fool or weakling, fell in a dead faint when they brought
him the news; and he was one who had had the strength of character

to haul his drunken troops off Dundee at the height of their spree and march them many leagues to the safety of the heather, and to lead them later in mid-winter over twenty miles of snowy mountains in a night. Some spring of hope died out of the exiles; and Montrose from then on was a death-wished man.

Intrigues, delays, and misunderstandings continued between the new King Charles at The Hague and his mother Henrietta Maria in Paris. Doubtless everybody was still suffering from devastating shock; an affliction whose physical and mental results were not then fully understood. The prince had offered the Parliamentarians *carte blanche* to spare his father's life, so that he must have desperately feared its loss, 'yet the barbarous stroke so surprised him that he was in all the confusion imaginable, and those about him were almost bereft of their understanding,' Clarendon reported.

Preparations for a landing in Scotland continued; Montrose went to Sweden and to Denmark to recruit men and help; the King of Denmark (which then included Norway) being King Charles II's near kinsman. Elizabeth of Bohemia continued her process of jollying him along, from henceforth by letter. She and Montrose shared the fear that her nephew, the young Charles II, was about to be duped by the Covenanting lords, specially Lauderdale, 'who haunts him like a fury,' Lord Byron reported. Montrose besought the king not to be deluded by Scotland's current rulers who had sold his father and in a few cases perhaps connived at his death.

Montrose was at this time a handsome thirty-seven-year-old widower, personable enough to lend credibility to the rumour put about by his enemies that he had seduced Queen Henrietta Maria and boasted of his success, two events most uncharacteristic of either of them, and unsupported by any evidence. Far more likely is the tale that he fell in love with the Queen of Bohemia's daughter, Louise, and she with him. 'He was exceeding constant and loving to those who did adhere to him, and very affable to such as he knew,' wrote his follower, Thomas Saintserf, 'though his carriage, which indeed was not ordinary, made him seem proud . . . Of exceeding strong composition of body, and an incredible force, joined with an excellent proportion and fine features . . . a quick and piercing grey eye . . . He was a man of very princely carriage and excellent address, which made him to be used by princes, for the most part, with the greatest familiarity.' Queen Elizabeth of Bohemia persuaded him to have himself painted by Gerard Honthorst, but this was after the king's death; Montrose sat for the picture in black armour, by him a helmet cascading with black plumes. To his usual device, *N'Oubliez*, he added *Nil Medium*—no half measures. The queen attempted to laugh him out of this mood: letters flowed to him at Hamburg, where he had gone, and where he left Archie Napier to collect and organize the hoped for imperial volunteers.

Elizabeth Stewart, Queen of Bohemia, from whom all subsequent rulers of the kingdom of Great Britain were to descend, was one of those characters who affirm that life is essentially an enjoyable thing. Brought up *en princesse*, with her spirited and amusing brother, Henry, and her poor little brother, 'baby Charles', who could steal no limelight since he could not speak till he was four and then only stammeringly, spoiled and fêted for her beauty by such poets as Sir Henry Wotton, married to the Palatine Elector and swept into a kingdom, she seemed to have it all her own sweet way. Everything devastatingly changed overnight; her brilliant brother, Henry, had died of a fever almost on her wedding day; her kingdom was lost in one appalling battle under the White Mountain and she and her husband driven out to a life of penury in the Netherlands. Presently her husband died young, and baby Charles, now king of England, was beheaded. Money grew ever tighter. Everything failed except Elizabeth's spirit. For her, life, however it developed, was a thing of delight: people, whoever they were, could be made into sources of interest or joy.

> You meaner beauties of the night
> Which poorly satisfy our eyes
> More by your number than your light,
> You common people of the skies
> What are you when the sun doth rise?

Wootton had written in her praise. She was exiled, poor, mockingly diminished as 'the Winter Queen' for her short season of reigning, but she remained throughout her life the undimmed Queen of Hearts, whom all the poets once, and not wholly from sychophancy, had celebrated: 'the eclipse and glory of her kind.'

There had been a time during the crisis in Bohemia when her husband had to beseech her not to be melancholy; but once disaster had actually befallen, she remained vigorously cheerful. She adored her son Frederick, but he was drowned; she also adored her sons Rupert and Maurice, but they were always off fighting, refused to settle, and produced nothing but natural children whom she never saw. Her second son Charles Lewis she could not do with, after he made friends with Oliver Cromwell, and, succeeding as Elector Palatine, became difficult about money. She complained that he was mean, which was true; and he complained that she was extravagant, which was truer still. His mother's court, Prince Maurice mocked, was 'vexed by rats and mice but worst of all by creditors'. She was said to prefer her dogs to her daughters, who retaliated in the time-honoured way by running away from home to become abbesses. Sophia married—oh dear!—the boring Elector of Hanover.

Elizabeth's loves and hates were faithful. She disliked Christina of Sweden almost as much as she hated Oliver Cromwell, and that was saying a great deal. 'Your humblest slave,' wrote Sir Thomas Roe to her, 'who loves you, and will love you, infinitely and incessantly, till death.' Lord Craven, acting as honorary chancellor of her court, fended off life's buffets and paid her debts with unflagging persistence. She left him all her papers and many of her pictures: Rupert and Maurice had the money. When at last in 1660 the long exile ended and she could float back to England, Pepys, who then saw her, thought her plain but jolly. What she had was charm; and bunches of city gentlemen were known to give up their cushy jobs to go and fight for her. By 1660 she was going on seventy, and died quite soon in her house in Leicester Square, supported, it was said, in the arms of her nephew Charles II, charming as usual but perhaps not altogether unrelieved that there went one major family financial problem.

But now, in 1648 in Holland, she took a hand in the lightening of Montrose's spirits and in the rapproachement, which she saw as the young king's best hope, between her nephew Charles, endeavouring to wean him from those dour but powerful Covenanters to whom she mockingly referred as 'the godly Brethern'. Montrose himself had gone in for some plain speaking to the king about them. 'Contrary to all duty, gratitude, faith and hospitality they sold your royal Father over into the hands of his merciless enemies, complotted his death, connived at his murder, and have been the only rigid and restless instruments of all his saddest fates,' he wrote, exactly a year before his own saddest fate. But the rigid and restless instruments pressed on with the young king's seduction.

*

'Inglesbie saith that they are all up again in Scotland,' the Queen of
Bohemia cheered Montrose when he went off recruiting for the king,
'that the English rebel Parliament can get no soldier to go for Ireland;
but it is thought they will send their rebel army for Scotland, without
doubt to help 'the Brethern' there. I wished Jamie Graeme amongst
them with all his followers,' she teased him, for Montrose had had
all his honours removed by the Brethern and was always referred to
by them as James Graham *tout court*. 'I can add nothing but my
wishes that you may persuade the King for his good. I pray you tell
my Highlander (Seaforth) I hope yet that his people will have another
bout . . .'

Letters flowed to Montrose at Hamburg, where he had gone to
establish a depot, and where he left Archie Napier to collect and
organize the hoped for imperial volunteers. 'All is walking abroad
and shooting,' she complained from Rhenen in August . . . 'I pray
God keep the King in his constancy to you . . . it will be a great
charity in you to let me know the news you receive . . . the place
being very barren of all news. We have nothing to do but walk and
shoot. I am grown a *good archer*, to shoot with my Lord Kinnoull.
If your office will suffer it, I hope you will come and help us to shoot?'
It is most cruel hot weather since you went,' she mourned in September. 'There is no news, only that the King is still at St Germains
but constant to his resolution . . . and to all his friends. For all that,
I would he were well gone from there . . . I pray, my lord, commend
me to my Lord Napier. Assure him I wish him all happiness.'

But what was that charming, black-browed, randy, young Charles
up to, how swayed by his demanding mother and by importunate
Lauderdale? The battle for the young king's soul went on; but
Elizabeth was generally able to be flippant—'Culpepper (King
Charles's Presbyterian adviser) is gone for Muscovy. The spices and
aquavitae will burn him quickly up.' There was talk of 'new commissioners sent to the King from the '*Godly brethern*,' to cross wicked
Jamie Graeme's proceedings. But I am assured, from a good hand,
that it will do no good . . . I have heard nothing of Rupert, they say
he is at sea . . . I conjure you to be confident that I am ever your
most affectionate constant friend . . .'

'Those that govern in Edinburgh make show to wish to have their
King,' she reported ominously in October. Would he fall into the
trap? By mid-November she heard from Paris that 'Rupert was gone
out of Kinsale and passed by St Malo three weeks ago with six good

ships. But whither, God knows . . . Cromwell's money prevails much in Ireland, for Wexford was betrayed to him. There be many glad and some sorry that Rupert is out . . . I assure you there is nothing left undone to hinder your proceedings. I hope God will prosper you in spite of them.' The future seemed menacing, uncertain. Cromwell had triumphed in Ireland, and Rupert was about to alienate still further the City of London, that powerful body.

In December she heard from the king in Jersey, and felt better: 'who assures me he is not changed in his affections or designs . . . Robert le Diable [Rupert] is about Scilly with seven good ships.' Had Montrose seen the proclamation 'against Morton and Kinnoull' and all adherents of 'that detestable bloody murderer and excommunicated traitor' James Graeme? What manners! 'The Turks never called the Christians so.' Wynram had been sent by Argyll to counteract Montrose but had not yet arrived—'the *godly Windrum*, I hope he will find *visage de bois* when he comes . . . There has been many synods held at Dort and at Rotterdam. Now there is one at Amsterdam, where the great-tongued Lord is, and high-nosed' (Lauderdale). No news had reached her, when she wrote Montrose her final letter in early January, of any waverings in Charles's constancy. 'Since Rupert was at Cape St Vincent off the coast of Portugal, I have not heard of him. But upon those four ships he has taken be many merchants of London bankrupt as I am informed.' Communications with England had been diminished—'Colonels Banfield and Penruddock are both prisoners in the Tower . . . Penruddock they say has been racked. All Banfield's letters and cyphers are taken . . . I pray God send you better conditions, and safety in Scotland . . .'

But Montrose was away up the Baltic, chaffering with the King of Poland, and with Queen Christina of Sweden, one of his admirers, aiming for troops, while others were at work nearer to King Charles, bringing an offer of an immediate £300,000 if he would come to terms with the Edinburgh government. Would he, could he, look such a gift horse in the mouth? On the first day of 1645 George Wishart, once chaplain to Montrose and now minister to the Scots congregation at Schiedam in Holland, wrote a warning letter to Archie at Hamburg—'My Lord Napier'—and he told how Lanark and Lauderdale were hard at work at the Hague bringing pressure to bear. 'All their present hopes are of Windrum's treaty, and offers to the King, which they magnify as very great, glorious, and advantageous to his Majesty, seeing he may by them get present possession of that whole Kingdom [Scotland] at so easy a rate as the forsaking of one man, who, as a bloody excommunicated rebel, is so odious to all men, that the King cannot be so demented and bewitched as to prefer him to the present enjoyment of the affections and services of a whole nation of most true and loyal subjects. Such are the charms whereby these old wizards go about still to fascinate the world, abroad and at home . . .'

The old wizards had fascinated and foxed the young king, confident that his advice to them to 'use moderation' would take effect, and youthfully unaware that moderation was the last thing that ever entered their minds. 'Depend upon my kindness and proceed with your business with your usual courage and alacrity,' the king adjured Montrose from Jersey in mid-January. He did not expect 'to give the least impediment to your proceedings' by negotiating with the Covenanters in Edinburgh, 'as we conceive that your preparations have been one effectual motive that hath induced them to make the said address to us, so your vigorous proceeding will be a good means to bring them to such moderation in the said treaty, as probably may produce an agreement, and a present union of that whole nation in our service. We assure you that we will not, before or during the treaty, do anything contrary to that power and authority we have given you by our Commission.' You are there to bring pressure— land in Scotland and bring it. Charles enclosed the Garter for Montrose, for 'singular courage, conduct, and fidelity . . . as becomes a Knight and Companion of so noble an order.' There was plenty of damned merit about this Garter. 'As I never had passion upon earth so strong as to do the King your father service, so shall it be my study, if your Highness command me, to show it redoubled for the recovery of you,' Montrose answered him.

Kinnoull, sent ahead to Scotland, reported over-optimistically back to Montrose, 'Your Lordship is gaped after with that expectation that the Jews look for the Messiah, and certainly your presence will restore your groaning company to its liberties and the King to his rights.' Left behind to await Montrose's summons, Archie fretted to be away, writing to King Charles at Breda for his exit permit. 'My Lord Napier,' the answer came, 'as I have ever been confident of your great affection to my service, I pray you continue

James Graham, 1st Marquis of Montrose, by Honthorst. *By kind permission of the Earl of Dalhousie.*

Archibald Campbell, Marquis of Argyll. The Newbattle portrait. *By kind permission of the Marquis of Lothian.*

Nephew and follower of Montrose, Archibald, 2nd Lord Napier, aged sixteen and probably in his wedding clothes, from an engraving after the painting by George Jamesone. *By kind permission of Lord Napier and Ettrick.*

your assistance to the Marquis of Montrose, which your being
with him will much the more enable you to do, and therefore I am
well pleased with your repair to him, and very sensible of your
good endeavours for my service, which I shall ever acknowledge as
your very affectionate friend. Charles R., Breda, the 15th April
1650.'

A wild wind lashed the North Sea all that spring scattering
Montrose's fleet, and the king's letter reached Archie too late.
Nor had the summons he awaited from Montrose ever come, the
call to reinforce him at Inverness, or Speymouth, maybe. Montrose
had landed at Kirkwall earlier in the month, from whence he had
besought his monarch 'to have a serious eye now at last upon the too
open crafts are used against you.' But Charles, twenty years old and
over-confident, had pressed on with the signing the treaty of Breda,
whose terms gave royal authority to the Covenanting Parliament and
a safe exit to Montrose. His hedging letter to Montrose had been
widely published throughout Scotland by the Covenanting government who had received it, though Montrose had not. The king's
belated letter to Montrose telling him to lay down his arms never
reached his general. Montrose landed in Caithness on April 12th,
to find the clansmen of the north on whom he had confidently
counted were biding their time. The Munros, the Rosses, and the
Mackenzies would wait and see, the men of Strathearn who would
certainly have risen with him were waiting for him there. With his
small and untrained body of Orkneymen, he was defeated at
Carbisdaile near the end of Loch Shin and fled disguised into the
wilds of Sutherland, appealing to the local laird, Neil McLeod of
Assynt, whom he thought his friend, for help in escaping down the
Naver to the sea and thence to Orkney.

But Neil McLeod of Assynt sold him for £25,000 to the Covenanters, on the day the Treaty of Breda was signed, one condition
of which was a safe exit for Montrose and his army. The only ray of
light connected with this event is that the £25,000 was never paid.
McLeod had broken the sacred law of the Highlands; and neighbours in his remote region noted with gloomy relish that his castle of
Assynt was presently burnt down, and that his descendants perished
utterly from out of the land. The ruins of his castle still stand beside
the glittering loch.

*

Captured, Montrose expected no mercy and received none. An over-indulgence in Old Testament reading had dried up the milk of human kindness in the Scottish heart. The Covenanted Scots felt immeasurably chosen. At Perth they had fought, incredibly, under a banner inscribed 'Jesus and No Quarter.' Against this it must be said that, although he spared Perth, Montrose had not hauled the Highlanders off vanquished Aberdeen before they had slaughtered a hundred citizens and doubtless raped many more; but at least he had previously warned this city to send their old men and women away.

Exhausted, famished, and in high fever from his wounds received at Carbisdaile, he was sent south under escort, riding in rags to emphasize his disgrace, and with his feet tied under the belly of a small shaggy pony with a rope for rein, exposed to the ridicule of the righteous through every village and town on the route. The death wish had lifted, he was cheerful and serene. The Reverend James Fraser, by no means an adherent, rode with him; he noted that Montrose 'being in the custody of his mortal enemies yet expressed a singular constancy and in a manner carelessness of his condition' as the procession crossed the river Conan and moved towards Beauly. After him on foot trailed his forty fellow prisoners, the rags and the ignominy were reserved for Montrose. At Muirtown both ministers and provost comforted him; at Forres and Elgin old friends who had been at St Andrews with him came 'to wait on him and divert him all the time, with allowance of the General' (David Leslie). At Keith it was Sunday, and the minister, Mr William Kinanmond, preached to him on the text of Agag (he who was hewn in pieces at the instigation of the prophet Samuel), 'in such invective, violent, malicious manner that some of the hearers who were even of the swaying side, condemned him. Montrose, patiently hearing him a long time, and he insisting still, said Rail on, and so turned his back on him.'

At Dundee, which had suffered much at the hands of his army, there was generosity. 'So far from insulting over him, the whole town expressed a great deal of sorrow for his condition, and furnished him with clothes.' The night was spent at Kinnaird Castle, where Montrose said goodbye to his two youngest children, lodged with their grandfather, Lord Southesk, who sat comfortably on the fence throughout the troubles, with his legs on the Convenanter side. 'Neither at meeting or at parting could any change of his former countenance be seen not suitable to the greatness of his spirit,' Fraser applauded. Not wanting to run the risk of taking him upstream and thus nearer to the Highlands, his captors ferried him across the Forth and landed him at Leith on a fine afternoon in late May. Ahead of him, dark against the sun, loomed the heights of Edinburgh, stronghold of his most implacable and bitter foes.

XII

It is difficult to understand the extreme malignity with which the Council in Edinburgh treated Montrose unless one considers what went before. For a century or more Europe had swum in a tossing river of debate which had ever and again turned into a sea of blood. To Scotland their religious settlement was felt to be a very frail thing. The Protestants of Bohemia had been extirpated, the nearby Netherlands had drenched in blood under Spanish Catholic rule, the advent of King Charles and his bishops had felt to them like the thin end of a terrifying wedge. They were very frightened; and therefore very cruel.

They reacted with fevered enthusiasm against everything that had gone before. Because the Bible in English had been publicly burnt under the rule of Mary of Guise they elevated it into an object whose every least syllable was sacredly to be observed; because this queen's French soldiery had marched up and down St Giles in scarlet cloaks and gilt morions to drown out the voice of their preachers, they hated glowing accoutrements and inordinately loved sermons; because St Giles had been crowded with fifty altars and gorgeously decked images they hated altars and even condemned the mild stone faces of medieval worthies.

Edinburgh's great church, elevated by King Charles I into the status of a cathedral, had held a great wooden statue of its patron, St Giles, and this upon his saint's day in September, had been annually taken in procession around the streets of Edinburgh with drums and trumpets, a garlanded bull, candles, bagpipes, and all kinds of jollity. But as soon as the more thoughtful Scots had actually got hold of the gospels in English and read them, they perceived that this was not what Christianity was essentially about. The notion that the bull and bagpipe element could peacefully co-exist with the thoughtful realizations, that they could even form an essential element in religion to certain minds and certain ages, the idea that man is feeling as well as reason, flesh as well as spirit, entered into no one's consideration. It was exactly the kind of carry-on against which the prophets of Israel had so expressly warned them: it deflected attention from the God who was a spirit and must be worshipped in spirit and in truth. It was idolatry and backsliding, it was a kind of Amalakite performance in the temple of Baal. Upon one St Giles's day in the 1550s the people of Edinburgh had seized the great image of St Giles and cast it into the Nor' Loch, the great sheet of water that lay in the chasm that now stretches between the Castle Hill and modern Princes Street. From thence they had subsequently lugged it out and burnt it. They were Napthali, the hind let loose; the people freed from the prison of ignorance and superstition where they had long lain captive.

Two books, *Napthali* by Sir James Stewart, printed in 1667, and *A Hind Let Loose* by Alexander Shields, printed a few years later, set forth the extreme Covenanters as they felt themselves to be. Napthali was the tenth of Jacob's twelve sons: in the patriarch's final blessing to the men who would head the tribes of Israel he had proclaimed, 'Napthali is a hind let loose: he giveth goodly words.' The Covenanters felt that they alone spoke the truth, had cleared away the clutter. They represented that element in religious feeling which is present also in the early Fathers and will probably exist for ever, the element which prefers to approach God with extreme simplicity, and in spontaneous words which can never be dead or mumbled meaninglessly, the element that prefers the white-washed chapel and the unmoneyed and unglorious ministration. It was to this that Montrose had signed on in the first Covenant: it was from this that, seeing to what abuse it might lead, old Archie Napier had held back from signing, although in principle it was his way also. It was this that Argyll had so skilfully employed for political ends, and in which he may indeed have sincerely believed.

Six years earlier on June 4th in 1644 a characteristic sermon had been preached in Edinburgh, and was reported on by Henry Guthrie, Bishop of Dunkeld, and regarded by his opponents as 'a rotten malignant'. 'Mr Andrew Cant, by the commission of the General Assembly, was appointed to preach at the opening of Parliament, wherein he satisfied their expectation fully. For the main point he drove at in his sermon, was to state an opposition betwixt King Charles and King Jesus (as he was pleased to speak), and upon that account, to press resistance to King Charles for the interest of King Jesus. It may be wondered that such doctrine should have relished with men brought up in the knowledge of the scriptures; and yet, such was the madness of the times, that none who preached in public since the beginning of the troubles had been so cried up as he was for that sermon.' It was no use their opponents talking about King David or King Solomon. To the purists kings were clutter too.

In the Solemn League which both English and Scottish Puritans signed there are the long declarations of sin, of inadequacy, of lack of endeavour, that seem to go beyond Christian repentance and into the realm of hysterical self-blaming, that presage the utterances of communist self-confessed traitors in Russia or China of late. There is the same aggrieved self-righteousness and pre-occupation with the sins of others, the same overriding fear of surrounding and largely imaginary enemies. All the horrors they commit are 'for the preservation of ourselves and our Religion from utter ruine and destructione'. Scotland to them was 'a hind let loose from the yoke of Tyrannical slaverie . . . the sin, shame and miserie of this age . . . in our Israel.' 'We are a perverse and crooked generation,' they were wont to insist, when someone perpetrated the mildest sexual peccadillo. 'BACK-SLIDDEN SCOTLAND,' *Napthali* apostrophised it in 1667; and to such in 1650 Montrose was the most backslidden of all—'that treacherous and truculent traitor, gathering an Army of wicked Apostates and Irish murderers;' he was 'that bloody villain Montrose, with his cut-throat Complices . . .' who, 'resolved to bring home that pest [Charles II] and thereby Precipitated themselves and us into ineluctable miserie.'

'Landing in the west Highlands with a party of bloody Irish papists he overran the whole country,' complained James Kirkton, a Kirk minister, 'and beat the Covenanters' forces in six bloody conflicts. His war, I believe, was the most cruel in the world. The behaviour of his soldiers was to give no quarter in the field and ordinarily when they came in the country they deflowered the women and butchered the poor men . . . and barbously mangled the carcase. He made two hundred widows in St Andrews and Kirkcaldy.' So much had propaganda done against Montrose in the years since he had left Scotland; and even the far more moderate Robert Baillie had written that there would be no peace or honour in Scotland 'until these wormes be chirted out'.

*

The Committee of Estates in Edinburgh had contemplated doing the chirting out the moment Montrose stept ashore; he who had once been the Covenanters' young (and extremely effective) champion, their David against the Goliath of superstition and idolatry that glowered across the North Sea from the Continent, and who had turned against them. (It never occurred to the hind let loose that the hounds had in fact largely kennelled themselves.) In any case they must hurry to condemn and execute him before specific orders could arrive from King Charles, before the protests of Europe could gather to prevent it. Sir William Fleming had already arrived from Breda with the terms of the treaty; but perhaps nothing now could have saved Montrose but an unequivocal declaration that unless he was set free the whole bargain was off.

On arrival at Edinburgh he was met at the Nethergate by the magistrates and the hangman and 'tied upon a cart bareheaded and driven by the hangman to the Tolbooth prison; the reason of his being tied to the cart was in hope that the people would have stoned him, and that he might not be able by his hands to save his face,' another eye-witness reported.* To their eternal honour the people of Edinburgh did not respond to this hope. 'In all the way there appeared in him such majesty, courage, modesty, and even somewhat more than natural, that those common women who had lost their husbands and children in the wars, and who were hired to stone him, were upon sight of him so astonished and moved that their intended curses turned into tears and prayers.' The long Royal Mile was crowded this bright afternoon with the retainers of the Covenanting lords, with Kirk ministers, with bitter widows of his wars, with every slum dweller and beggar from the warrens behind the High Street, but no gibes or jeers came from these enemies, no sound but that of sobbing broke the stillness. One voice alone shouted an insult and followed it with a peel of hysterical laughter—Lady Jean Gordon, now Lady Haddington, who was a daughter of Huntly, recently executed, and a niece of Argyll, and thus torn all ways. She was notoriously scandalous, and a voice from the crowd cried up at her 'that it became her better to sit upon the cart herself for her adulteries'.

Argyll had made up a party for the event, which included his honeymooning son and daughter-in-law. 'The Lord Lorn, and his

* Wigton MS.

new lady were also sitting in a balcony, joyful spectators, and the cart being stopt when it came before the lodging where the Chancellor, Argyll and Warriston sat—that they might have time to insult—Montrose, suspecting the business, turned his face towards them. Whereupon they presently crept in at the windows; which being perceived by an Englishman, he cried up, it was no wonder they started aside at his look, for they durst not look him in the face these seven years bygone!'

M. de Graymond, French Resident in Edinburgh, reporting home, was stirred out of his diplomatic detachment by the whole proceedings. Montrose, a royal commissioner, a marquis, a knight of the Garter, being 'paraded the whole length of the Canongate and through the town to the prison! . . . Few were there present who did not sympathize, or forbore to express by their murmurs and mournful sighs how their hearts were touched by the nobility of his bearing, amid such a complication of miseries . . . It has occasioned much talk here since, that the procession was made to halt in front of the Earl of Moray's house where among other spectators was the Marquis of Argyle, who contemplated his enemy from a window, through partly closed blinds . . .' Graymond described Montrose's sentencing at length, apologizing to Mazarin for his interminable letter—'*Je demande, tres humblement, pardon a votre Eminence, si je me suis un peu trop laisser emporter dans cette longue narration;*' but Montrose's whole aspect and quality and the savage brutality of his sentence—'unknown heretofore in Scotland—seemed to me a subject deserving profound reflection.'

For three hours the procession moved slowly through the streets, arriving at the Tolbooth prison at seven in the evening. Here Montrose was at once confronted by interrogators from Parliament. He declined to answer them until he knew what terms they were on with the king: after long delays and consultations he was told of the treaty—though not of its terms; and with what thoughts we know not, asked for a delay in the questionings until the morrow, as he had had a long journey, and 'the compliment they had put upon him that day had been somewhat tedious.' The fever from his wounds had abated, but they were not yet healed and he looked deathly pale.

The next day was Sunday, when to try and to execute Montrose would be to break the Sabbath. Throughout the hours till Monday morning the preachers vilified him from their pulpits and the appointed Kirk ministers wrestled for his soul. No friends, no relations were allowed to visit him, and for the account of the proceedings in prison we are indebted to Patrick Simson, minister at Renfrew, who reported his eye-witness account to the Rev. Robert Wodrow. He was sorry, Montrose said, to have offended the Church of Scotland—'I would with all my heart be reconciled with the same,' but if it meant 'calling that my sin which I account to have been my duty, I cannot, for all the reason and conscience in the world'. He had sinned greatly in his lifetime against God, but not, he believed, against Scotland.

Simson's account breathes a reluctant admiration for the prisoner's logic and powers of reasoning when rebutting his accusers—'he discoursed handsomely, as he could well do.' As for taking papist Irishry to fight for him, for consorting with that rollicking and ruthless giant from the Islands, Colkitto; that was because the king's own subjects had refused him this their duty, and 'we see what a company David took to defend himself in the time of his strait,' he quoted at them from the Old Testament. Yes, his men had plundered the country, but the ministers must know that 'soldiers who wanted pay could not be restrained from spoilzie, nor kept under such strict discipline as regular forces;' but he had done all he could to keep them back; and if bloodshed could have been prevented thereby he would rather all that was shed had come out of his own veins. What about breaching the Covenant, the Covenant he had signed 'Montrois' in his flourishing hand, the Ministers asked him?

'The Covenant which I took I own it and adhere to it. Bishops I care not for them. I never intended to advance their interest. But when the King had granted you all your desires, and you were every one sitting under his vine and under his fig tree—that then you should have taken a party in England by the hand, and entered into a League and Covenant against the King, was the thing I judged my duty to oppose to the yondmost.'

The voice of France now spoke out loud, clear, and civilized. Spurred on by de Retz, a letter was sent on behalf of Louis XIV, still a minor, pointing out to the Estates that Montrose had acted within the king's commission and should be set free: there were no grounds on which the King of France's 'dear friends' of the Scottish Parliament could condemn or execute him, since that body were now bound by the treaty of alliance they had signed with the king who

7*

had commissioned him to do what he did in landing in Scotland. The message of France arrived a week too late.

All the elements of Greek tragedy were now present—the weeping, powerless chorus of the city's women, the doomed hero, the wronged tyrant implacably seeking revenge, the ministers and elders of the Kirk driven by the fires of religious rage. It was as if all Edinburgh were held in the grip of some potency it could neither understand nor combat, as if the Fates themselves had joined company with Macbeth's three witches and now rode howling over the Castle Hill, over the Parliament House and the Tolbooth prison and the house-high gallows which men were now hard building at the Mercat Cross.

Through the short darkness of the summer nights the black-robed ministers continued to drag at Montrose's soul like ravens, to hammer at the obduracy that would not recant, or go back upon his long adherence to the king. All the techniques were used; he was cajoled, adjured, threatened; told he was a faggot burning in hell fire —one of the ministers could already see him there. One sentence of exasperation was finally jerked from Montrose when morning came and they would not let him shave himself, or be shaved. If he had wanted to break God's law and do away with himself, he would have done it a week ago. No razor? 'I thought they would have allowed that to a dog.' As a result, Sir James Balfour was able to record next day that Montrose in the trial chamber looked 'pale, lank-faced, and hairy'.

Lady Napier, she who had been Elizabeth Erskine and was the wife of exiled young Archie, had been turned out of Merchiston three years ago and was now living, rentless and in some distress, in or near Edinburgh with her five small children—Archibald, John, Jean, Margaret, and Mary. Poor and pressed by debts, it was she who provided and somehow was able to convey to Montrose the splendid clothes in which he walked from the Tolbooth this morning of May 20th to face his trial. It was ten o'clock, and the ministers had already been at him since eight, accusing him of everything from sedition to sodomy. He had replied, one of them complained, 'in a manner too airy and volage': clearly he had been associating too much with the Winter Queen and had acquired a Continental frivolity quite unbecoming to his situation.

Standing in the place of delinquents in Parliament he heard from

Loudoun, the Chancellor, 'a long discourse declaring the progress of all his rebellions. He pleaded his innocency,' Sir James Balfour reported, and the Wigton MS gives his answer: 'Since you have declared to me that you have agreed with the King, I look upon you as if his Majesty were sitting amongst you; and in that relation I appear in this reverence—bareheaded.

'My care has always been to walk as became a good Christian and loyal subject. I did engage in the first Covenant and was faithful to it. When I perceived some private persons under colour of religion intend to wring the authority from the King and to use it for themselves, it was thought fit, for the clearing of honest men, that a bond [Cumbernauld] should be subscribed, wherein the security of religion was sufficiently provided for. For the League, I thank God I was never in it; and so could not break it. How far Religion has been advanced by it, and what sad consequences followed on it, these poor distressed Kingdoms can witness. When his late Majesty had by the blessing of God almost subdued those rebels that rose against him in England, and that a faction of this Kingdom [Scotland] went in to the assistance of the rebels, his Majesty gave commission to me to come into this Kingdom, to make a diversion of those forces which were going from this against him. I acknowledged the command was most just, and I conceived myself bound in conscience and duty to obey it.

'What my carriage was in this country many of you may bear witness. Disorders in arms cannot be prevented; but they were no sooner known than punished. Never was any man's blood spilt but in battle; and even then, many thousand lives have I preserved. And I dare here avow, in the presence of God, that never a hair of Scotsman's head, that I could save, fell to the ground. And as I came in upon his Majesty's warrants, so, upon his letters, did I lay aside all interests and retire.

'And as for my coming at this time, it was by his Majesty's just commands, in order to the accelerating the treaty between him and you; his Majesty knowing that whenever he had ended with you, I was ready to retire upon his call. I may say that never subject acted upon more honourable grounds, nor by so lawful a power, as I did in these services.

'And therefore I desire you to lay aside prejudice; and consider me as a Christian, in relation to the justice of the quarrel; as a subject, in relation to my royal master's commands; and as your neighbour, in relation to the many of your lives I have preserved in battle. And be not too rash; but let me be judged by the laws of God, the laws of nature and nations, and the laws of this land:

'If otherwise—I do here appeal from you, to the righteous judge of the world, who one day must be your judge and mine, who always gives good judgements.'

'This he delivered with such a gravity and possessedness as was admirable; the sentence . . . he heard with a solid and unmoved countenance.'

Loudoun had been quick to answer, 'punctually proving him, by his acts of hostility to be a person most infamous, perjured, treacherous, and of all that ever this land had brought forth, the most cruel and inhuman butcher of his country; and one whose boundless pride and ambition had lost the father [Charles I], and by his wicked counsels had done what in him lay to destroy the son likewise.'

'He made no reply,' continues Sir James Balfour, 'but was commanded to sit down on his knees and receive the sentence, which he did.' He was to be hanged, his head cut off and set upon an iron spike at the top of the Tolbooth, his legs and arms to be severed and sent for display in some public place in the principal towns of Scotland— Glasgow, Stirling, Perth, and Aberdeen; the rest of his body to be buried as garbage, or if he repented, his trunk was to receive burial.

'And immediately arising from off his knees, without speaking one word, he was removed thence to the prison. He behaved himself all this time in the House with a great deal of courage and modesty, unmoved and undaunted, only he sighed two several times,' wrote Balfour. 'At the reading of the sentence he lifted up his face, without any word speaking.'

Sitting mumchance at this sentence, under Argyll's forceful and astygmatic gaze, were, beside Loudoun and Balfour, Lords Eglington, Roxburgh, Buccleuch, Tweedale, Torpichen, Burleigh, Balmerino, Forrester, and Balcarres. Of these Burleigh and Balcarres, as well as Argyll, had been soundly beaten by Montrose in battle and might still be smarting; and Torpichen was yet a minor. As Montrose left someone heard him murmur that these were fitter to be hangmen than he was to be hanged. As a proud nobleman, sprung from kings, he had thought to have a nobleman's death, a clean quick stroke of the axe; and not to dangle like a felon from a rope. But a passionate ideology had infected them all: no one spoke up for the death to which by age old custom he was entitled. He had always been exceedingly proud; long ago when he was a boy, crooked old Lord Rothes had told him his pride would hang him high. But however he went, he would go in his best clothes and with his best mien.

The Reverend Robert Traill and the Reverend Mungo Law were neither of them ministers for whom their flock or acquaintance felt much love or sympathy—'two such venomous preachers as no man that knows them can name them without detestation,' one contemporary wrote. These, leavened by Robert Baillie, were to make a last bid to reclaim Montrose for the fold. 'By a warrant from the Kirk we staid awhile with him about his soul's condition. But we found him continuing in his old pride,' Robert Traill complained to his diary, 'and taking very ill what was spoken to him, saying "I pray you, gentlemen, let me die in peace".' Traill saw him take Robert Baillie a little aside, but coming out of the Tolbooth Baillie told the others that Montrose spoke 'only concerning some of his personal sins, and nothing concerning the things for which he was condemned'. At a time when a good word spoken for Montrose could land a man in prison for weeks, and when anything to his discredit was worth a fortune, it is to Baillie's lasting credit that he had the grace to keep silent on Montrose's personal sins.

Throughout the night a dozen guards stayed with the prisoner, puffing tobacco, a thing which he much disliked. Like Raleigh, whose *History of the World* he so much admired, Montrose wrote verse on his last night of life. As poetry, it is less absolute than Raleigh's, but in feeling it is the same—'Let them bestow on every airt* a limb'— in its belief that God would gather up his severed and far-scattered limbs, would make him once again a whole being, its certainty that beyond the shame and torture of his death the world of reconciliation and joy awaited him. Amongst a steady hail of sanctimonious injunction he made his peace with God. It was reported that he prayed long, amidst the din, and afterwards slept like a child.

In the morning he combed out his long brown hair. Traill had arrived punctually; the scene shocked him. 'Why is James Graham so careful of his locks?'

'My head is yet my own: to-night when it will be yours treat it

---

* *airt*, a point of the compass, a useful word it is sad to have lost.

as you please.' Even voluble Warriston was silenced by the deplorable levity of this remark.

Edinburgh lay under a May morning sky, the air brisk and brilliant, the guardian hills enthroned around. Through them the North Sea breeze blew fresh, to be caught and thrown aloft by the cliffy hill along whose central ridgeway Montrose now walked to die. Going eastward from the Tolbooth to the Mercat Cross he could see the far blue firth where escape and freedom lay. He was thirty-eight; full still of life and thought and action. On either side the grey stone houses towered above him, then as now, six or seven storeys high. Faces lurid with excitement clustered thick at every window to see him passing by. Elizabeth Napier, who had known him so long, had fully understood his wish for a brave show; but John Nicoll, notary public, cared not at all for Montrose's glorious array. What a waste—when his clothes must in the established manner become the perquisite of his executioner in a few minutes time! 'In his going down from the Tolbooth he was very richly clad in fine scarlet [a cloak over a dark suit] laid over with rich silver lace, his hat in his hand; his bands and cuffs exceeding rich; fine white gloves upon his hands; his stockings of carnation silk; his shoes with ribbons; serks [shirt] with pearling about, above ten pounds the ell; provided for him by his friends, and a pretty cassock put upon him on the scaffold. To be short,' Traill indignantly told his diary, 'nothing was here deficient to honour his poor carcase, more beseeming a bridegroom than a criminal going to the gallows.'

To James Fraser, among the crowd on foot, it seemed otherwise. 'He stept along the streets with so great state, and there appeared in his countenance so much beauty, majesty and gravity as amazed the beholders: And many of his enemies did acknowledge him to be the bravest subject in the world; and in him a gallantry that graced all the crowd . . . His friends and well willers being debarred from coming near, they caused a young boy to sit upon the scaffold by him, who wrote his last speech in brachography, as follows. The young man's name was Mr Robert Gordon, son to Sir Robert Gordon of Gordonstoun, from whom I got the same.'

Montrose's trial by his peers in Parliament had been more of an abuse session than a trial: he had been given no defence counsel and offered no chance to produce the king's commission which legalized all he had done. Now at last he could speak directly to the people, and used none of the personal abuse and denunciation that his enemies had feared. His words, emanating from this proud, well-combed, well-clad and handsome figure produced such an effect that when he died a great sob came up from all those watching hearts.

'I am sorry if this manner of my end be scandalous to any good Christian here . . . They who know me should not disesteem me for this. Many greater than I have been dealt with in this kind . . . And this measure, for my private sins, I acknowledge to be just with God. I wholly submit myself to Him. But in regard of man, I may say they are but instruments. God forgive them; and I forgive them. They have oppressed the poor, and violently perverted judgment and justice. But He that is higher than they will reward them.

'What I did in this kingdom was in obedience to the most just commands of my Sovereign. And in his defence, in the day of his distress, against those that rose up against him. I acknowledge nothing; but fear God and honour the King . . . With God there is mercy, which is the ground of my drawing near to Him . . . I am sorry they did excommunicate me, and in that which is according to God's laws, without wronging my conscience or alliance, I desire to be relaxed . . .

'It is spoken of me that I would blame the King. God forbid. For the late King, he lived a saint and died a martyr. I pray God I may end as he did. For his Majesty now living, never any people, I believe, might be more happy in a king . . . He deals justly with all men. I pray God he be so dealt withal, that he be not betrayed under trust as his father was.

'I desire not to be mistaken; as if my carriage at this time, in relation to your ways, were stubborn. I do but follow the light of my conscience, my rule; which is seconded by the working of the Spirit of God that is within me. I thank Him I go to Heaven with joy the way He paved for me. If He enable me against the fear of death, and furnish me with courage and confidence to embrace it even in its most ugly shape, let God be glorified in my end . . .

'I have no more to say, but that I desire your charity and prayers. And I shall pray for you all. I leave my soul to God, my service to my Prince, my good will to my friends, my love and charity to you all . . .'

Messrs Traill and Law had accompanied Montrose to the scaffold, and now made a last bid to reconcile him with recent developments in his Kirk, exhorting repentance and submission. Montrose would not, but asked them to pray a last prayer with him, at this final moment of his life. This they refused. Napthali, a hind let loose—to run in what dark forests, to drink at what dread subterranean streams? They told him to pray apart, aloud, and they would listen. 'I have already poured out my soul before the Lord,' the boy Robert Gordon heard Montrose say, 'who knows my heart, and into whose hand I have committed my spirit, and He hath been pleased to return to me a full assurance of peace in Jesus Christ my Redeemer, and therefore if you will not join with me in prayer, my reiterating it again will be but scandalous to you, and me.' Praying by himself, he was 'perceived to be mightily moved all the while. When he had done he called for the executioner and gave him gold and forgiveness.'

Among the town council accounts for this week in May of 1650, which include—Item, paid to David Sandys, wright, and others, for making of a large scaffold for the execution £6 13*s*. 4*d*, Item, paid to the wrights for making a high new gallows and double ladder for the same execution, £6 13*s*. 4*d*—there is no mention of payment to Allan Robson, the executioner, whose fee, by an ironic tradition, always came from the victim. Montrose, who all his life had been lavish to the poor, the blind, the beggars, and the unfortunate everywhere, gave him four gold pieces, 'for drinking money,' Robert Gordon heard him say. No doubt Allan Robson would need every penny. He was in tears as he went about his task. He had signed on; but no one had explained to him that the job would involve killing men like Montrose.

'With an undaunted courage and gravity he went up to the top of that prodigious gibbet,' the Wigton MS continues. His final words were a plea that God's mercy would light on Scotland. Robson did his task, and three hours later cut down the body and dismembered it. 'The weeping hangman who with his honest tears seemed to revile the cruelty of his countrymen,' one spectator thought.

The shock waves were prodigious, and rippled as far away as Paris; from whence the poet Abraham Cowley wrote home to Henry Bennet in horror at the news: 'I thought that they would have contented themselves with the revenge of simply putting him to death, without such extraordinary circumstances of cruelty, I am confounded with the thoughts of it.' An anonymous Englishman, probably a spy reporting home, saw Montrose on the scaffold and realized what his death might do. 'His countenance changed not; but the rest that came in with him a Saturday are in great fears. I never saw a more sweeter carriage in a man in all my life. It is absolutely believed that he hath overcome more men by his death, in Scotland, then he would have done if he had lived.'

Argyll had troubles of his own, and had perhaps not enjoyed winning round four and the execution as much as he had hoped. Unlike Montrose, he had had a sleepless night, and then just as he was nodding off, the drums had rolled through Edinburgh calling the guards to arms, in case an attempt should be made to rescue Montrose from the scaffold. (This had given the prisoner his last laugh— 'What, am I still a terror to them? Let them look to themselves, my ghost will haunt them.') 'I confess I am weary,' Argyll told Lord Lothian, his emissary to King Charles in Holland, 'for all last night my wife was crying; who blessed be God is safely brought to bed of a daughter, whose birthday is remarkable in the tragic end of James Graham at this Cross. He was warned to be sparing in speaking to the King's disadvantage or else he had done it,' Argyll added, getting in a last posthumous thrust of malice at his rival. Sacrilegeous, too, he must be painted, for what we doom we must necessarily damn— 'not so much as once humbling himself to pray at all upon the scaffold.' No remorse here; though eleven years later Argyll was to say that he had pleaded for mercy for Montrose. No one corroborated his tale: it seems unlikely. Argyll had the terms of the Treaty of Breda: he could with perfect legality have freed Montrose. But this was the rival chieftain who had raged into his heartlands and smoked him out of Inverary, the brave general who had made Argyll a laughing stock in front of both their clans. 'Stone dead hath no fellow,' as Lord Essex had said a year ago when there was talk of reprieving Lord Strafford, and stone dead it must be.

Late in the darkness of that night Elizabeth's Napier's servants stole across the Boroughmuir. Montrose had bequeathed his heart, that talismanic thing, to Elizabeth Napier and her husband 'for the unremitting kindness shown to him in all the different turns of his life and fortune'. Her servants found the newly turned earth and took the heart from the headless and dismembered trunk where it lay in the felons' pit on the Boroughmuir, at grave danger both to her and to themselves.

A month later King Charles was at the mouth of the Spey river in Morayshire. 'About ten or eleven o'clock we came to anchor after much tossing,' wrote John Livingstone, a Covenanting preacher. 'The King hath granted all desired, and this day hath sworn and subscribed the two Covenants, and with assurance to renew the same at Edinburgh, when desired.' No tears, no indignations, no recriminations, could bring the king's commissioner alive again. Forced to swallow Montrose's death, the king had now swallowed the Solemn League and Covenant as well, which promised to enforce Presbyterianism upon the entire British Isles, willy nilly. Charles was just twenty; had believed that when he told the government in Edinburgh to practise 'a just and prudent moderation' they would obey him. In the event they had defied him. But he had had enough of frustration and beggary, of dependence on the charity of France, of advice and disapproval from an increasingly difficult mother. He would accept the throne of Scotland from any hands, on any terms. These were the crooks who had double-crossed his father; they would learn that two could play that game.

Away in the Low Countries, young Archie Napier grieved alone. Better far to have died with Kinnoull in the north Highlands in the failed campaign, better to have suffered at Edinburgh with Montrose. The light of his life had gone out; and who now could save Scotland? Not, he was perhaps beginning to suspect, the charming young man with the swarthy long face and the black hair who was now its king and who had compounded with the Covenanters. Charles had become a sophisticated European monarch and not a Scots king. He would use Scotland as a springboard to his throne, and go back on the Covenanters exactly as they had, by Leslie's hesitation at Worcester, betrayed him. There is a limit to loyalty and Archie would not, for any ends, compound with the men who had ruined his family and basely killed without trial the noblest spirit in Scotland. Restless, unreconciled, he moved from town to town, short of money, dogged by Commonwealth spies and desperate for home. ('Yet, loving brother, never embrayce dishonorabill agreyment.') From Cromwell's 1654 Act of Grace and Pardon, Lord Napier of Merchiston was expressly omitted.

In the year of Montrose's death young Archie had been excluded by decree of the Estates 'from entering Scotland from beyond the seas until he gave satisfaction to the church and state' in May, and in June 'debarred from having access to his Majesty's person' by the same Covenanting body. By 1656 the yearly value of his remaining estates was valued at £600 and his forfeits and charges amounted to £9,786 18*s*. 4*d*. It was a bleak outlook. The Estates of Scotland, who did not know what she had been up to with Montrose's heart, allowed Archie's wife Elizabeth £100 a year out of his estates, later increased to £150. By 1655 King Charles was back in exile again, and young Archie was with him at the Hague: Elizabeth and the children had joined him; perhaps life had taken on a more cheerful hue. But they had followed the court to Cologne in October of that year: it was said that Archie and his wife and children were living there in great poverty. This, maybe, forced Elizabeth's return to Scotland soon after. Early in 1658 young Archie was still living in the Low Countries, applying in April of that year for permission to leave Brussels and go to Flushing in the hope of entering the Duke of York's service, for that young man had now a great command. But illness put a term to that project.

In the spring of 1658 young Archie lay dying of a fever. The king was to go back to his own two years later; home would have opened to Archie; restoration, comfort, reward perhaps; a chance to rebuild his life, retrieve his home, bring up his family in happiness, live out a full life with plain, friendly, loving Elizabeth. He lay at Delftshaven, where the Rhine snakes past Rotterdam and moves its last slow miles to the sea. The loneliness and futility of exile wept out of him like the sweat of his ailment; the lost cause, the lost land, the lost life, all assaulted him in that moment early in the process of dying when the failure in achievement rises up to sicken the soul. The King of Spain had offered him command of a regiment; he might have found glory and activity among the Spaniards instead of rotting away idle in Holland, or seen those fabled islands Columbus had discovered. But it would have meant leaving the king's cause, the cause of Scotland; and what was the point of fighting in other people's wars? He had all the honour he wanted already; and in a dream he was a nineteen-year-old again, riding with Nat Gordon and two trumpeters and a single troop of horse to the gates of Edinburgh and causing that strong city to surrender.

There had been something miraculous about the year on the hills with Montrose;—larger than life—the speed, the perils, the triumph and even the sadness. Nor had it been a life without food for the mind. Montrose's follower Thomas Saintserf had told how 'His spirit was so eminent for speculation and for practice, that his Camp was an Academy, admirably replenished with discourses of the best and deepest sciences, whose several parts were strongly held up, under him, the head, by those knowing noble souls, the Earls of Kinnoul and Airley, the Lords Gordon, Ogilvy, Napier and Maderty. Such noble discourses banished from his quarters all obscene and scurrilous language, with all those offensive satirical reflections which are now the only currency of wit amongst us . . . nor did this proceed from a narrowness in his heart, being to all who knew him one of the most munificent, as well as magnificent personages in the world.'

To have fought with Montrose was almost enough; and yet perhaps as fever burnt young Archie out of life on this alien strand, he saw more clearly the territory of his childhood, mountainy Lennox with the gleam of its great level water of Lomond, the cloud shadows racing up the ben whose ferny hollows sounded to falling streams, Kilpatrick woods so thick with running deer, and wild now with spring winds or silent under rain. Others, not he, would rejoice in Gartness, green in the lea of the Campsie hills; would lie snug in the strong tower of Merchiston while the winter tempests howled outside, would plough and harvest the red Lothian fields.

Outside in the streets the alien voices hawked the foreign food he did not want to eat; bells called the hour from churches whose worship was estranging. He was thirty-two, and for the last dozen years his life had been as empty as a shell; waiting and longing for the knock at the door, the voices ringing with hope and with excitement, the call that never came. All had added up to unanswered letters, to expeditions that never set sail; had turned to trickery and policy and false promises, where once it had seemed noble and clear—hard duty, simple devotedness. Was it a world in which Argyll forever triumphed, Montrose forever bled? Had life fooled him somewhere on his way, that the red sky at morning had clouded into a long rainy afternoon?

To the westward, where he longed to sail, the dunes stretched away towards the sea. 'The passionate desire I had to do you service,' he had written to the king when he was a twenty-year-old. The words echoed away from dune to dune, growing fainter—'the passionate desire I had to do you service . . . service . . . service'—till the sound of it spilled into the sand; and maybe peace and comfort came in the end to young Archie in his lonely dying and maybe not.

Part V

Survivors of the Volcano:
Scotland and England

XIII

Since the 1640s Scotland, and Edinburgh in particular, had been going through a series of appalling emotional hiccups. The capital city, with the wind from the North Sea, was always more extreme in religion and politics than Glasgow, lying under its south-west wind. (Even now, girls' bottoms don't get pinched in Edinburgh, while in Glasgow . . .) The death of their Scots king at the hands of the English had been the cause of profound shock. 'The guilt and stain due to the act should not, with reason, be imputed to the generality of the Scots Nation,' Guthrie, once Bishop of Dunkeld, had protested. 'The third part of the nobility was not present, having been secluded for their known affection to the King . . . and for the gentry, burghs, and commonalty throughout the land, Fife and the western parts of Galloway being excepted, there were a hundred for one, all the Kingdom over, that abhorred it.' Even James Kirkton, that stoutly Kirk-ridden Kirk minister, had thought the beheading of Charles was 'to the great regrate of Scotland . . . I never heard his enemys blame him for the common vices of princes, except the two bastards in his youth, and his swearing in his old age. People generally think his greatest unhappiness was he mistook wilfulness for constancy, his condescensiones always coming too late, granting unprofitably to his people to-day that which would have abundantly satisfied yesterday, and the next day that which would have satisfied this day, but all out of time.'

Perhaps even the act of execution itself had been plotted in Edinburgh? Guthrie thought it had. 'While Cromwell remained in the Canongate those that haunted him most were, besides Argyll, Loudoun the Chancellor, the earl of Lothian, the Lords Arbuthnot, Elcho and Burleigh; and of ministers, Mr David Dickson, Mr Robert Blair and Mr James Guthry. What passed among them came not to be known infallibly; but it was talked very loud that he did communicate to them his design in reference to the King, and had their secret assent thereto.' Suspicion lived on, jumpiness, heads nervously turned to look behind in the narrow streets as the evenings darkened: what plots went on up those steep staircases on the first floor where the gentry and nobles inhabited, what treacheries did those high stone houses harbour? Then had come the execution of Montrose: even the provost, Sir James Stewart of Coltness, had protested, 'what need of so much butchery and dismembering?' He was an ardent follower of Argyll, but not afraid to say that 'heading, and publicly affixing the head, has been thought sufficient for the most atrocious state crimes hitherto. We are embroiled, and have taken sides; but to insult too much over the misled is unmanly;' all the same, he had had to give the orders and see the scaffold put up. It seemed as if no one could opt out of the guilt and terror of it all.

Then had come the return of young King Charles a month later; the news of his landing had arrived in Edinburgh on June 20th 'lait at night', wrote John Nicoll, Writer to the Signet, 'all signes of joy were manifested throw the whole kingdom, namelie and in a speciall maner in Edinburgh, by setting furth of bonfires, ringing of bellis, sounding of trumpetts, dancing almost all that night throw the streets. The poor frail wyfes at the Tron sacrificed their payments and creels and the verie stooles thai sat upon to the fyre.' The jolly bonfires seemed hardly to have died down and their ashes to have blown away before Charles was defeated and in exile once again and the terrible Protector was at Dunbar, conquering Scotland as completely as ever had Edward I, driving all before him.

'A great armie in a multitude of garrisons bydes above our head', poor Robert Baillie, who was a bit of a Kerensky, mourned in 1658. 'Deep povertie keeps all estates exceedingly at under . . . The Countrey lies very quiet; it is exceeding poor, trade is nought; the English has all the moneyes. Our noble families are almost gone; Lennox has little in Scotland unsold; Hamilton's estates, except Arran and the Barony of Hamilton is sold; Argyll can pay little annual rent . . . and he is no more drowned in debt than in common hatred, almost of all, both Scottish and English; the Gordons are gone; the Douglasses little better; Eglinton and Glencairn on the brink of breaking; many of our chief families estates are cracking; nor is there any appearance of any human relief for the tyme. What is become of the King and his family we do not knowe.' Well, but who began it all, Mr Baillie? Always keep a hold of nurse, in the shape of the existing framework, for fear of meeting something worse.

If it was like this in Glasgow, which managed to keep its beautiful cathedral out of the hands of the destroyers, how did poor Edinburgh fare? Cromwell's unspeakable Roundheads had put out the eyes of one man, 'ane simple sodger,' and stripped him naked, 'becaus upon his bak thair was drawn with quhyte chalk the wordis I AM FOR KING CHARLES . . . The College Kirk, the Gray Freir Kirk, and that Kirk callit the Lady Yesteris Kirk, the Hie Scule, and a great pairt of the College wer all wasted, thair pulpitts, deskis, lofts, seattes, winddis, dures, lockes, hinges, and all uther their decormentis wer all dung down to the ground by these Inglische sodgers, and brint to asses,' Nicoll recorded. Not all the English were like this. 'Ane gallant Englische gentillman had his lug (ear) nailed to the gallows and thereafter cut from him, for drinking the Kingis health,' and 'twa Englisches' for the same offence were stripped, lashed, and parted also from their ears.

And then had come the great, the glorious, the blessed deliverance, as it seemed to some; though emphatically not to others. King Charles was finally proclaimed in May 1660; and the church bells, bonfires, trumpets, drums, cannons, and dancings round the fires excelled themselves in fervour; Edinburgh 'using all other tokens of joy for the advancement and preference of their native King to his Crown and native inheritance. Whereat also there was much wine spent, the spouts of the Mercat Cross running and venting out abundance of wyne, plaiced there for that end, and the magistrates and counsell of the town being present, drinking the Kinges helth, and breaking numbers of glasses.'

For now it was the end of the kill-joys, and as Nicoll unjealously remarked 'at this time our gentry of Scotland did look with such gallant and joyful countenances as if they had been the sons of princes . . . and it was the joy of this nation which for so many years had been overclouded, and now to see them upon brave horses, prancing in their accustomed places, in tilting, running of races, and suchlyke.' The pop-stars, in their brave Rolls Royces, prancing in their wonted places, the enjoyers, the life-enhancers, the glittering undeservers. In July and August of next year 'ther were sundry Commedies actit, playing and dancing at the Cross of Edinburgh and at the Netherbrow and in the Canongate.' Summer, it seemed, had come again.

*

Even the burial of Montrose's scattered limbs had been made the occasion of a prolonged and slap-up party at government expense. In Montrose's grand procession walked all the lords of Scotland, rapidly deserting to the winning side: for kings may come and kings may go but land goes on for ever, or at least until Lloyd George. The accolade for humbug—or for repentance, who knows?—must go to William Drummond, Earl of Roxburgh, who had been on the committee which organized Montrose's degrading entry into Edinburgh—the hangman's cap stuck on awry, the bound arms to hinder protection from stones and filth, the weary trundle through the crowded streets—who now bore his bier. Absent from these jollities was 'pale Argyll', the mighty rival who had encompassed Montrose's death, and who waited now in prison for an execution unmourned by any save his Campbell clan. The drums rolled out and the trumpets shouted and every Graham in the land had the field day of their lives, carrying Montrose's banner, his accoutrements, his Garter. The procession displayed some seventy items, including 'Twenty-Five poor in gowns and hoods . . . A great Mourning Banner . . . The great Gumpheon of black taffety, carried on a lance by William Graham younger of Duntroon, another spriteful cadet of the House of Clarisse . . . the great Pincel of mourning, carried by George Graham younger of Cairnie, who from his first entry of manhood, accompanied his chief to the wars . . . the defunct's servants two and two in mourning . . . the Lord Provost and Burgesses, Members of Parliament, . . . A Horse in Close Mourning, led by two lacqueys in Mourning.' Behind the coffin walked the new Marquis of Montrose and his younger brother Lord Robert Graham, 'in hoods and long robes carried up by two pages, with a gentleman bare-headed on every side;' and next to them nine of the nearest in blood, three and three, in hoods and long robes, carried by pages, viz.—the Marquis of Douglas, the Earls of Wigton, Marischal, Southesk, Lords of Drummond, Maderty, Napier, Rollo and Baron of Luss.

After came the body of Sir William Hay of Dalgetty, and 'it was observed that the friends of both the deceased had wedding countenances, and their enemies were howling in dark corners like howlets. . . . Never funeral pomp was celebrated with so great jollity; neither was it any wonder, since we now enjoy a King, Laws, Liberty, Religion, which was the only cause that the deceased did so bravely fight for. And who would not be good subjects, since there is so great honour paid to their memories?' demanded Saintserf. He noted that all Montrose's scattered limbs had been gathered together, 'save only his heart, which inspite of the traitors, was by the conveyance of some adventurous spirits appointed by that noble and honourable lady, the Lady Napier, taken out and embalmed . . . and sent by the same noble lady to the now Lord Marquis, who was then in Flanders' and who had given it back.

'The solemnities being ended, the Lord Commissioner, with the nobility and barons, had a most sumptuous supper and banquet, with concerts of all sorts of music.' Round five to Montrose.

The Napier under the hood and long robes had been the third Archie, great nephew to Montrose, third Lord Napier, and aged eighteen. This part of the funeral may have seemed quite jolly; a grislier part had fallen to him earlier, when with almost equal ceremony, the scattered parts of Montrose had been gathered together and carried to lie in state in the chapel of Holyrood House. With three Graham cousins, on Friday, January 4th, 1661, to Archie III had fallen the melancholy task of climbing a scaffold, built six storeys high, to the top of the Tolbooth, and taking the remains of Montrose's head from its spike; from whence the joined body was marched in procession 'with sound of trumpet, discharge of many cannon from the Castle, and the honest peoples' loud and joyful acclamation'. A disapproving Puritan divine noted with satisfaction that Graham of Gorthie had dropped dead next day, but perhaps the emotion and the six-storey climb up the scaffolding, and not the wrath of Jehovah, contributed to this.

Even before this event, the childhood of the third Archie cannot have been too full of cheer, brought up fatherless at Merchiston through troubled times with the looming Covenanters steadily chiselling away at his inheritance; the lonely anxious mother, aware of commitments and of starving tenants driven out of Menteith by encroaching Campbells, striving to do her best by everyone and to make ends meet. Then there had been the visit to his father in the Low Countries, the trail to Cologne with the other crowds of exiles, the poor lodgings, the shabby clothing, the struggle to make do. He was Master of Napier, but sometimes not master of enough to eat. It cannot have been a carefree childhood. Then, when he was sixteen and back in Scotland, had come the news of his father's early death, and now he was in charge of the family, to gather up its wrecked inheritance as best he might.

To King Charles in exile, he had written to announce his father's death and express his own loyalty. 'I am sorry that the meanness of my fortune does not suffer me to wait upon you. I beg your speedy order to put me in a condition to do you service.' Send me, please, the fare, or I can't enlist. But before it came, if indeed it came at all, Archie III, refusing to take the Oath of Engagement to Cromwell's government, had been seized and imprisoned in Stirling Castle. Four hundred years since John de Napier so nearly starved in its defence against Edward I, and here he was, back again. What thoughts and feelings went through his sixteen-year-old head, his restless active sixteen-year-old body, pacing perhaps for an hour daily, along the narrow walk on the battlements, looking out at the Highland hills, at the Lowland plains, from Stirling, where all the roads of unbridged Scotland met? Was this a life sentence, was the king exiled forever? And if so, how long could he, Archibald third Lord Napier, who had seen and known so little of the stirring life beyond his prison, hold out in loyalty?

It was another Scotland that he saw. The power of the great lords who had had it all their way for so long had been broken under Cromwell's iron rule: they had found themselves obliged, like other people, to keep the laws of God and man. In spite of the toing and froing of armies, local reforms had gone on—Scotland was divided into formal shires on the lines of her ancient sheriffdoms, Parliament was to meet at least every three years, there was even a tentative beginning of religious toleration, even for Jews. After years of godly rule followed by the dragooning of Cromwell's major generals, Scotland was prepared to go easy under a mild monarch and would even, in the euphoria of 1661, accept the return of bishops. But Charles II, in his later years, and James VII and II, when he came to reign, pushed it too hard, denouncing the Covenant and fining absentees from church. In a renewed fear of popery the Scots took to conventicles, meetings for worship in the field; against which troops were finally employed, blood was shed, and many Scots shipped overseas; the killing times, when they could cry, as their great co-religionist in England, Richard Baxter wrote,

I preached, as never sure to preach again;
And as a dying man to dying men.

It was a Scotland still dour, still strict: universities were sternly disciplined; undergraduates who were mostly under the age of eighteen rose at five in the morning, had to be in bed by ten, and were not allowed to speak to each other, even for casual conversation, except in Latin. Life was real, and life was earnest.

The great lords, with their excessive clannishness, which had once been so necessary a protection in lawless ages, had done for themselves. If Huntley had really joined with Montrose, and not been 'a back-friend' as even his own clansmen had called him; if Hamilton had joined with either or both of them, and not left his royalist effort until too late, none of them, nor the king they fought for, would have been beheaded; as they all, at different times were; (Huntly proclaiming that if he had known he was going to die for the king he would have fought rather more consistently for him earlier on). His eldest son Lord Gordon had died at Alford, Nathaniel Gordon had been beheaded by the Covenanters after Philiphaugh, Aboyne the brave, the intransigeant, always suspicious of treachery, had died of a broken heart abroad: the new Huntly was Lord Lewis Gordon, also gallant, tricky, flighty; who as a boy of thirteen had ridden into Aberdeen with a thousand men at his back and ridden out with two thousand more enlisted to his standard. Such as he would ride no more. Many were ruined, and all were diminished. It was said that Stirling of Keir was the only gentleman in Scotland that had come through the troubled times with both his property and his loyalty intact.

But the human race is notably resilient. By his skill and courage in Marlborough's wars, Argyll's son redeemed the name of Campbell from the odium into which it had fallen. The chaplain, George Wishart, who had been with Montrose and written the history of his wars was now prosperous; but as Bishop of Edinburgh he did not forget the months he had spent under the Covenanters as a rat-ridden captive in the Tolbooth. It had made him, he said, the friend of prisoners everywhere; and he would not sit down to a good dinner at the episcopal table in Edinburgh until he had sent out some of it to the poor men now languishing in the dreaded Tolbooth. John Napier of Kilmahew and his brother-in-law Colquhoun of Luss, recovered from the conflicts of Glenfruin, were members for Dunbartonshire in 1672, and, way ahead of the Chartists, persuaded the free-holders of that shire to pay them £5 Scots a day for attendance at the Edinburgh Parliament (which was only 5s. English); but what we make on the swings we lose on the roundabouts, and in 1685 John Napier was fined £2,000 for non-conforming, though most of his neighbours had done a prudent switch. The Haldanes of Gleneagles had earlier signed the Covenant, thus enabling themselves to remain at Gleneagles until they turned into physicists.

For by now the party was almost over; 'the killing times', when restored loyalists took things out on the Covenanters of Galloway would soon be done; Scotsmen henceforth were to slay each other mainly in the pages of the *Quarterly Review*, or in long factious books discrediting each others' pedigrees and published at immense private expense. As if realizing this, the main branch of the Napiers for the next two generations had but daughters surviving to inherit.

Not that there was much to inherit. The battered tower of Merchiston had gone: what remained was the heart of Montrose in a steel box made from the blade of his sword and encased in a gold filagree casket which the Doge of Venice had sent John Napier the mathematician; an admirable possession but not one that pays the household bills. King Charles was aware of indebtedness: 'Whereas to our certain knowledge our right trusty and well-beloved servants, the Lady Napier, and the now Lord Napier, have been very great sufferers during the late commotions in Scotland, from the first beginning thereof, both by the plundering of their goods, long exile, and did constantly adhere to us beyond seas, where their sufferings were also very great, all of which they have cheerfully endured for their duty to our dearest father and us; we do think it just now for us to give them some recompense for their fidelity and loss . . .'

This was charming; but like so many Stewart professions, rested upon the laurels of its charm. There is a family legend, undocumented and probably untrue, that Archibald, 3rd Lord Napier, was offered a dukedom by a grateful Charles II on his restoration, which he refused; on the sensible grounds that there is no point in being a duke if the Roundheads have snatched your land; it simply adds on to the hotel bills. But as the Stewart Dukes of Lennox had now died out, this might have been the moment for restoring that long-usurped Honor of Lennox, the earldom so hotly disputed for by its heirs the Napiers two hundred years before. But no; this was to be reserved for Charles's bastard by Louise de Kérouaille, who was made Duke of Richmond and Lennox. In the event the Napiers were promised £3,000, which was never paid.

Scotland was possibly a subject on which King Charles's thoughts did not care to dwell, looking back from the splendour and safety of his throne. Landing in the home of his fathers while it was totally under Covenanter rule, he had had a sad time. Obliged to listen to a three-hour sermon daily and three of them on Sundays, and discouraged from any form of amusement, he had been reprimanded for toying with ladies and for smiling on the Sabbath, and pointedly shown the hacked-up pieces of Montrose, one of his few disinterested supporters, hung up on the gates of every considerable city. When crowned at Scone in 1651 he was instructed by the Kirk ministers to repent of such a wealth of sins and wickednesses that he was heard to murmur, 'I should repent also that I was ever born.' The only permissible pleasure was golf; a game which he detested. Betrayed in the end by Leslie's refusal to take the Scots into action at Worcester, and barely escaping with his life from that battle, it was little wonder that he veered from then on into the warm bosom of Rome (not to mention a few other warm bosoms), and felt little interest in such true friends as he still possessed in Scotland. The grand design of King Charles II was to avoid further exile: he had had enough of the compromises, the intrigues, the lapsed promises, the false flatteries, and of being sustained by variable and grudging allowances from his cousin of France. He would settle for the throne of England, a quiet political life, and the peacefulness of a silent betrayal—a steady £166,000 every year from France to spend on worthy objects like the Navy, his mistresses and their children, Chelsea Hospital, and the founding of the Royal Society.

His brother James, that too ardent Roman Catholic, could, if he liked, 'travel'. Charles would stay king, and with the loss of as few lives as possible; for he was a civilized, amiable man; and the moment anyone starts judging him, he turns round with that charming ugly face and says something so funny that we are obliged to shut up. Let others hug their principles; Charles preferred to hug Lady Castlemaine. In Scotland, as well as in his southern kingdom, he had seen enough of professional goodness. 'At Domesday,' he replied to Lord Halifax, attempting to engage him in moral argument about his extra-marital activities, 'at Domesday we shall see whose arse is the blackest.' This sunny, resilient, and excellently non-fanatical man was impossible to trust, and nearly impossible not to like. The old Whig jingle sums him up succinctly, if bitterly:

> Here lies our sovereign lord the King
> Whose word no man relies on;
> Who never said a foolish thing
> And never did a wise one.

His descendants are now as the sands of the sea, and that pleasing dark Medici mug still sometimes gazes into the paddock at race-meetings up and down the land, happily intent upon the horses and upon the ladies that he so much loved.

At the Restoration the third Archie and his mother had been in high favour, but being in high favour is quite another thing from getting your land and money back. The government had wisely decided to let sleeping dogs lie; which was splendid for everybody except the faithful dogs. For Scots lords there was in any case no getting back that entire local command which Cromwell had destroyed. What went on with Archie III, behind those bird-wing brows and fine eyes, the beaked nose over a firm chin and full curving lips? From the flowing periwig above the seventeenth-century armour a long handsome face looks out; intelligent and proud. Too proud to be a landless duke? A more cynical character might have reckoned that once you are a duke it is easy enough to marry some land, more especially with a face as pleasing as his, more especially in an epoch when many only sons died young, making heiresses of many landed girls. He looks intelligent enough, but what he does not look is either shrewd or ambitious. He may have simply been too lazy; or too proud. The currency of dukedom was suffering from a slight debasement. In France St Simon was protesting at the number of royal bastards who were being made dukes by Louis XIV; in Britain Charles II was following the French king's example. This custom, though time-honoured and well within their rights, was coming to seem rather jungly, as if the Shah of Persia and the Aga Khan should now have four simultaneous wives.

As against his casual acceptance of the material destruction of their house, it must be said that Charles II granted Elizabeth Napier a pension for life—though it took nine years to arrive—and that James VII and II and Queen Anne continued it. Also that when the third Archie applied to King Charles for an alteration in his peerage —he was unmarried, and his only brother John had been killed in a

Merchiston Tower Romanticized—late eighteenth century. Painting by Alexander Naesmith. *By kind permission of Oscar and Peter Johnson Ltd.*

Merchiston Tower Utilized—mid-twentieth century. Stripped down to the 1460 form in which Sir Alexander Napier built it; with the iron staircase recently added. *By kind permission of Edinburgh Corporation and Napier College of Science and Technology.*

Archibald, 3rd Lord Napier, by Sir Peter Lely. King Charles's Restoration rescued him, as a boy of seventeen, from imprisonment in Stirling Castle. *By kind permission of Lord Napier and Ettrick.*

Elizabeth and John Napier, about 1700, by Wissing. John died as a lieutenant in the Navy in 1704 and Elizabeth became Mistress of Napier and married Sir William Scott of Thirlestane. *By kind permission of Lord Napier and Ettrick.*

sea fight against the Dutch—the king agreed, and in handsome terms. 'Remembering the constant love and fidelity to us and to our august father, and to our interests and service, the very many true and faithful services shown to us' by Archie III himself, his father, and his grandfather, 'and the great calamities which they suffered throughout that time of national commotion and tumults,' Carolus Rex had 'determined by our regard for their family, that the honour, title, and dignity may remain in perpetuity . . . in his heirs whomsoever, failing the heirs male of his body,' and that whoever inherited the title was to take the surname and arms of Napier as well, so that it should never die out. The Duke of York wrote from London to Queensberry to say that this was not to be a precedent to others; it was a thing *sui generis*. 'I must tell you,' he added chattily, 'the Earl of Essex cut his own throat in the Tower yesterday, to prevent the stroke of justice.' Perhaps the killing times were not quite over yet.

And perhaps the third Archie was bored in this so different Scotland. Or the death of his only brother unsettled him, made him long for adventure, for change, for fame. Two years later he sought to enlist as a soldier of fortune, with the Swedes, who at this moment had been jockeyed by Louis XIV into fighting the Dutch, who had killed Archie's brother John. He wrote to the Swedish ambassador in London, in October of 1674, offering to raise a Scottish regiment and help to drive the invaders out of Charles XI of Sweden's realm, greatly stretched by his conquering great grandfather, Gustavus Adolphus. But maybe the King of Sweden would have none of Archie and his Scots regiment: there is no record that he ever went to the Baltic. It is possible that it was his canny sisters, two of them married and with sons, who urged upon Archie, an apparently unrepentant bachelor, the perpetuation of his name. What if he went stravaguing off over Europe, there maybe to be minced by Cossacks, lanced by Poles and left for the wolves in goodness knew what scuffle in some dark sandy forest beside the Vistula? Tom Dalyell, who had fought for the Russians, had learnt from them some very nasty tricks which he was now practising upon the luckless conventicles: he was known as the Beastly Muscovite and the Russians were clearly not a people with whom to tangle.

Still a bachelor, the third Archibald died in 1683: his peerage descended through his sister Jean to her son, Sir Thomas Nicolson of Carnock, who died at the age of seventeen in Paris, and thence through Archie's second sister Margaret, Lady Napier in her own

8

right, to her daughter, Elizabeth, Mistress of Napier; pretty, oval-faced and graceful, and married to William Scott of Thirlestane, who took her name; and that was one hatchet successfully buried. Elizabeth's only brother John followed his uncle John and went to sea, where he was equally unlucky, dying as a very young naval officer on board H.M.S. *Deptford*, off the Guinea Coast, already beginning to be known as the white man's grave. All this marrying did not seem to alter that strangely persistent face; the Napiers continued with their arched eyebrows, full curved lips, beaked noses, oval visages. Even if it disappeared for one generation it kept cropping up again. The Stewarts had now become a cause too lost even for the Napiers; their return as kings to a land so alienated from them in thought and feeling no longer made sense: in the Jacobite incursions of the Fifteen and the Forty-five they took no part; not even, as so many Scots families did, sending a younger son to participate, so that whether Stewart or Hanoverian won, the house of Whatsit would not perish from the land.

William Scott's forbear, John Scott of Thirlestane, one of the many Border lairds of that name, had gained the motto of 'Ready, aye Ready,' and the right to a border of fleur de lys round his shield and a bunch of spears above his helmet, from King James V at Fala in 1542, 'beand willing to gang with us into England, when all our nobles and others refuised, he was readdy to stake all at our bidding.' His grandsons, William and Walter, had gone with their cousin Buccleuch to rescue Kinmont Willie from Carlisle, an enterprise so dangerous that only younger sons were allowed to go, though Buccleuch himself led it. Summoned into England to answer to Queen Elizabeth, who asked him how he dared, and getting around her by telling her, 'I know not the thing that a man dare not do,' Buccleuch had been seen off at the Border by a thousand of his followers, Scotts and others, who never thought to see him alive again.

The records of old are so full of battle, murder and sudden death, so riddled with fierce and grappling litigation, that it is a relief to know that our forbears had their softer side, that they could be douce as well as dour. John Scott of Thirlestane, William's forbear, writing in 'the zier of God 1632', declared, 'Maistres and dair suethart my most humbell servis being rememberit to your santifeit person. I thought goud to remember my most humbell selfe to you,

I sweir I haive beine so Inamorat with you sene our last meiting that I am ravisit with your favor; thairfor suit hart I will intreit you most earnestly as I sall remaine your most humbell serviteur als to do that much favor to me as to cum to Pibelles upon Sant Petres day and I sall meit you thar God villing and I sall shaw unto you the haill mistrey of my love quich I entertaine for your sweit sake; thairfor Misteres I will Intreit your faver to halld me apardinnit for my Importunantei, for my affection is mor ardent than my pen is abell to expres for the present, so thinking your sweitnes will aparden my boldnes and your wisdom will pitie my distres cummitis your odori-firous and suiet person to the allmightis protrection and restes your most humbell servitour forewer. Yours to Command Johann Scott of Thirlestanes.' Did she meet him in Peebles upon St Peter's day, to be shown the whole mystery of his love? We do not know. It was the glorious first of June, and alas, a few months later she married Sir David Ogilvie. *Nil desperandum;* Ogilvie is killed in the Civil War, and John Scott, though a royalist too (against the grain of his family, for Buccleuch was a Presbyterian and had voted for the death of Montrose), and in spite of being sequestrated as a malignant, fined and restrained, survived the war, married the widowed Lady Ogilvy and lived, as far as the early mortality of the times allowed, happily ever after.

James II and VII, in his two Declarations of Indulgence, had given complete religious freedom to all, Roman Catholics, Covenanters, and Quakers; but had then by suspending the burgh elections and nominating only Catholics as magistrates and councillors, shaken Scottish nerves to such a degree that they were almost as ready to welcome the Bloodless Revolution that displaced him as they had been to welcome back his brother; and settled down to a life of no bishops and of all frustrated Presbyterians now being as Presbyterian as they wanted. The union of the two kingdoms in 1707 was in some respects not fair, but it was a common sense arrangement and one that was freely negotiated. The English wanted recognition for the Hanoverian succession (Elizabeth of Bohemia's daughter Sophia was now in the lead, followed by her son, eventually George I), and the Scots, who had had an enormous venture to Darien in the Panama isthmus, in which the English had disagreeably declined to co-operate and which had disastrously failed, needed financial aid.

Give and take was the sensible order of the day. The most baffling
part is the consent of the argumentative and independent Scots to the
abolition of their Parliament—surely a mistake. Edinburgh, to
whom the genius of the brothers Adam would soon add a splendid
new town, retained the irrefutable dignity of a capital city, whatever
the politicians might say.

Very slowly, farming improved, and with it, general prosperity.
Scotland's last famine had been brought on by seven bad harvests
running in the 1690s—the 'Seven Ill Years'—which wrought great
misery all over northern Europe: some figures suggest that in
Finland one in three died from it. Sir Robert Sibbald, who originated
Edinburgh's Botanical Gardens and founded her School of Medicine,
said sadly that during these years death was visible in the faces of
the poor: Fletcher of Saltoun feared that as many as one in every
five in Scotland died. As against this horror, by the 1720s witchcraft
cases cease and the beastly practice of burning to death confused and
muttering old crones with malign expressions. (They were not always
old: in the 1620s Alexander Napier of Loriston with others of his
colleagues in the Court of Session knocked off for a lunch interval
in which the daughter of one of them, her father consenting, met this
fate.)

The end of reiving created a bad pocket of unemployment on the
Border: Sir Walter Scott in his youth noted the many deserted farms,
crumbling small manors, and even whole villages. The Scotts, the
Elliots and the Armstrongs must take off for other fields to conquer;
two of them eventually taking off for the moon. And what would
the new way of life hold for the Highlanders? The two Jacobite
rebellions, the Fifteen under the lazy Old Pretender who only arrived
on the scene when it was practically over, and the Forty-five under
his much more dashing and lively son the Young Pretender, Bonnie
Prince Charlie, had so thoroughly alarmed the English that tartan
was proscribed as the garment of sedition, and all suggestion of
enrolling Highland soldiers in the British army was rejected. It was
William Pitt who raised the Highland regiments to play their
inimitable part: Highlanders and Islanders could now stop dinging
and banging at each other and set happily to work on the French,
and in due course on the Russians, the Germans and the Japanese.
Unlucky honest James VII had done for the Stewarts in Scotland
by his attempt to employ Roman Catholics in positions of power:
to reign as a Catholic one had now, like Charles II, to confine it to

the last few hours of life. By the end of George II's reign it was fairly generally recognized that the king over the water had better stay there. The front line of the Stewarts considerably died out at the end of the eighteenth century, in the person of Henry, Cardinal York, the Young Pretender's brother, who lived to be eighty-one, longer than any Stewart who reigned. Turned by Napoleon into a displaced person, he was obliged to accept from George III a pension of £4,000 a year—it was a humdrum end to so much splendour and so much disaster.

'The world's tragedy and time are near at an end,' Raleigh had written prophetically from his imprisonment in the Tower of London; and in a sense he was right; individual human life was coming to have a new value. Highlanders had been killing one another since the dawn of time, but the massacre of Glencoe, in which a party of Campbells murdered a party of Macdonalds who had hospitably received them, caused a wave of horror all over the British Isles that was new, and not due alone to the treacherous nature of the attack. The universities prospered, social mobility increased, bright new minds found utterance. By 1696 in a series of acts of Parliament every parish was ordered to have a school house, and a schoolmaster whose salary was paid by the local landowners, of whom Charles II had noted that 'there was no nation or kingdom in the world where the tenants had so great a dependence on the gentlemen as in Scotland.' It was a dependence that in the main suited both sides, unless the laird was outrageously bad. His tenants addressed him with dignity, and as an equal. Far more grinding was the tyranny of the Kirk, which ruled supreme. The two church services on Sunday were mandatory; and in the interval between them children were not allowed to play, since this was the Sabbath Day; and had to be kept indoors, which if they were peasants, consisted of a one-room or at most a two-room cottage, shared with the family livestock as often as not.

Elizabeth's son, Francis, 6th Lord Napier, who succeeded his grandmother Margaret, replenished the family stock, with the aid of two indefatigable wives. By Lady Henrietta Hope he had William, Charles, Francis, John and Mark; by Henrietta Maria Johnston from Dublin, daughter of General Johnston, Governor of Quebec, he had George, James, Patrick, another John, Stewart, Hester and Mary.

His early Georgian face, in its modified wig, is a placid long oval: nothing in the fine eyes seems to search for innovation. Yet he had his ten sons educated by the famous philosopher and historian David Hume, whom the Kirk distrusted so deeply for his progressive ideas that they kept him firmly out of all university employment. And Francis Napier spent what little he had on enormously expensive surveys and plans for the Forth-Clyde canal; finally opened in 1791 very greatly extending Scotland's trading possibilities.

He had also bought back Merchiston: the Napiers were now complete with their tower and their legend. When they were forced to part with it to Covenanting Mr Cant in 1647 they had, needless to say, done nothing to make it larger or grander during the two hundred years they had lived there; but the Lowises, who bought it very soon from Cant, had more or less gutted the medieval interior and made it rather smarter and more mansion-like, and considerably easier to live in. Unluckily they did it very badly and shoddily; and once such an ancient and demanding structure is parted from the land whose revenues keep it standing, it has no prolonged future as a private house. Always loved, always longed for, it had to be sold after the death of Francis, whose ten sons and whose canal plans had cost a pretty penny.

In the 1960s Merchiston met a lucky if unromantic fate. Stripped of all seventeenth- eighteenth and nineteenth-century wings, fronts, and other accretions it was reconstructed within by Edinburgh Corporation at great expense, and restored to the original stark fifteenth-century outline which Sir Alexander Napier had given it in the 1460s, and permanently implanted, like a sword in the stone, into the glass and concrete cubes of Napier Technical College. It had been bought back by William John 9th Lord Napier, in 1818, and let shortly before his death in China, to the founders of Merchiston Castle School, to whom it was finally sold by the Napiers in 1914.

'Merchiston Castle', Henry Cockburn complained in 1845 in his *Memorials*, 'has been greatly injured by a recent and discordant front' (built on by Merchiston School); and it would be possible now to say that the Tower had been greatly injured by a recent and discordant Technical College. But it is surely better than crumbling into ruin; and logarithms John would undoubtedly have approved a plan that his noble mathematique science should here be enthroned. It is better to be the haunt of vice-principals and filing cabinets than to be the haunt of bats and owls; and since it could no longer echo to the

sound of those innumerable familes of Napier children it is well that
it should echo to the voices of Edinburgh's intelligent and lively
young.

Dying, Francis Napier had told his married daughter Hester
Johnstone how the forfeit of land under Cromwell and the 'un-
expected expenses he had been at in plans for the Canal' would mean
the loss of Merchiston, but he left to her his other precious possession,
the heart of Montrose. This now underwent a series of strange
adventures, described by Hester's son, Alexander Johnstone.

'When I was about five years old, my father, my mother and myself
were on the way to India, in the fleet commanded by Commodore
Johnston, when it was attacked off the Cape de Verde Islands, by the
French squadron under Suffren. One of the French frigates engaged
the Indiaman in which we were, and my father, with the captain's
permission took command of four of the quarterdeck guns. My
mother refused to go below, but remained on the quarterdeck with
me at her side declaring that no wife ought to quit her husband at a
moment of such peril, and that we both should share my father's
fate. A shot from the frigate struck one of the guns, killed two of
the men, and with the splinters which it tore from the deck, knocked
my father down, wounded my mother severely in the arm, and
bruised the muscles of my right hand so severely that it is difficult for
me to hold a pen. My mother held me during the action with her
right hand, and with the other she held a large black velvet reticule,
in which she, conceiving if the frigate captured the merchantmen the
French crew would plunder the ship, had placed some of the things
she valued the most, including the pictures of her father and mother,
and the gold filagree case containing the heart of Montrose. The
splinter must have struck the reticule, the gold filagree box was
shattered to pieces, but the steel case had resisted the blow. The
frigate which attacked us was called off, and the next day Commodore
Johnston came on board the Indiaman and congratulated my father
and mother in the highest terms for the encouragement they had
given the crew of the ship.

'In India, at Madura, my mother found a celebrated native
goldsmith, who partly from the fragments she had saved, and partly
from her description, made as beautiful a gold filagree box as the one
that had been destroyed. She caused him also to make her a silver

urn, like the one in the picture, and to engrave on the outside of it, in Tamil and Telugu, the two languages most generally understood throughout the southern peninsular of India, a short account of Montrose's life and death . . .

'My mother's anxiety about it gave rise to a report that it was a talisman and that whoever possessed it could never be wounded in battle or taken prisoner. Owing to this report it was stolen from her . . .

'My father was in the habit of sending me every year, during the hunting and shooting season, to stay with one of the native chiefs who lived in the neighbourhood of Madura, for four months at a time, to acquire the various languages and practise the native gymnastics. One day when I was hunting with the chief who was rumoured to have purchased the urn, my horse was attacked by a wild hog which we were pursuing, but I succeeded in wounding it so severely with my hunting pike that the chief soon afterwards overtook and killed it . . .'

The chief, pleased with Alexander, had asked him what present he would like, and had been told that if the rumour of his having it was true, Alexander would like above all things to be able to restore it to his mother; and he told the chief its tale. The chief expressed his sorrow that the talisman had been stolen, said that a brave man should always honour the wishes of another brave man, whatever his race and religion, and gave the heart back to Alexander together with other presents. When, later in life, this same chief rebelled against his overlord, the Nawab of Arcot, and was captured after a brave fight and about to be executed, he had asked his servants to do what had been done for Montrose, and to keep his own brave heart in his family.

'My father and mother returned to Europe in 1792,' Alexander continues, 'and being in France when the Revolutionary Government required all persons to give up their plate, and gold and silver ornaments, my mother entrusted the silver urn with Montrose's heart to an Englishwoman, of the name of Knowles at Boulogne, who promised to secrete it until it could be safely sent to England. She died shortly afterwards, and neither my mother or my father in their lifetime, nor I myself since their death, have ever been able to trace the urn, although within the last few years I have received from the French Government the value of the plate and jewels which my father and mother had been compelled to give up to the municipality of Calais in 1792. To her last hour my mother deeply regretted the loss.' *

William, 7th Lord Napier, 'bred to arms' and having no notion of the bad state of his inheritance (his father, what with the canal, etc., left debts of £10,000) had been 'put to unavoidable expense' (probably in other words living it up), in the army; but provided generously for his daughters as far as the entail permitted, and raised £4,000 by selling his commission in the Scots Greys; but he, too, had a deeply valued possession 'my library of books which are considerable and numerous' and these, as well as the pictures and portraits were 'always to be transmitted with the honor and titles of Napier'. In the end William, sadly, had to sell the books himself. The Napiers never economized on the number of their children; and the percentage of survival was high. This was festive, but did not make for the accumulation of this world's goods.

The 6th, 7th and 8th Lord Napiers were all soldiers, their epoch being one of colonial expansion and consolidation. The consolidation was not always solid: the eighth brought back a funny story against himself after he had been at the Saratoga surrender in 1777 as an ensign and taken prisoner by the Americans. Fascinated as egalitarians often are by lords, an old American lady had walked twelve miles to see Francis, 8th Lord Napier, imprisoned after the battle at Cambridge, Massachusetts. Eager, footsore, and confronted suddenly by a long-legged nineteen-year-old boy in a battered ensign's uniform, she had commented, 'Well, if that's a lord, I don't want to see another until I see the Lord Almighty.'

Francis, 8th Lord, came back to a Scotland healed of the wounds of her blood-stained past; Napthali, the hind let loose from fear, had now to drink refreshment at a clearer stream. Scotland was basking in a golden age of art, of architecture, of intellectual and industrial achievement, with the swords of at least inter-clan warfare beaten into ploughshares, and the spears into tool-making machines. Her writers were speaking good words, her doctors finding good cures, and Francis forgot Saratoga and his nineteen-year-old disgust and humiliation in defeat, and the stupidity and unnecessariness of the war in the first place, and settled to the joys of family life—'I have experienced so much warmth of heart in the character of Lord Napier' his cousin by marriage, Lady Sarah Napier, reported, 'I know so well how he, his wife, and all his family have existed on domestic happiness for years back'—and to a distinguished career in Scottish public life, having fathered William, Francis, Charles, Henry, Maria, Charlotte, Anne, Sophia and Caroline. He enjoyed

8*

an honorary degree from the University of Edinburgh, was Grand
Master Mason of Scotland, a representative peer in Parliament,
Lord-Lieutenant of Selkirk and High Commissioner to the General
Assembly, and had married a beautiful woman, Maria Margaret
Clavering. His eldest son William John, 9th Lord Napier, of whom
more later, was born at Kinsale in Ireland in 1786, his second,
Francis, was lost at sea in the *Hussar* frigate. Among his cousins, sons
of George Napier whose father had been Francis, 6th Lord, were five
remarkable brothers, Charles, George, William, Richard and Henry.

Lowland lairds were far from being the sole sufferers from adherence
to the Stewarts. After the Jacobite rebellion of 1745 the Highlands
suffered as grievously as the Napiers by their loyalty to the king
had suffered a hundred years earlier. Many an emigrant ship set sail
from the west coast, amidst weeping and heartbreak, filled with
economically rather than politically dispossessed lairds and tenants.
Clan feuds still held sway here; Campbells in triumphant Whig
oppression; Stewarts expressing themselves as willing to shoot down
a Campbell as a blackcock. Wearing of the kilt was almost more
rigorously suppressed than possession of arms. 'Is it all fear on both
sides?' asks R. L. Stevenson's David Balfour of the wandering
minister Henderland, master of Gaelic and avid for snuff.

'Na,' said Mr Henderland, 'but there's love too, and self-denial
that should put the like of you and me to shame. There's something
fine about it; no perhaps Christian, but humanly fine.' And no doubt
the imagined Henderland was as typical of this age as were the many
canting ministers of whom we hear more. 'There are two things that
men should never weary of,' thinks David Balfour, 'goodness and
humility; we get none too much of them in this rough world among
cold proud people;' and Mr Henderland, to him, exemplifies both
virtues. 'Though I was a good deal puffed up with my adventures and
with having come off, as the saying is, with flying colours, yet he soon
had me on my knees beside a simple poor old man, and both proud
and glad to be there.' The Highlander gives David, a hungry fugitive,
the only silver coin he has. Through thick and thin, though still
banging it out bravely with their enemies, the Highlanders retained
those wholly unsubservient and unhurried good manners which they,
and the dwellers in the west of Ireland, retain to this day. Clans lived
with laird, ate often from his table, took their manners from him. It

was a democracy within a hierarchy; and the loyalty, until the lairds began to be seduced by Edinburgh's rising standard of living and by the demand of their wives and daughters that they should keep up with the McJoneses to the detriment of their tenants, was absolute. Even in the eighteenth century over most of Scotland the power of kin was stronger than the power of law: many sheltered the proscribed Macgregors, and their name survived.

In Edinburgh the Scotts may be said to have had the last word. It is the memorial to their great and good Sir Walter that hugely pierces the luminous haze that lies across the great central chasm which renders Edinburgh uniquely dramatic amongst capital cities. John Napier of the logarithms has no memorial in the land whose prime intelligence he once was.* His fame was always of a more international kind, and he contributes nothing to the tourist trade. Also he was too clever by half; and with all those suspect mathematical figures and that black cock which might easily have been classed as a familiar, let alone his dangerous habit of pacing his fields at night accompanied only by a large dog, was lucky to die in his bed. His benignity saved him; aided by his being so considerable a landowner and so firm a pillar of the church. Fame has come late. The Russians have recently called a mountain after him, on the newly photographed backside of the moon. Well they might; it was his calculations that started them off on the road there. They spell it Neper, admittedly; but it is the thought that counts.

Sir Alexander, third of the fifteenth-century Napiers of Merchiston, who probably knew his fellow citizens well, had provided against just such a contingency. At St Giles, in that great church whose stalwart columns of grey stone glow with a kind of golden sheen, whose strength and holiness express the strong wholeness of Scotland's spirit, as the extreme delicate beauty of the crown spire echoes the beauty of her hills and dales, Sir Alexander had placed his own memorial, so high up that not even the most ardent Covenanter would climb up to hack it down. On the corbal of the half-pillar to the south of the high altar in St Giles' great church are his arms of Lennox, cadenced, the saltier engrailed cantoned with four roses, and under the shield are four cherubims. Some have joke faces, but the face looking outwards down the side-aisle is the face

* Written in 1966: he now has his technical college.

of Alexander Napier; a long oval, high-arched eyebrows and a jutting nose. With a pointed beard improbably reposing upon a pair of cherub's wings, and an extremely cynical expression, he confronts the worshippers and the tourists of this most beautiful and least yielding of cities.

XIV

The Napiers in the south had emigrated, according to the more flippant amongst their descendants, because their nervous systems were no longer able to stand the strain of life around the Border or along the Highland line. Recovering in the unruffled scenery of the south-west, they built themselves charming stone houses in Dorset and Somerset, most of which, growing bored or restless, they subsequently gambled away. (Not the least now, do young men, no longer called upon to gamble their lives in war, tend to chance them away on roads or gamble away their livelihoods; and it is time someone thought up a cheerfuller and more constructive substitute for war.) Like most roving Scots in the south, the Napiers seemed to have no difficulty in making good. No longer obliged to cry Ready, Aye Ready, and follow James V of Scotland over the Border with a plump of spears, they bought themselves a small but sufficient fishing fleet, and 'supplying the several adjacent abbies with fish,' amassed a comfortable competence just before these were dissolved. This done, and their first flush of house-building over, they seemed to lose impetus; joined by further cousins from the north and living in their beautiful little stone manor houses at Swyre, looking down over the yellow cliffs of West Bay, at Puncknowle, Baglake, Minterne Magna, Middlemarsh, Melbury Osmond, and Long Crichel in Dorset, and at Tintinhull in Somerset, a property that had belonged to the executed Sir Thomas Wyatt. The west country lapped the Napiers in its immemorial mild calm; lucky enough to settle in a place where, apart from a brush or two in the Civil War, and Monmouth's rebellion (in which they took no part), nothing very disagreeable occurred until the bombing of Yeovil by the Luftwaffe in 1943.

They did not sit quite still. Sir Richard Napier, son of Sandy and first cousin to logarithms John, settled in Bedfordshire and stuck to science, astrology, and being unlike other people—'He did practise physick; but gave most to the poor that he got by it,' according to John Aubrey. 'A person of great abstinence, innocence and pietie, his knees,' Aubrey added, 'were horny with frequent praying,' and he claimed to be in constant communication with the archangel Raphael, whose observations he somehow failed to record. 'He died praying upon his knees, being of a very great age.' Rather more humdrum was his nephew, another Richard, a fellow of All Souls and one of the founder members of the Royal Society; where he enjoyed the company of King Charles II, Robert Boyle, Christopher Wren and Isaac Newton. 'A great pretender to virtue and astrology, made a great noise in the world, yet did little or nothing towards the public,' Anthony á Wood reported disparagingly; and Richard Napier seems to have left no records, though he and his uncle Richard kept writing to each other on serious seventeenth-century subjects like 'Whether man hath libertem arbitrium—that is, freedom of will; and how far it extendeth.' What sounds a slightly priggish fourth son of his (but maybe it's just his way of speaking) was sent to Padua University, writing home to his parents in September of 1659 to tell them that 'the future desire of my heart shall be, to please you, to serve my country, and to improve myself in every kind of literature. That it may please Almighty God to have you and my dearest lady mother long and forever in his safe keeping prays, from the bottom of his heart, Filius Tuus Obedientissimus, Robertus Napierus.' But perhaps he relaxed as the term went on.

He too made good. There is a tablet to him at Padua University— To the young and distinguished Roberto Napiero, an Englishman by birth, and of a noble family, who, while he had the government of the University of Padua [an annual appointment] in order that he might put an utter end to the furious strifes which were raging, did not only hold those everlasting reins of Justice, but held them with a tight and steady hand. The Archi-Lyceum of Artists have placed these Arms: 1662.

Another Robert Napier, the first Richard's more orthodox brother, was a successful Turkey merchant and a High Sheriff of Bedfordshire and bought Luton Hoo in 1600, was member for Bedfordshire 1611 and for Corfe Castle in Dorset in 1625. When he appeared at court to receive a baronetcy from King James I there were mutterings from jealous English courtiers; for who, after all were these Napiers? This was a remark liable to enrage James. In Scots eyes the English aristocracy were a Norman rabble most of whom had exterminated each other in the Wars of the Roses, whilst the Scots in general had been living on their land since about 500 A.D. and very adequately defending it from Angle, Dane and Norman. English patronizing he would not have. Who were the Napiers? 'By my saul,' King James crossly replied, for so did he pronounce his immortal member, 'By my saul they are all gentlemen these many hundred years.'

Settling first at Swyre, Puncknowle and Bexington, James Napier (son of Sir Alexander Napier of Merchiston by a sister of Robert Stewart, Earl of Atholl) had Edward Napier of Hollywell, Nicholas Napier of Tintinhull, and James of Baglake. At Puncknowle people kept digging up Roman coins, it was the kind of knoll the Romans liked living on, and in Domesday Book it had been held by a settler with the persuasively Norman name of Hugh Fitz-Grip. It was not a totally cosy situation; in 1440 Bexington village had been sacked and burnt by the French, and all its inhabitants reft away to France from whence they had had to buy themselves back. But beautiful it certainly was. Edward left a son William, only seven years old, but this did not prevent him being seized of the manor of Swyre, of 17 messuages, 6 cottages, and 640 acres annual value £71 8s. 3d, held of the queen in chief part of a knight's fee; and advowson of the Church, held of the queen by free soccage. Casting aside soccage and all, he left these dreaming vales as soon as he was able and set off abroad. 'Here lyeth William Napier,' his stone announced fifty-eight years later, 'who after xv yeares travell in forayne landes married Anne Shelton, the daughter of William Shelton of Ongar Park, esquier, by whom he had VI sonnes, and now his sole being with God his bodie here resteth in Jesu Christ.' His younger brother Robert went west and became Queen Elizabeth's Lord Chief Justice of Ireland, returning to Dorset to settle at Middlemarsh.

George, John, Andrew, Robert, Edward, William, sons of William; and Launcelot, James, Thomas, Robert, Edward, sons of Nicholas: Dorset, never a thickly populated county, seems in the seventeenth century entirely saturated by Napiers. Robert Napier, son of William Napier of Swyre, in an English reply to the quiverful of logarithms John, was the father of William, Andrew, Robert, Edward, Shelton, Edmund, John, Arundel, Anne and Catherine. Dorset, like some majestic sea swelling hugely between green troughs where delectable villages lay hidden from Atlantic winds, cradled in every second vale a crop of little Napiers, harboured in due course a harvest of grown-up ones. Sadly the letters of grief drone on, in the marbles of the grey stone churches: 'Alice, wife of Launcelot Napier, 1597 . . . Magdalen, wife of Sir Robert Napier, 1635 . . . Sir Nathaniel Napier, of much esteem and honor in this county . . . Sir Gerard Napier Knt and Bt who was Deputy Lieutenant to King Charles ye 1st and never deserted him, and loyall to King Charles ye II and esteemed by him for his Loyalty and good service to ye Crowne, May 14th 1672 . . . here reposeth ye most virtuose, most obliging and charitably good Lady Blanche Napier . . . carried to joy ease and happiness unspeakable there to live in the blest habitation of angells to all eternity' (in 1695); '. . . the Rev. Nathaniel Napier, rector of Sutton Walrond 36 years, born of an illustrious family but paid the common debt to nature, 1722. En mortalitas exemplar! . . . James Lennox Napier, 1736, knight of the shire for Meath in Ireland . . . John Tregonwell Napier, rector of Chettle . . .' Sir George, Sir Charles, Mistress Anne Napier of Melbury Osmund . . . One could hardly walk down a village street in Dorset without falling over a Napier baronet or a Napier parson, yet by the mid-nineteenth century all were gone.

At Swyre one of the Napiers had the Lennox Legend engraved in stone on his memorial, placing it as near as possible to the altar, as if it had been the Lord's Prayer or the Ten Commandments. At Puncknowle a note of Scots melancholy seems to creep into the memorial to Sir Robert Napier; perhaps of nostalgia, of enclosement in this downy Dorset valley, this easy country so far from the windy bluffs of Edinburgh. 'Man is a dream of a shadow,' his son Sir Charles Napier recorded, startling the other parishioners by having this dictum of Pindar's inscribed in the original Greek, and adding in Latin, 'We do not speak great things but live them,' he continued in English, 'Reader whereas thou hast done all thou canst thou art but an unprofitable servant Therefore this marble affords no Roome for fulsome flattery or vaine praise.' The sculptor, a Scot called Hamilton, threw in a stone skull or two to ram home the point, but no one was ever so unworldly as to omit the Lennox arms carved with a great flourish above. The house the Napiers built at Puncknowle was so beautiful that it was recently sold, plus three hundred not very sumptuous acres, for around a quarter of a million.

Sir Robert Napier, returning from Ireland and knighted by Queen Elizabeth some time before 1593, restored Middlemarsh, derelict since 1536. In the parish of Minterne Parva, it was 'a little manor and hamlet with a large old stone building' which had been the retiring place of the Abbots of Cerne Abbey. The seventeenth century was one that liked to spell things out loud and clear; and on the chimney piece in a large upper room Sir Robert inscribed, 'Faith and Hope in Christ and Charity to our neighbour are inseparable.' The house was presently burnt down, but the Dorset almshouses which he and his cousin John Napier built and endowed in Dorchester, 'ten poor men to have their habitation and maintenance therein,' are still there and known as Napper's Mite. To this end he bestowed 'the manor of Little Puddle alias Little Piddle . . . that it should not be alienated or sold, but held in the heirs of his name and blood forever continued to the uses aforesaid, and to perform . . . all things else which should be thought agreeable with his purpose, tending only to the glory and honour of God and to the relief of the poor.' In November 1667 Sir Gerard Napier 'devised all his manor of Stert in the parish of Babcary in Somerset' to pay for reading divine service to the old men, and for new clothes for them all every two years, with 'any excess to be shared among them.' James Napier's charity was the leper hospital at Goderthorn by Bridport, but Mistress Anne Napier preferred children; six little Dorchester ones 'out of poor families', to be educated at Trinity School and supplied with blue dresses from the rent of her lands in the parish of Melbury Osmond.

It is a far cry from the rigours and ardours of Montrose's campaigns, in which their cousins were now battling, but at least one Napier managed to find himself a satisfyingly lost cause, even in peaceful Dorset. He became a Roman Catholic, than which no cause was more thoroughly lost in seventeenth-century England, with Foxe's Book of Martyrs a best-seller to be found in every house, and treasured alongside the Bible. Even in death he declined to mingle, except with his own family. 'In the name of God Amen, I John Napier of West Baglake in the Countie of Dorsett and parish of Longbriddy Esquire . . . for matter of buriall of my poore Carcasse, the times are such as whether Anabaptist, Brownist, and such heretikes will give it Christian Buriall no man knoes: But if it please my sonn Henry Naper to burye me by my wife Elizabeth in Puncknowle Church they shall doe a deede I much desyre them to doe for me For that there lyeth my wife and twoe children maids both who dyed Infants . . . But if my Carkes will not be permitted I charge my sonn Henry to doe his best endeavours to bury my body in the very Alley as he goeth from his house to the Dyall in his garden at Baglake and that he Wall my grave Round and lay a flat stone on me And this is all the Pompe of buriall I crave.' But like so many wills this one did not come off, and they planted him at Swyre amongst a lot of second cousins, which is not at all the same thing. (For three hundred years the people of Litton Cheney believed that John Napier's body *was* in the very alley—alas, poor papist.) His charming house at Baglake was swiftly confiscated by the authorities to compound for his recusancy fines.

For even in quiet Dorset the volcano erupted; and the Civil War took its toll, less ruinous to all than it had been in the north, but often sharply squeezing even to the most prosperous. Such was Nathaniel Napier of Middlemarsh, son to Sir Robert by Magdalen his wife, and knighted by James I at Newmarket for no discernible reason (but perhaps a useful sum had been passed, or the king was in a relaxed mood after hunting), High Sherriff in 1621 and member for Dorset in 1626; who built Crichel House on a manor which had belonged to a family—surely Saxon—called Cifrewast, and put up a memorial to the last of the Cifrewasts in the church. His fourth son, James, lighted out for Ireland and founded a family there: his eldest, Sir Gerard, was M.P. for Wareham and Melcombe Regis and made a baronet in 1641. The Crichel Napiers were famous in the family for being more intelligent about money than anyone else; they always seemed to have it, and Gerard bought Baglake, his cousin Henry's house near Litton Cheney by paying part of his recusancy fines.

By 1641 the fires of the Civil War were beginning to smoulder, and Royalist Robert Napier had his farms at Puncknowle and Bexington, value £300 per annum, sequestered by the Commonwealth authorities, and poor Henry Napier, late of Baglake and already crippled by recusancy fines, also fell by the way. Even canny Sir Gerard plumped for the king and had his lands sequestred, 'being a colonel in arms'; though he managed to compound for them for nearly £3,000. He spent another £10,000 bolstering the cause of Charles I, and was disabled from being the member for Melcombe and declared a delinquent. To Charles II in exile Sir Gerard sent 500 badly needed gold pieces, but he sent them by a Sir Gilbert Taylor and somehow they never arrived. However it is the thought that counts; and in 1665 a restored King Charles and Queen Catherine came to stay with him at Crichel. His second son Sir Nathaniel, carried away by the gaiety and relief of the Restoration, re-furbished Middlemarsh and 'much beautified and adorned the house and gardens' at Crichel, and fathered William, Gerard, Robert, Lennox, Nathaniel, Margaret, Blanche, Catherine and Elizabeth. Possibly finding home a little noisy, he became a great traveller, but returned to become member for Dorchester, representing part of that borough all through the reigns of William and Mary, and of Anne, and be made a baronet. Known to contemporaries as 'a gay ingenious gentleman, well-versed in several languages, and with a good understanding of architecture and painting', Sir Nathaniel and his fifth son Nathaniel were both members for Dorchester at the same time in 1700 and 1701, which must have been confusing for the Speaker, and, come to that, for the other members of the House.

In 1700 Middlemarsh, too, burnt down; the Napiers seemed destined never to hang on to their property. Nothing now is left but a piece of the old house built into a farm; and during the sway of Sir William Napier, 4th bart, Crichel also was burnt down. Sir William rebuilt it 'in great splendour' and be it added, with superb taste; and commemorated what he felt was the miraculous saving of his own life and the lives of his family by a large annual gift to the poor of the parish. His father Nat had succeeded his namesake and fellow M.P., and marrying Catherine, daughter of William, Lord Alington, begat also Sir Gerard Napier, who was trustee for the Frampton family and famous for being the only person in Dorset who got out of the South Sea Bubble in time, whereby both these families are still living in their same houses. Gerard married Bridget Phelips of Montacute and had Sir Gerard, 6th and final bart, painted by Gainsborough and dying childless at twenty-six, leaving his wife Elizabeth, daughter of Sir John Oglander of Nunwell, to live out forty-nine years of widowhood at Bath.

Full stop; but Diana Napier, daughter of Sir Nathaniel, 3rd bart, had married Humphrey Sturt, son of a rich lord mayor of London; and as she had also become heiress of the Alingtons, Crichel was given a new financial lease of life. Their son Henry's renewals at Crichel caused the Reverent John Hutchings to raise a disapproving eyebrow: 'so immensely enlarged that it has the appearance of the mansion of a prince more than that of a country gentleman,' he pointed out severely in his *Survey of Dorset*. The Napiers of Crichel were now Sturts (and would presently be Martens). Diana Napier's youngest grand-daughter, eccentrically christened Eliza-Bizarre, and deb of about the year 1790, was known as 'the lovely Bizzy Sturt'.

How many unexplained and perhaps sad lives do these old records contain; and how did handsome Gerard's childless widow get on in her forty-nine years at Bath—first as young Lady Napier, gay and garrulous maybe and swinging her panniered skirts; then middle-aged Lady Napier, inclining to good works and gossip; and then as old Lady Napier, loved only by a rather bossy and crotchety maid and tolerated by an overfed dog? She at least had independence and wealth, the power to go where she wished: far more dismal may have been the lot of the daughters at home, parent-bound as any Chinee and staring wistfully at the sad rain falling, from windows at Tintinhull, at Merchiston, at Luton Hoo, at Fintry or Culcreugh, as the years slowly rolled by. Henrietta, *d.* unmarried 1667; Anna, 1695, Agnes, 1709, Mary, 1765, Marcia Charlotte, 1850—looking after parents, aunts, old servants; the unsung and unhonoured saints of many a lonely village or chilly manor house. But maybe half of them were as jolly as minnows; apple-cheeked and happy with spring and summer and nephews and nieces and decorating the house and the church for the joyful festivals of family or religion. Close and valued members of a family, perhaps they lived and died happier than in full emancipation, with a bed-sitter in Earls Court and a bottle of sleeping pills ever to hand.

In Scotland life sounds appreciably grimmer; an atmosphere of stern severity prevailing. Anything in the nature of a shotgun marriage would find itself recorded in the parish register: 'the whilk day Robert, lawfully procreated betwixt William Napier of Culcreugh and Lady Bessie Houston, his spouse' was christened in 1695 in the parish of Fintry (where Isabella of Lennox had first built a church in the thirteenth century); 'This day ane male child called John, lawfully procreated betwixt Alexander Napier of Culreuch and Mrs Margaret Lennox his spouse was baptized before these witnesses, Sir John Houston of that ilk, Knight, John Lennox of Woodhead, and Archibald Napier of Boquhable' in 1686 in the same church. Product of this sternly moral environment, which Robert Burns was shortly to mock, was Robert John Napier of Culcreuch, born 1765, commanding at the siege of Mangalore in the East Indies and among the innumerable Napier colonels reported on in this epoch by the historian Mark Napier; and Alexander Napier of Blackstone, colonel of the Black Watch, to whom Sir John Moore wrote for a sketch and approval when he took a Highland soldier as supporter on his coat of arms: 'Under an officer who understands them, they will conquer or die on the spot . . . but it is the principles of integrity and moral correctness that I admire most in Highland soldiers, and this . . . makes their courage sure, and not that kind of flash in the pan which would scale a bastion today and tomorrow be alarmed at the fire of a picket. You Highland officers may sleep sound at night, and rise in the morning with the assurance that your men, your professional character and honour, are safe.' And perhaps Colonel Alexander Napier did sleep sound and rise with assurance, for all his Spartan upbringing; though this is all we know about him: he was killed at Corunna.

Dorset is paradisal; and long may it so remain. In earlier centuries it all belonged to the Church, and a kind of dreaming other-worldliness still haunts its countryside. On the flinty fields of those remote uplands where Thomas Hardy saw poor Tess hoeing turnips all the day, there is still no tumult but of lapwing and of lark: the woods are deep and quiet as when Bathsheba slept in them to salve her broken heart. There is an untouched quality in that huge marmoreal sea of downland whose waves are still clothed only in windswept tree or turf. Paradisal; but not affording very much to bite on, for the active or the young. (Sergeant Troy, it will be remembered, felt obliged to light out.) By 1850 all the Napiers had moved on to the Americas or the Antipodes, or succumbed to the quiet of it; younger, or natural, children fading imperceptibly into the landscape like so many Red Indians. Natural children, probably, or when Sir Gerard Napier died in 1765 and Sir George about the same time, some busybody would have disorganized their lives by raking them out, and pointing out to them that they were baronets, once if not twice over. Silently, over the centuries, they faded into the deep rural simplicity of Hardy's Dorset, verderers of those still woods; until in the twentieth century the only parishioner of Minterne Parva was a quiet old man called Stephen Napier, whose son, Herbert, was Captain Gerald Digby's keeper, much liked by all and addressed affectionately by Napiers as Cousin Herbert when they went to shoot at Lewcombe. Such lush and sheltered vales are not likely spring-boards to ambition; (though against this it must be admitted that the Churchills were cradled in Minterne Magna). In this gentler soil, would the passions and energies of Scotland transmute themselves to something slightly other, though not less valuable, or would they not survive at all?

In Somerset, just across the border, the Napiers continued. James Napier of Puncknowle had married a sister of John Russell of Berwick St John, that alert young man who paved the way to a stupendous Bedford fortune by being the only person in Dorset who could speak Spanish when some vital infanta was blown ashore at Weymouth. Perhaps this strongly possessive Russell strain had a sobering effect on their second son, Nicholas Napier of Tintinhull, for in this small village of Somerset the Napiers stayed put, doing nothing much for six generations except to cherish their land and build three charming houses out of the local stone; one of them, called the Mansion, now belonging to the National Trust, so beautiful in its style and proportions that in the 1930s an exact reproduction of it was built in America. Here Nicholas Napier's descendants, five successive generations of Thomas Napiers lived, steeped in rural calm and spelling their name wrong—Napper, perhaps in irritation at the English habit of pronouncing the correct version N'pier. The third Thomas Napier, married to Lydia à Court, launched into public life in 1635 so far as to join Sir Robert Phelips of Montacute in his refusal to pay Ship Money; riding from Tintinhull—a Saxon name roughly meaning Hill of Discussion—to Ilchester, where he 'gave scandalous words to the Sheriff'. After this fuss they beat the assessment down by sixpence, but after another year on the hill of discussion they thought better of it and paid up without petitioning; and Thomas, like all the rest, was for the king when it came to the crunch. The song and dance over Ship Money was considerable: previously only dwellers in sea-port towns had paid for the Navy, rather as though only occupiers of ground-floor flats should pay for the police, and Charles I's attempt to tax everybody for the ships practically sparked off the Civil War. Somerset was a poor place to make a stand anyway, as it is extremely close to the sea on both sides; but it was one of those times when people all over the country suddenly feel that their ancient liberties are being eroded by unsympathetic bureaucrats.

Thomas Napier of Tintinhull Mansion Esquire, son of ditto, son of ditto, son of ditto, son of ditto—what were they like? Swinging their full-skirted coats they turn unknown faces away from us, and trudge the green landscape in their well-filled waistcoats; shooting the sitting bird with cumbersome fowling pieces; or, with very long leathers and heavy stirrups, splosh their horses through the muddy fields of Somerset in pursuit of the elusive deer or fox that threatens corn or fold. English gentlemen in the seventeenth and eighteenth centuries lived in rooms furnished at most with one picture, one looking-glass, one table and three or four stiff chairs, all of them fine; used superb silver; ate too much invariably and generally drank excessively as well; rode horses of flawless beauty, married plain wives, and were accompanied everywhere by hideous but obviously cherished mongrel dogs. Their children tended to live off-stage, brought up for the greater part of the day by large households of illiterate but cheerful servants who were always being told not to laugh so loud; a jolly backstairs life in which they were kindly teased by grooms and shouted at by gardeners, comforted by flocks of print-clad Betsys, schooled by the parson, indulged by Mamma, and permitted, as soon as they could tote a weapon, to join their father's following of besotted mongrel dogs. They had few toys, no jaunts, and no games but what they invented for themselves. What they did not lack, in hall or cottage, were a great many people who took an interest in them. Cold and discomfort were appalling, floors were bare, and still only the robust grew up. Roads were mud or dust and exeats rare; very few inlanders, rich or poor, had ever seen the sea. Yet diarists and visitors alike unite to comment on the cheerful faces of the English countryside in these centuries before the Industrial Revolution, like some sinister whirlpool, sucked them off to groan and fester in its unspeakable slums. And in the pictures that come down to us people do not look harassed, nervous, or bored, and the children, however doomed, to all appearances are loaded with spontaneous joy.

Were the Napiers of Tintinhull like Fielding's Squire Western? Did they share the pride and disregard of other human beings which were soon to cause so many of their counterparts on the other side of the Channel to get themselves chopped? They seem less aloof, less callous and inhuman; in 1800 Jane Austen's Mr Knightley was properly kept in order by his gardener, William Larkins. It was not till later, in the nineteenth century, that Charles Napier complained of the appalling habit that had crept in with the *nouveaux riches* of talking to the less fortunate as if from a higher plane. Life was strictly hierarchical, rich were no less rich and poor were no less poor, but in the country at least a kind of practical common sense in living together obscured the boring distinctions of class. People died of damp and disease in their poor cottages, but not of loneliness, and not by suicide. The air they breathed was healthy, and the food they ate, though sparse enough, was fresh and good.

Did the Thomas Napiers love their wives and children, cherish their tenants, read books, travel, enjoy music? Had they any ideas, beyond a stout patriotism, outside their own valley? Were they immune to the grace and beauty of the house their forbears had built and did it excite in them only the fondness of a well-used habitat, a vague undiscriminating pride of possession? Nothing remains but a child's name scratched with a diamond on a window-pane; nothing but a legend of final profligacy, and some extremely plain tombs.

Here, if they had had enough work to distract them from gambling, they might still be; large, and beetle-browed, and never going to London so long as it was humanly possible not to. But when Queen Anne's wars were over, and on the many days when it was impossible to shoot or hunt, they had begun to spend the long dark winter afternoons and evenings losing money to their neighbours. Dinner was at four, and then what? It's a long time till bedtime, even if dinner lasts a couple of hours. It was an age when all England see-sawed in a wild ocean of gambling. Anyone master of five shillings endeavoured instantly to convert it into ten, whether they had anything further to fall back upon or not.

> When the bonny blade carouses,
> Pockets full, and spirits high—
> What are acres, what are houses?
> Only dirt, or wet, or dry

wrote Samuel Johnson; and so it was in Somerset. With the fifth Thomas the land went, the silver, the furniture; eventually the houses. There was even a story that the last of the Thomas Napiers lost a daughter to Phelips of Montacute, who lived a mile or so away. Certain it is that the last Thomas Napier used to bet with Phelips on which of two raindrops would first reach the bottom of the window. But the tale that the Napiers lost Tintinhull Mansion, arguably the most beautiful small manor house in England, on the fall of a raindrop is not true. The trustees of nine-year-old John Napier sold it in 1789.

In the 1750s the Mansion was still there; but younger sons had to live. From this nadir, this dead-end preoccupation with midnight card tables and streaming window panes, Andrew, youngest grandson of the last Thomas Napier, was sharply rescued by the necessity of earning something with which to buy his horses if not his bread. He became a smuggler on a large and successful scale; an activity which he concealed by selling cow-hides under the unexceptionable facade of a hide-merchant in Cheapside. The love of a good woman seemed called for; and as so often, it was to hand. By some curious alchemy, there are always enough good women with a small but useful income to go round the handsome scamps. Smuggling Andrew Napier married a local Somerset heiress called Letitia Berkeley, with whom he acquired the manor of Pylle, near Shepton Mallet, where he went to live. Miss Berkeley, nice, prim, and on the bossy side, was descended from Robert Fitzhardinge to whom Queen Matilda gave Berkeley Castle for his help in her war against Stephen in the twelfth century: she was thus sprung from Lady Godiva, but nothing in her expression can have encouraged any pleasantries on this subject. Painted as a widow, dour and elegant in deep black and a muslin ruffled cap, she sits sombrely beside an urn with 'Andrew Napier 1770' engraved upon it. There is something overwhelmingly respectable about the ex-Miss Berkeley, in trim authentic widowhood, with every frill more beautifully goffered than the last: did she feel safer with scampish Andrew Napier safely inside that urn? It was probably she who persuaded her husband to consult the family records and brush up his spelling, to put down roots again and bring up his children and abstain from midnight adventures with barrels of brandy in coastal lanes, to re-adapt to the role of respectable country squire.

But his portrait, wearing a coat of apricot velvet, long-faced, beak-nosed, arched eye-browed, with jowls rather heavier after a century or so amongst the lush pastures of Somerset than his Scots contemporaries, reveals a gleam of unmistakable mockery in the eye —the solid imperturbable scamp never quite tamed or chastened by the good woman, the scamp prepared to play along but thinking it all pretty funny. Scotland in the eighteenth century had still its stray upheavals, was still recovering from its political and religious earthquakes: England had already recovered and was looking around for further mischief, for a further release of energy. It worked this off by acquiring an empire in the most unplanned manner in which this has ever been done; hopping from Canada to India to Australia and back more in a burst of spirits and a desire to out-gun the French than from any deep soulful mission to perpetuate a way of life. Like Andrew Napier, d. 1770, England at this epoch, though now respectably married to Scotland, had a certain unrepentant gleam in its eye.

Mark Napier, the Scottish historian, grandson of the sixth Lord Napier, when tracing the ramifications of his family, noted in his measured early nineteenth-century terms that 'the branch of Tintinhull, older than the Crichel branch, is represented to this day in lineal male descent by a Napier, and I believe is the only branch of all the English cadences of which this can be said.' The present incumbent, a Colonel Napier (Andrew's elder brother), had, he noted with evident satisfaction, been wounded twenty-seven times and was wholly disabled in two limbs. He had paid the subscription and could be said to have joined the club.

Edward Berkeley Napier, son of Andrew's timely match, also married an heiress, another Letitia, daughter of Henry Martin, who left them owners of the manor and lands of Pennard, and of East Pennard House, a solid Georgian mansion looking westward across the Vale of Avalon. Here, rooted like comfortable oaks in this smiling country that seems forever bathed in autumnal light and glinting with the steel of Arthur's knights, the Napier parents dearly hoped that the Napiers would solidly remain. But things rarely work out according to the dreams of parents, which is just as well, or the world would long ago have become perfectly static. Sons do not stay quiet on rich acres, in snug little businesses, or with safe hereditary manual skills, they go to Australia or Arkansas, open boutiques in the Seychelles or restaurants in the Andes, or book flights for the planets. Sometimes, aware that life is short, they live it up while the going is good, especially in times of piping peace. Gerard Berkeley Napier, son of Edward and godson of a Crichel cousin and inheriting this comfortable Pennard set-up when he was quite young, made no attempt to settle, and died at the age of twenty-nine from a hunting fall, though not before he had had five children by his wife, Mary Paul. This tragic crash provoked a sharp reaction in at least one of his family. The third and youngest of these orphaned boys was Gerard John, a square-chinned little boy with clear grey eyes set deep under arched brows. His father, during his brief life, had spent money like water; as far as the estate was concerned, his demise came just in time. Gerard John, born in 1821 and outliving Queen Victoria by a few months, was the instigator of a changed pattern of life; as was indeed his monarch. He kept extremely careful and meticulous accounts, never overspent, and became an admiral and the father of two more. The younger of these, Trev Napier, born in 1867 and serving at Jutland, was known in the Navy, on account of his remarkable height, as Long Napier.

The disruptive forces of civilization have failed to break up the tribal patterns of the Scots, or to unlock the chains of clan: there remains a mysterious capacity to exercise remote control over their distant cousins which is enjoyed by no other race. Separation seems unable even to affect their features, though it must have been coincidence that Gerard John, with his arched brows, beak nose, and powerful jowl looked so exactly like his contemporary Lord Napier in Scotland (William John, Captain R.N., well known at the newly founded United Services Club in London for determinedly eating what he liked, whether it agreed with him or not, because he was not going to yield to a mutiny on board *his* craft). A common ancestry in the murk morning of recorded British history, a mutual survival from that remote Macbeth world, through five hundred years of life lived *à l'outrance* amongst the weeping hills and the interminable winter nights of home, form a bond which time and place seem powerless to break. By 1800 the relationship between the Napiers in Scotland and the Napiers in Somerset was sufficiently remote, but even a century later they were writing to each other as Dear Kinsman and experiencing that singular cohesion; and it was in the meteoric wake of four young Merchiston Napiers, Charles, George and William, and their first cousin, another Charles Napier, that Gerard John left the lulling fields of Avalon and went to sea in H.M.S. *Racer* in the spring of 1833.

He was by now as stoutly English as the next man. But the difficult country still had its pull, was still exemplar of the proposition that a tough row to hoe makes life more exhilarating; that a short life, full and merry, may be better value than a long haul of frustration and safety—was still Scotland the Brave. She was exemplar, too, of the truth that people in general, with patience and a deeply held faith whose central tenet is love, with a few human beings in every generation prepared to stick their necks out in the common interest, will in time stop dropping each other down oubliettes and start inventing cures for fever; that the longest and the darkest nights may sparkle with life and discovery, as well as with passion and imagination; and the black spells of the witches' cauldron be broken by the vigour of an indefatigable hope.

Rockingham, 1966.
(Revised 1971.)

Family Trees

Notes

Notes

Notes

ALWIN MACARCHILL—witnesses many charters of King David I, between 1124 and 1153, a generous benefactor of monasteries, 1st Earl of Lennox about 1154, died soon after, first so-called in a charter of 1208 made by his son.

ALWIN, 2ND EARL OF LENNOX—enormous benefactions to the Church, marries daughter of 2nd Earl of Menteith. He was left a minor, and David, Earl of Huntingdon, younger brother to King William the Lion, was granted wardship of the earldom by the king. Alwin's benefactions extended particularly to the Cluniac Abbey of Paisley, and included the lands and church of Kilpatrick, the reputed site of St Patrick's death. Alwin left nine sons and one daughter. One son was perhaps the legendary Donald of 'Nae peer'? Alwin died circa 1225.

MALDWIN, 3RD EARL—huge benefactions continue, gives land to Glasgow Cathedral. Confirms land grants to Paisley Abbey——'devoted and bestowed by our ancestor to God and Saint Patrick in ancient times, free from every temporal exaction.' Charters confirmed by Alexander II at Stirling, 1227. Also to the monastery, one net on his water of Leven, and protection when going into the solitary places where this would lead the monks. Stands surety for the peace settlement between Alexander II and Henry III of England. Gives Dumbarton Castle, once a Roman outpost, to the King Alexander, and sells the barony of Colquhoun to the first chief of that ilk in 1249. Maldwin married Elizabeth, grand-daughter of Alan, hereditary Lord High Steward, ancestor of the Stewarts, and died circa 1250, having made further grants to the Abbey of Arbroath.

MALCOLM LORD—predeceased his father, whose only son he was. A slight dispute with the Abbot of Paisley over land is compounded for 50 marks. D. 1248, leaving.

MALCOLM, 4TH EARL—grants more land and goods to the Church.
The king gives him free forestry over the earldom of Lennox.
On St Valentine the Martyr's day in 1273 grants more fishing
rights to Monastery of Paisley. Benefactions continue through-
out his forty years of ownership. Swears support to little Queen
Margaret, the Maid of Norway, appears before the English
Council at Brigham to arrange her marriage. Confirms the
Macfarlanes (descended from Gilchrist, 5th son of 2nd Earl,
and his son Farlane), in their land of Arrochar. D. *circa* 1290.

MALCOLM, 5TH EARL—is resistance hero in struggle for Scottish
independence. Befriends Wallace when a fugitive. By royal
consent allows a dispute between Robert Reddehow and Joanna
his wife against the Abbot of Paisley to be heard in his court.
Two years later, in 1296, Robert, Bishop of Glasgow, sends a
deputation to admonish the Earl of Lennox and the bailies of
his court for allowing the case. Malcolm has supported Bruce,
as much the most worthy candidate, in his claim to the throne;
and everyone's attention is now distracted from a dispute over
eleemosynary lands in 1297, by the departure of King Edward I
of England to France, after, he hopes, settling the Scottish
succession; and Malcolm, plus Earls of Buchan, Menteith,
Strathearn, Ross, Atholl and Mar, form commission for
administration of affairs of Scotland, which soon takes the form
of invading and devastating Northumberland and Cumberland
and laying siege to Carlisle. Malcolm shelters Wallace, who had
taken Dumbarton Castle from the English, in his castle of
Faslane. Wallace eventually captured and executed in 1305.

Malcolm, 5th Earl swears fealty at Bruce's coronation in
May 1306; meets him as a fugitive this summer and feasts him;
goes with him to fight against English collaborators in north-
eastern Scotland. In the spring of 1314 Bruce and Malcolm of
Lennox are besieging Dumbarton Castle, once more in English
hands. Menteith who is holding it for the English offers to
surrender it only if Bruce will grant him the earldom of Lennox.
Malcolm, asked by Bruce, agrees; perhaps hoping to get it
back later. Bruce wins castle without this difficult clause.
Menteith, repentant, is offered forgiveness if he will go in the
front rank at Bannockburn, agrees, fights well there.

Evidently the war had caused a closing of ranks between the
Church and the civil power: in 1318 Malcolm, on terms with the

Abbey of Paisley, makes a further charter in its favour. In 1320 Malcolm seals Scotland's independence charter, the Declaration of Arbroath. In 1321 Bruce, now King Robert I, renews Malcolm's earldom, gives him back Dumbarton Castle 'for his good deeds and services often before rendered to us . . . which castle, King Alexander, our predecessor, held for a time according to his own good pleasure, from Maldwin Earl of Lennox.'

Malcolm supports Bruce's five-year-old son, King David II, when the king dies in 1329. In 1332 Edward III of England invades and crowns a Balliol at Scone; Malcolm, now old, leads his men going to join the army in the relief of Berwick, assailed by the English, and is killed at the battle of Halidon Hill 1333.

DONALD, 6TH EARL—supports King David II against Balliol and the English. But David, abandoned at Neville's Cross by Walter, the High Steward (married to Bruce's daughter and perhaps already with an eye to the main chance), is captured and imprisoned by the English. Donald, 6th Earl is one of the Council who appoints a commission to arrange with the English for the king's ransom. Grants a number of charters, one of which stipulated as the terms of the lease 'to be held of the grantor for rendering to the king's common army, when occasion required, one cheese for each house in which cheese was made in the said lands'. Donald's charter of free forestry was renewed by the king. He died *circa* 1364, leaving an only child

MARGARET, LADY OF LENNOX—married to Walter Lennox of Faslane, great grandson of Aulay, 4th son of 2nd Earl of Lennox. Walter known as Lord of Lennox, swore allegiance to King Robert II (son of Walter the Steward and Marjorie Bruce) at his coronation at Scone in March 1371, and acknowledged his son, now legitimized (he was a son of the pre-marital Elspeth Muir and not of Euphemia Ross) as lawful heir. His name was still spelt Levenax in the Act of Settlement. Granted renewed right of 'weapon-schawing' and armed muster of vassals, also priority for his own earl's court over the sheriff's. He and his wife resigned the earldom in 1385 but kept the life rent. He was still alive in 1388. He and his wife had four sons, Alexander, Alan, Walter, and the eldest, who became

DUNCAN, 8th EARL—married Ellen, daughter of Archibald Campbell of Lochawe and appears, in the teeth of the times, to have led a quiet life, though he certainly did not die a quiet death. He had a charter of weaponschawing from Robert II, 1387. His name appears on no public acts, and only on grants of local feudal charters, to John Kennedy and to Walter Buchanan. The sole exception to this is its appearance on the list of the Scots nobles who welcomed the ransomed King James I at Durham on his return home to his kingdom from captivity at Windsor. Retribution for any real or supposed treachery during the king's absence was swift. Duncan, 8th Earl was beheaded at Stirling in 1424 with his son-in-law Murdoch Stewart, Duke of Albany, who had been acting as Regent and also acting suspiciously, and his two grandsons, Walter and Alexander Stewart. A third grandson, James, also in rebellion, escaped to Ireland after burning Dumbarton. Duncan left three daughters, co-heiresses to the earldom

1) ISABELLA, COUNTESS OF LENNOX in her own right, and Duchess of Albany. In 1391 Duncan had signed a contract at Inchmurrin with Robert Stewart, Earl of Fife and Menteith and later Duke of Albany, a younger brother of King Robert II, for a marriage between Albany's son, Murdoch Stewart, and Isabella Lennox. Duncan subsequently resigned his earldom and had it renewed to pass through daughters. The marriage contract here signed would, it was hoped, unite the earldoms of Lennox, Menteith, and Fife. Albany subsequently lived to be 81, the oldest royal Stewart on record until Henry, Cardinal York, in the eighteenth century. All this while only the young imprisoned James I stood between Albany and the throne of Scotland. Albany's dukedom was sequestered in 1424, and Isabella's three sons all died unmarried, though James in his exile in Ireland produced an alleged seven natural sons.

2) MARGARET, married Robert Menteith, and had one son, Murdoch Mentieth of Rusky, who died young, leaving two daughters, Elizabeth, married to John Napier of Merchiston, and Agnes, married to John Haldane of Gleneagles.

3) ELIZABETH, married to John Stewart, Lord Darnley, by whom she had a son who did not die young and whose son Matthew, greatly increased his bargaining power in the long run by being married to Elizabeth Hamilton, grand-daughter of King James II.

Isabella enjoyed the earldom for her life-time, but clearly recognized her next sister, Margaret, as her eventual heir: her numerous grants to the Church are made 'with the consent and assent of our dearest sister-german, Margaret', who also signs with her in them. But when she died, long after both her younger sisters, the earldom of Lennox fell in dispute. The title of earl, and half the land went to Lord Darnley, who, as a Stewart, was naturally the preferred candidate of King James IV. He had also supported that young man in the rebellion in which his father, King James III, had been defeated, and eventually slain. John Napier, on the other hand, had stood by the reigning king, and his young son was therefore in some danger of losing his Napier inheritance, let alone the Lennox one. It was perhaps for this reason that Elizabeth Napier lay low, and did not for long dispute the Honor of Lennox. The Haldanes disputed longer; and some doubt has since been expressed as to whether she or Elizabeth Napier was in fact the elder sister, but Elizabeth held the messuage of Rusky, the principal dwelling of the domain, which was invariably the perquisite of the eldest among sisters.

James's eldest natural son, also a Stewart, who was a powerful figure and who became Lord Avandale, enjoyed the Lennox revenues while the dispute went on, but leant to the side of his kinsman, Darnley, and warmly supported him in his contention that Agnes Haldane was in fact a natural child herself. It has sometimes been maintained that James's seven Irish sons were not illegitimate, in which case of course they would have been the undisputed heirs, in the form of their eventual descendants, the Lennoxes of Woodhead, but at the time no one claimed, or even suggested, that James's sons were in the running.

The logical and fair conclusion would have been for the Napiers to have had the earldom of Lennox, and the Haldanes the earldom of Menteith, and for the Stewarts to have contented themselves with being Lords Darnley; but the Stewarts by now were unstoppably on the up and up, and had perhaps to dree their weird, while the Haldanes did well enough as scientists and the Napiers as soldiers and sailors.

The Stewart Lennoxes continued, unimpressively, through the sixteenth and seventeenth centuries. Since Matthew, 4th Earl, had, with the Macdonalds, joined forces with Henry VIII's invasion of Scotland, the name of Lennox had become more or less synonymous with craft, and was employed by Shakespeare as the name of one of Macbeth's dubious contemporaries. Matthew was declared guilty of treason and forfeited, but Mary Queen of Scots was persuaded by Elizabeth to allow Matthew and his son Darnley back to her realm in 1564. Both were Roman Catholics, and Elizabeth's motives are obscure: she did not want Darnley as suitor for herself, and perhaps thought it was safer to have Mary married to a Catholic so futile as Darnley, rather than a more powerful Continental co-religionary. After Darnley's death his father Matthew strove in vain to bring his murderers to book, was made Regent on behalf of his grandson, the boy King James VI, and was killed at Stirling soon after, in 1581.

Lennox's younger son Charles, seemingly a nonentity, was next heir to the throne if James died childless, but died himself in 1576, leaving only a daughter, Lady Arabella Stewart. This luckless girl, constantly in financially choppy waters, and pleading for a regular income both from Queen Elizabeth and James VI and I, whose first cousin and next heir she was until his marriage, fell in love with (or decided to marry) Sir William Seymour. As he was a grandson of Lady Catherine Grey, and hence in almost equal proximity to the throne, Elizabeth forbade their marriage. (William was descended from Henry VII's elder daughter, Arabella from his younger, as well as from King James II of Scotland.) King James VI and I upon his accession forgave Arabella for her ambitious engagement and treated her well: and Arabella and William made a solemn promise not to marry each other. But did, secretly, in 1611; a circumstance which they were unable to conceal effectively. They were separated; William was imprisoned and Arabella secluded. Arabella complained of physical prostration, and a relaxed guard enabled the couple to make plans for a separate escape to France. William arrived there, was eventually restored to favour and given back the forfeited dukedom of Somerset for his deeds in the Civil War: Arabella was captured at sea and sent to the Tower, where she died childless four years later.

The character of Esmé Stuart, 1st Duke of Lennox, is an enigma. Fourth Lord of Aubigny in France, he was a grandson of John, 3rd Stewart Earl of Lennox, and spelt his name Stuart, in the French manner, which Mary Queen of Scots had also popularized in Scotland. When the Hamiltons were forfeited, he came in line for the throne through the marriage of Elizabeth Hamilton, grand-daughter of King James II, to his great grandfather, Matthew, 2nd Earl of Lennox. All contemporaries agree upon Esmé's redoubtable charm, his manifold accomplishments. In middle age he was sent by the Guises to the court of their young kinsman, to convert King James VI and I, Esmé's cousin, to Catholicism. James was then thirteen, and all he was converted to by charming Esmé was a preference for the male sex. He doted upon Esmé, and made him Duke of Lennox. Lennox was extremely tactful with the Kirk: twice did he make solemn and open professions of allegiance to the Reformed Church; but as it was by then common knowledge that he was an emissary of the Guises, everybody thought he was foxing. When James was captured by the Ruthvens, extreme Protestants, Esmé attempted unsuccessfully to rescue him, and finally returned thankfully to France, pausing in London to tell the French ambassador that he thought the young King James so constant to the Protestant faith that he would die rather than forsake it. Esmé died a few months later, in 1583, professedly as a Protestant, but was *still* suspected of foxing. People do not as a rule fox on their deathbeds; but did Esmé hope to persuade the Protestant Council in Scotland to admit his sons to the Lennox inheritance in Scotland?

His son Ludovic, 2nd Duke of Lennox, was made Duke of Richmond also by his faithful kinsman King James, now also King James I of England. Ludovic's younger brother, Esmé 3rd Duke, had a cagey and enigmatic son, Charles, 4th Duke, who supported King Charles I with money throughout the Civil War but never fell foul of anyone else: 'He never acted for the King or against him,' a contemporary reported. This careful hedger of bets left a son, Esmé, 5th Duke, who died in Paris, aged eleven, succeeded by his first cousin Charles, 6th Duke and 10th Sieur d'Aubigny, who performed a useful if unhonoured service at the court of his cousin, King Charles II. He married that admired young woman, La Belle Stuart, whom

King Charles in his cups admitted that he found more amenable to his advances after marriage than she had been before. Charles, 6th Duke died childless; the descendants of his sister in time resuscitated the title of Darnley—an odd one to want—and the dukedoms of Richmond and Lennox were brought into play again for the king's natural son by Louise de Kerouaille. Perhaps by then he felt he would have no more sons and so gave both to this dearly loved little boy.

Faintly chastened by illegitimacy, the male line of the Stewart Lennoxes continued in the families of the Dukes of Buccleuch, Grafton and St Albans, as well as Richmond, and hence in many others.

NOTES ON THE NAPIERS

DONALD, 'NAE PEER'—mentioned in charter of Hay of Lochwardine, whose daughter is recorded as having married 'Donald, son of the Earl of Lennox, from whom came the Napiers'. His connection is not directly documented and can only be reasonably inferred with his traditional descendant

JOHN DE NAPIER—witnesses a Lennox charter in 1280, has a brother, Matthew de Napier of Aglecleck, defends Stirling Castle in 1314 during its siege by Edward I of England—'the might of England against 200 men'—is sent into English imprisonment and fined three years' rent of his lands. Has Lennox arms. His son

WILLIAM DE NAPIER of Kilmahew in Dunbartonshire (part of the Lennox)—also has charter from King David of lands in Perthshire, from King Robert II in 1376, from Robert III in 1390; a safe-conduct in 1398 from Richard II of England to go into that country for himself and fourteen servants, as many horse as foot. His elder son Duncan remains at Kilmahew; his younger

JOHN DE NAPIER—goes to Edinburgh, is living there in 1368. His son

WILLIAM NAPIER—has a charter of lands in Haddington from Robert II in 1376, and of land in Edinburgh from Robert III in 1398, is Governor of Edinburgh Castle in 1401, pleads unsuccessfully as co-heir to the earldom of Lennox when Duncan, 8th Earl is beheaded in 1424. His son, or possibly nephew

ALEXANDER NAPIER—Provost of Edinburgh, acquires the lands of
Merchiston from King James I in settlement of a royal debt,
entertains French ambassador, Reginald Giraud who has come
to Scotland in 1435 to escort this king's daughter Margaret to
Paris for her marriage with the Dauphin; goes as a commissioner
to meet the English ambassador at Newcastle to arrange a three
years' truce. His son

SIR ALEXANDER NAPIER—builds Merchiston Tower, around 1460, is
Provost of Edinburgh, has carved head on pillar of chapel of
San Salvador in St Giles, which he endows; rescues Queen
Joanna, widow of James I from Stirling Castle where the
Livingstones have imprisoned her during her son's minority, is
awarded lands of Philde near Methven in Perthshire when said
son, James II, comes of age; Comptroller of the Household
1449–61. Also holds lands at Lindores, in Fife; in 1461 goes on
an embassy to England which he combines with a pilgrimage to
the shrine of St Thomas á Becket at Canterbury, signs three
year truce with England, is given safe-conduct by Henry VI
whenever he wants to come to England, becomes 'Maister of
Houshald' and Vice-Admiral of Scotland. Embassies for infant
King James to Bruges, Burgundy, Denmark, where he negotiates
royal marriage with daughter of King Christian: terms include
a mortgage on Orkney; 1468, escorts the princess back to
Scotland, dies 1473, buried in St Giles. Has John, Henry and
Janet, succeeded at Merchiston by

JOHN NAPIER—Lord of Council, Provost of Edinburgh, Master of
the King's Household, goes on embassy to Edward IV in
London on behalf of Margaret of Anjou, a refugee after the
battle of Towton at the court of Scotland; is awarded pension
by Margaret of 50 marks for life; marries Elizabeth Menteith,
grand-daughter of Margaret of Lennox and great grand-
daughter of Duncan, 8th Earl of Lennox (of which earldom his
father Alexander had already had settlement of a part); supports
King James III against the rebellion instigated on behalf of his
younger son, is killed with him fighting at Sauchieburn in 1488.
He leaves Archibald, George, John, Janet and Margaret, of
whom

ARCHIBALD NAPIER—succeeds him at Merchiston and other Napier
lands, fails to obtain Honor of Lennox, but is awarded one
quarter of earldom. Member of the royal household, three times

married, Archibald fought at Flodden in later life, survived it by seven years, left by his first wife, Catherine Douglas, Alexander, Catherine, Isabella, Mariota, Janet and Elizabeth, by his second wife, Elizabeth Crichton, John, and by his third wife, Alexander of Inglistoun, born after his elder brother

SIR ALEXANDER NAPIER—was killed at Flodden in 1513. Knighted in 1507, for him James IV made the Lennox and Rusky inheritances into a free barony, incorporated with his father's other properties and 'Merchamstoun near the burgh of Edinburgh cum turre et manere eundum', confirmed to his father by charter in 1494. Legally obliged by a general enactment of James IV to learn to read and write and study Latin and the arts, Sir Alexander was killed in the flower of his youth, leaving besides James and John, a four-year-old eldest son

ALEXANDER NAPIER—who succeeded to Merchiston etc, on the death of his grandfather in 1521. A Lord of Council but never well, he is repeatedly allowed by James V to go abroad in an attempt to acquire health—'our weilbelovit freynd the Lard of Marchaynston'. Alexander extricates himself from a Douglas marriage arranged for him during his minority and marries Annabella Campbell; appoints his first cousin Robert Napier to act for him when he goes abroad and gives him power of attorney when threatened with excommunication in 1542 by the Archdeaconry of Lothian for failing to pay a debt; redeems the Lennox property of Gartness alienated by his grandfather Archibald; returns from abroad in time to be killed fighting for James V against an invading army of English at Pinkie Cleugh in 1547. His two brothers James and John eventually emigrate, and Alexander is succeeded in his estates by his son

SIR ARCHIBALD NAPIER—Master of the Mint, marries Janet Chisholm when he is fourteen, has eldest son when he is fifteen and two more children before he is twenty, gets back his Lennox inheritance of the islands in Loch Lomond, appropriated during his minority by his cousins the Haldanes of Gleneagles, has them confirmed to him by Mary Queen of Scots on the additional grounds that his father, grandfather, and great great grandfather have all died in battle fighting for her family; is sent on embassy to England, where, according to Sir James Balfour who accompanies him 'his witt and knawledge is wonderit at be the Englischmen'. Appears to understand the necessity of further coinage if the trade of Scotland is to prosper, prospects for gold and silver for the Mint, is a Lord of Council. Has trouble in old age from slightly rakehell sons acquired by his second marriage, aged thirty-six this time, to Elizabeth Mowbray, but survives to be seventy-four, having, after staying loyal to Queen Mary and mustering at Carberry, given up the unequal struggle and concentrated on farm-improvement, geology, and religion, while the king's and queen's wars bang fitfully on around him. Knighted in 1565, he is appointed to a commission for ferreting out hidden Jesuits in 1589 after the scare of the Armada, but doesn't take part. Dies in 1608, leaving John, Francis, Alexander (Archie has been killed by the Scotts), William, Janet, Helen, Elizabeth and Marion. His eldest son

JOHN NAPIER—invents logarithms, the decimal point, a primitive tank, a submarine, and writes a scientific treatise on the Revelation of St John the Divine. Member of Council, a good landlord, has speculative ventures in doubtful company to discover minerals. For other details see text, where they are fully covered. Dies in 1617, leaving six of each, Archibald, 9th laird of Merchiston and first Lord Napier, and a baronet, John of Easter Torrie, nearly executed for assisting Montrose, Robert of Culcreuch, from whom the Napiers of Milliken, Alexander, William, Adam of Blackstone, and Joan, Jane, Elizabeth, Anne, Helen, and Margaret. Succeeded by

ARCHIBALD, 1ST LORD NAPIER—fully documented in the text and family tree, who died in 1645 and was succeeded by his son by Lady Margaret Graham,

ARCHIBALD, 2ND LORD NAPIER—to whom the same applies; who dies in 1658, and is succeeded by his son by Lady Elizabeth Erskine,

ARCHIBALD, 3RD LORD NAPIER—ditto, dies unmarried in 1683. Succeeded by his nephew

THOMAS, 4TH LORD NAPIER—dies unmarried in Paris aged seventeen in 1686 and is succeeded by his aunt

MARGARET, LADY NAPIER—dies in 1706, and losing her only son at sea, is succeeded by her grandson

FRANCIS, 6TH LORD NAPIER—buys back Merchiston, sequestered under the Commonwealth government, finances plans and surveys for the Forth–Clyde canal, has ten sons and employs David Hume to educate them; they are William, Charles,

Francis, John, Mark, by Lady Henrietta Hope, daughter of
Lord Hopetoun; and George, James, Patrick, a replacement
John, and Stewart, by Henrietta, daughter of General Johnston
of Dublin, Governor of Quebec, who also produces Mary, who
dies young, and Hester, who survives and is entrusted with the
heart of Montrose in its steel casket, which gets swept up into
the French Revolution and has never been seen since. Of these
ten sons all are in the Navy or the Army, the first John dies
young as a lieutenant in the 25th regiment, James is lost at sea
in the *Fox* frigate as a young lieutenant, Charles, Captain R.N.
is the father of Black Charlie and Fair Tom, and George married
Lady Sarah Lennox and is the father of Louisa, Generals
Charles, George, and William Napier, Richard and Henry,
Caroline and Cecilia, besides a previous two baby sons and a
little daughter all of whom, together with his first wife, die of
yellow fever at New York during the American War of 1776.
The eldest son of Francis succeeds as

WILLIAM, 7TH LORD NAPIER—'bred to arms' and having no notion of
the low financial state of his inheritance. Leaves the Scots
Greys, and endeavours to pay the debts of £10,000 involved in
his father's Forth-Clyde canal survey, and also to provide as
generously for his daughters as the entail permitted. Sells
his commission in the Scots Greys for £4,000 but has in the end
to sell Merchiston, and even his library, to him almost more
precious. Marries Mainie Anne, a girl with a turned up nose,
daughter of 8th Lord Cathcart; is deputy adjutant general
of the forces in Scotland; dies in 1775 leaving an only son

FRANCIS, 8TH LORD NAPIER—is an ensign at the Saratoga surrender
in the War of American Independence, and taken prisoner by
the Americans. Returns to Scotland and marries Maria Margaret
Clavering, daughter of a general, and either naturally beautiful
or made to look so in her portrait by Sir Joshua Reynolds.
They buy back Merchiston. 'I have experienced so much warmth
of heart in the character of Lord Napier,' reports Lady Sarah
Napier, his cousin by marriage, mourning for the loss at sea of
his second son, Francis, serving in the *Hussar* frigate in the
Napoleonic wars. He has an honorary degree from Edinburgh
University, is a representative peer in Parliament, Lord Lieuten-
ant of Selkirk and High Commissioner to the General Assembly,
Grand Master Mason of Scotland, and dies in 1801, leaving,

besides Charles, Henry, Maria, Charlotte, Anne, Sophia and Caroline,

WILLIAM JOHN, 9TH LORD NAPIER—born at Kinsale in 1786, of whom more later.

ETC.

Bibliography

Bibliography

Boswell of Auchinleck MSS
Napier and Ettrick Charter Chest
National Register of Archives (Scotland), Edinburgh
Wigton MS

Anonymous: Ballads
Baillie, Robert: *Letters and Journals, 1637–62* (ed.) David Lang, Bannatyne Club, 3 vols., 1841–2
Brown, P. Hume: *History of Scotland*, 3 vols. 1899–1905
Buchan, John: *Montrose*, 1928
Burton, John Hill: *History of Scotland*, 2nd edition, 8 vols. and index, 1873
Chronicle of Lanercost, see Maxwell
Dickinson, W. C.: *Scotland from the Earliest Times to 1603*, 1961
Douglas, Sir Robert: *The Peerage of Scotland*, 1764
Dunbar, William: *Poems* (ed.) W. Mackay Mackenzie, 1932
Fergusson, Sir James: *William Wallace*, new edition, 1948
Fleming, David Hay: *Mary Queen of Scots*, 2nd edition, 1898
Fordun, John: *Chronica Gentis Scotorum* (ed. and trans.) W. F. Skene, 2 vols. 1871–2
Fraser, Lady Antonia: *Mary Queen of Scots*, 1969
Fraser, Sir William: *The Lennox*, 2 vols., 1905
Fyfe, James G.: *Scottish Diaries and Memoirs*, 2 vols., 1928, 1942
Henderson, T. F.: *Life of Mary Queen of Scots*, 2 vols., 1905
Henryson, Robert: *Poems and Fables* (ed.) H. Harvey Wood, 1933
Hume, David: *History of England*, new edition, 8 vols., 1763
King James VI & I: *Basilikon Doron*, 1599
Lang, Andrew: *History of Scotland*, 3rd edition, 4 vols., 1903–7
Lindsay, Robert, of Pitscottie: *Historie and Cronicles of Scotland*, (ed) A. J. G. Mackay, 3 vols., Scottish Text Society, 1899–1911

LINKLATER, ERIC: *Edinburgh*, 1960
  Mary Queen of Scots, 1933
  The Royal House of Scotland, 1970
  The Survival of Scotland, 1968

MACKENZIE, WILLIAM MACKAY: *The Scottish Burghs*, 1949

MATTHEW, DAVID: *Scotland under Charles I*, 1955

MAXWELL, SIR HERBERT (trans.): *The Chronicle of Lanercost*, 1913

MITCHISON, ROSALIND: *History of Scotland*, 1970

NAPIER, ARCHIBALD, 1ST LORD: *A defence*

NAPIER, ARCHIBALD SCOTT: *A History of the Napiers of Merchiston*,
  privately printed, 1923

NAPIER, MARK: *'The Lenox of Auld'*, 1880
  Memoirs of John Napier, 1834
  Memoirs of Montrose, 2 vols., 1856
  Memorials of Claverhouse, 3 vols., 1859–62

NOTESTEIN, WALLACE: *The Scot in History*, 1946

PRYDE, G. S.: *Scotland from 1603 to the Present Day*, 1962

RUSSELL, GEOFFREY BURTON: *Mediaeval Civilisation*

SHIELDS, ALEXANDER: *A Hind let loose*, 1687

SPOTTISWOODE, JOHN: *History of the Church of Scotland* (ed.) M.
  Russell and M. Napier, 3 vols., Bannatyne Club & Spottiswoode
  Society, 1847–51

STEWART, SIR JAMES *et al.*: *Naphtali*, 1667

TERRY, CHARLES SANFORD: *History of Scotland*, 1920

THOMSON, J. MAITLAND: *The Public Records of Scotland*, 1922

TYTLER, PATRICK FRASER: *History of Scotland*, 2nd edition, 9 vols.,
  1841–3

WEDGWOOD, C. V.: *The King's Peace*, 1955
  The King's War, 1958
  The Trial of Charles I, 1964

Index